74 DAYS

Also available from Century

The Red and Green Life Machine

A Diary of the Falklands Field Hospital

RICK JOLLY

An Islander's Diary of the Falklands Occupation

JOHN SMITH

CENTURY PUBLISHING

LONDON

Jacket photographs courtesy of Rex Features
Photographs within text courtesy of Pete King, Ian Strange and John Smith
Map of the Falkland Islands courtesy of Royal Geographical Society

First published in Great Britain in 1984
by Century Publishing Co. Ltd,
Portland House,
12–13 Greek Street,
London W1V 5LE

British Library Cataloguing in Publication Data

Smith, John
74 days
1. Falkland Islands War, 1982—Personal narratives
I. Title
997'.11 F3031

ISBN 0-7126-0361-1

Photoset by Rowland Phototypesetting Ltd,
Bury St Edmunds, Suffolk
Printed in Great Britain by Redwood Burn Ltd,
Trowbridge, Wiltshire

To those who gave
and to those who were prepared to give their lives
in order that the Falkland Islands could be freed from
Argentine Occupation.

Acknowledgements

So many people have helped in so many ways in the preparation of this Diary for publication that it would be quite unfair to single out individuals. Each person who assisted in refreshing my memory on one detail, no matter how small, has contributed towards making this picture complete. The expansion of some of the events was necessary as during the time of the Occupation one had to be very careful about writing too specifically. The Argentines would not have looked kindly on our accounts and opinions of some of their activities. Therefore I offer my sincere thanks to all those who helped in any way.

Publication would never have been achieved without the valiant efforts of Rosemarie Allan who converted my scruffy notes into what has become this book. Pete King has contributed greatly with his photography and general enthusiasm.

Finally, I owe a great debt to Ileen and my family who encouraged me in writing during times when I was ready to throw the whole lot into the dustbin and give up.

Glossary

APC Armoured Personnel Carrier
BAS British Antarctic Survey
CAMP The countryside anywhere outside Stanley
DUKW Amphibious Landing Vehicle
ESRO European Space Research Organisation
FCO Foreign & Commonwealth Office
FIC Falkland Islands Company Limited
FIBS Falkland Islands Broadcasting Service
FIG Falkland Islands Government
FIGAS Falkland Islands Government Air Service
FIDF Falkland Islands Defence Force
GH Government House
GPMG General Purpose Machine Gun
HE His Excellency
KEMH King Edward Memorial Hospital
MET Office Meteorological Office
MOD Ministry of Defence
PATA Plant & Transport Authority
PWD Public Works Department
SATO South Atlantic Treaty Organisation
TOM (TEATRO DE OPERACIONES MALVINAS) Argentine designation of military operations in the FI
YPF (YACIMIENTOS PETROLIFEROS FISCALES) An Argentine organisation supplying petroleum-based products to the Falklands under an agreement reached between Britain and Argentina in 1974.

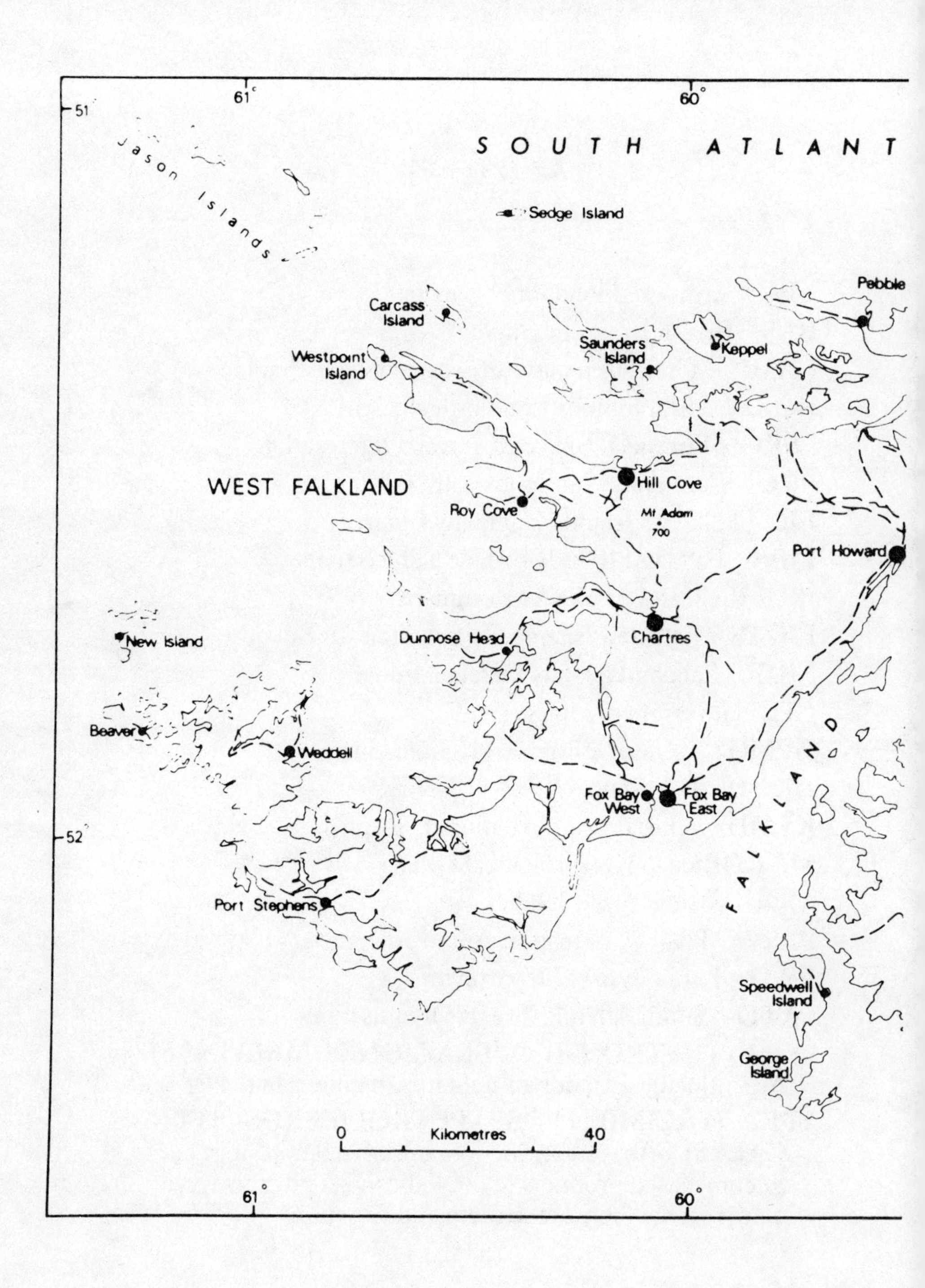

61°
60°
51
SOUTH ATLANT
Jason Islands
Sedge Island
Carcass Island
Westpoint Island
Saunders Island
Keppel
Pebble
WEST FALKLAND
Hill Cove
Roy Cove
Mt Adam
700
Port Howard
New Island
Dunnose Head
Chartres
Beaver
Weddell
Fox Bay West
Fox Bay East
FALKLAND
52
Port Stephens
Speedwell Island
George Island
0
Kilometres
40
61°
60°

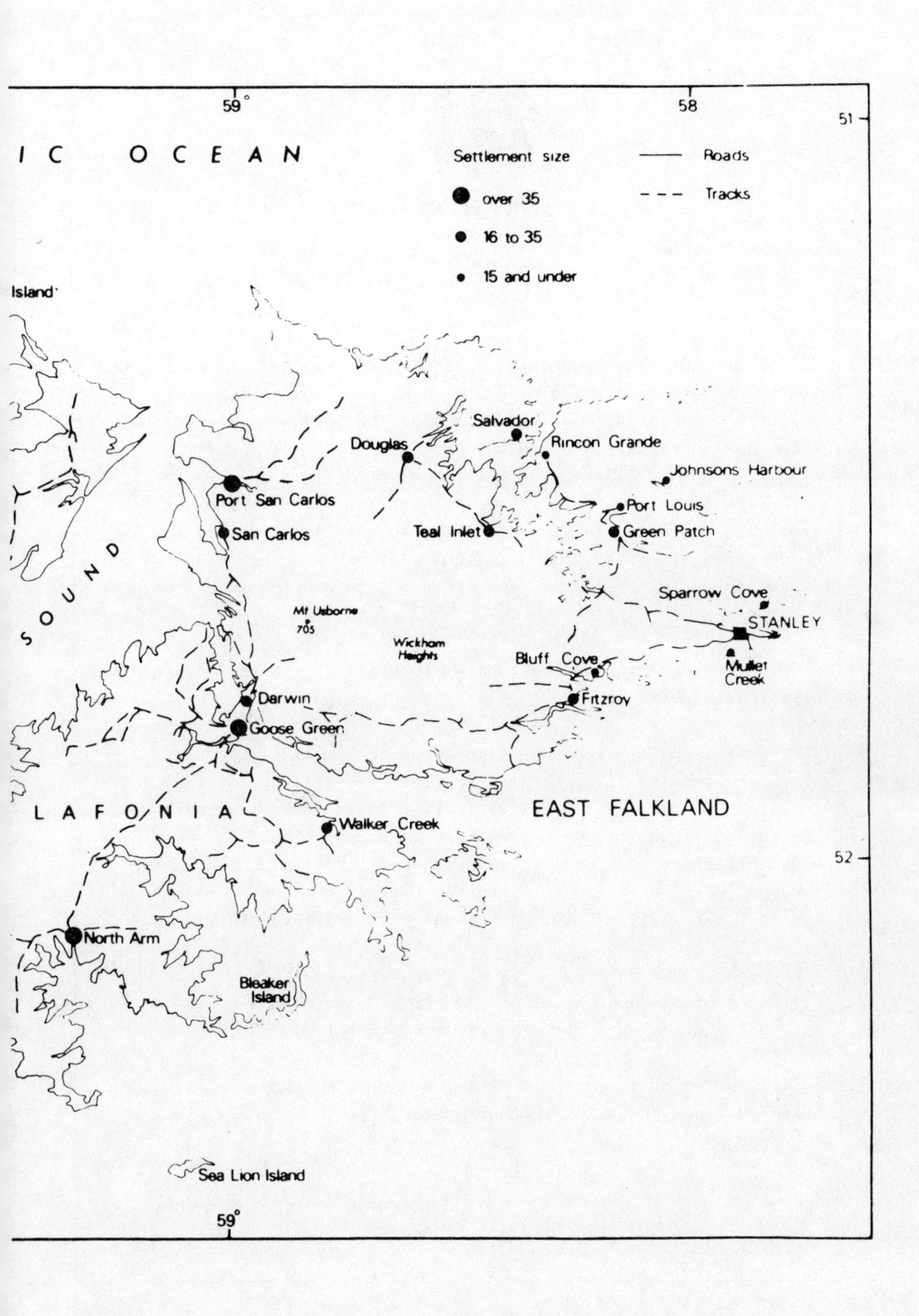

59°
58
51
IC OCEAN
Settlement size
over 35
16 to 35
15 and under
Roads
Tracks
Island
SOUND
Salvador
Douglas
Rincon Grande
Johnsons Harbour
Port San Carlos
Port Louis
San Carlos
Teal Inlet
Green Patch
Sparrow Cove
Mt Usborne
705
STANLEY
Wickham Heights
Bluff Cove
Mullet Creek
Darwin
Fitzroy
Goose Green
LAFONIA
EAST FALKLAND
Walker Creek
52
North Arm
Bleaker Island
Sea Lion Island
59°

10 DOWNING STREET

THE PRIME MINISTER

I met John Smith in January 1983 when I visited the Falklands. We stood together, in the middle of a cleared path through an Argentine minefield, discussing some of the native plants which were growing wild in the field.

John Smith is native to the Islands and his diary is unique in giving an insider's view of what life was like under occupation. He does not dramatise, he just gives a simple account of what happened to him, his family and friends from day one to day seventy-four.

My own memories of those days are still very much alive and will remain so.

I will never forget the night when information came through that it looked as if the Argentine fleet was heading for the invasion of Port Stanley. I will never forget the day I smiled my way through constituency engagements in Finchley knowing that that night British troops would be making their landing in San Carlos. I was 8,000 miles but only a heartbeat away from that silent armada, that hostile coast and those brave and loyal Islanders.

Perhaps the proudest moment of my life was at 10 o'clock on the night of 14 June when I stood at the Despatch Box to announce that white flags were flying over Port Stanley.

These events are history and John Smith's diary proves that history is not something that always happens to other people.

Margaret Thatcher

December 1983

Preface

When I first came to the Falklands 25 years ago, I was working on board the Royal Research Ship *Shackleton* with the British Antarctic Survey. Soon afterwards I married Ileen – who was born in the Falklands. We have four children, Jeremy 20, Martyn 19, Anya 16 and Tyssen 11. Jeremy is currently taking a year off before returning to England for more studies; Martyn is an apprentice electrician at the Power Station; Anya hopes to take up nursing and Tyssen is still at school. They are a great bunch. Ileen is devoted to the family and the house – she collects old china while I gather bits and pieces of historical interest. We like to share these things with people and our home is rather like a museum as a result. Our guests appear to enjoy the atmosphere, so our interests have resulted in a happy and profitable combination.

It is so very difficult to convey adequately the enormity of the impact which the events of 1982 had on the people of the Falkland Islands. First, the Argentine Invasion, then the Occupation, followed by the relief of the British Liberation with its subsequent changes on the life and people of the Islands. It is not just a change of circumstances or environment. It's a total capsize of life as it used to be prior to 2 April 1982.

At that time, probably the immediate impression on visitors to the Islands, besides the solitude and remoteness, was their cleanliness and orderliness. Port Stanley and the settlements were like something from a picture postcard. The air was dust free, the streets clean, the number of vehicles so few that exhaust fumes were soon whisked away by the South Atlantic winds. Pollution in a physical sense was almost unknown, but pollution of another kind was a very real threat always lurking in the background of our lives. This was a combination of pressure from Argentina to claim the Islands as her own coupled with what almost amounted to encouragement from certain sections of the British Government to assist her in achieving her objective.

Prior to April 1982 the total population of the Islands was only 1,800 but they were administered in much the same manner as other overseas British territories. The authority of Her Majesty the Queen was vested in the Governor with full colonial status and he was assisted by a staff appropriate to his office. The legislation and affairs of the colony were looked after by the Executive and Legislative councils, the majority democratically elected, the others in an ex officio capacity or appointed by the Governor. The administration was headed by a Chief Secretary, finances were controlled by the Chief Financial Secretary, medical affairs looked after by the Senior Medical Officer and so on. Admittedly, there were domestic and internal departmental squabbles, with feathers being ruffled occasionally, but it was and still is an enviable state of affairs which many governments are striving towards today.

In area the Islands are about the size of Wales, the coastline deeply indented with beaches and harbours not unlike the fiords of Norway. The capital, Stanley, occupies an area about half a mile long from east to west and a quarter of a mile from north to south. This is important to bear in mind while reading the diary. When the British naval, air and land forces were bombarding the Argentine positions around Port Stanley it tended to sound in most reports as if these were some miles distant. In fact they were just up the road or in some cases at the end of the garden, depending on where you lived.

Outside Stanley there are no roads. The people are scattered over some 30 or 40 sheepfarming settlements with populations ranging from a single family to bigger farms with about 120 inhabitants. Travel between the settlements is either on horseback, by Land Rover or by aircraft. Supplies are delivered to the settlements by the small coasting vessel *Monsunen* owned by the Falkland Islands Company (FIC). The company also carries in the baled wool to Stanley for shipment to and eventual sale in England on a Danish vessel chartered four times a year to bring out supplies and take home the wool. The selection of items carried to the Falklands on each voyage is vast, ranging from toothpaste to tractors. Contrary to popular belief, the Islands are not largely dependent on Argentina for the essentials of life. We did rely on Argentina for the supply of fuel and domestic gas which was agreed by the British and Argentine governments in 1974 with regrettably little explanation or reference to the people of the Falkland Islands. The Argentine

YPF (Yacimientos Petrolíferos Fiscales) company was allowed to instal a Plant at Port Stanley, which required a number of Argentine technical staff to be here permanently to look after it. This seemed to us to be the thin end of the wedge.

The political wedge was driven in even more firmly with the setting up of an air service to the mainland of Argentina, brought about by the FIC's withdrawal of the steamer *Darwin* on the financial grounds that it was no longer possible to economically maintain their monthly passenger and mail service to Montevideo. The inter-island service was to be continued with a smaller vessel. The British Government said that it would provide an air link with the mainland and a sea link. At that point the Argentines quickly seized the opportunity to step in with the offer of a sea plane service, followed up by the building of a temporary airstrip which would solve the problems until such time as the permanent airfield was completed. The sea link proposed by Britain never materialised.

The Argentine air link was provided by LADE (Lineas Aéreas Del Estado), whose role in the Argentine Air Force is similar to that of our RAF Transport Command. On completion of the temporary airstrip F-27 Fokker Friendship Aircraft were used; once the permanent airfield built by Britain was operational, the F-27s were alternated with pure jet Fokker F-28s. It was a fine enough airport but because of its short length could take only aircraft which were capable of the relatively short flight between the Falklands and the mainland of Southern Argentina – yet another stage in the plan to ensure that now the Islanders were totally committed for entry and exit to their own home by way of Argentina. This state of affairs was of course highly pleasing to the Argentinians, who added insult to injury during the flights by giving the instructions for use of the life-saving equipment only in Spanish! The lesson was quite clear: if you wished to be saved, you should learn Spanish.

An even odder situation brought about by the air link was that when the Governor wished to journey to and from his colony he did so by courtesy of the Argentine Air Force. This was of course especially handy for the Argentine Government during times when talks on the Falklands were taking place in New York, Rio or indeed anywhere else, as the delegates from the Falklands could never leave unnoticed either by the local population or by the Argentines. Like the YPF company, once LADE was established it needed to be looked after from the Falklands end by a team of experts, headed by a Vice-Commodore of the Argentine Air Force. The Argentines brought their wives and families and quickly absorbed themselves into the Falkland way of life, with exchanges of invitations to official and social functions on both sides. Their children attended our schools. The small Argentine community quickly became part of the scenery. The Comodoro even received permission to erect what was described as a 'modest bungalow' in Stanley. It turned out to be quite a vast, rather splendid wooden building, specially flown in by several Argentine C-130 Hercules transports, thus speeding the construction as well as proving that C-130s with heavy loads could safely use our new runway. This increasing driving in of the wedge was conducted with such tact and skill that there was very little that we could do to prevent it, although it was perfectly clear to the locals that the ultimate aim of the exercise was eventually to win us over. The Argentines also took the opportunity to learn as much as possible about each and every Islander: a file was opened on each one of us containing information on our political views, character, attitudes towards them, activities, work, background, hobbies, friends, visitors, even personal idiosyncrasies. It was all so very easy to do and, as we were later to find out, very thoroughly done, making it extremely difficult to pull the wool over their eyes during the Occupation.

Despite these storm clouds gathering on our horizon, life continued as normal – a full life both in Stanley and the Camp. To live here one has to be very self-sufficient. If the plumbing bursts you get in among the pipes and sort things out. If the chimney falls down you build a new one. This 'do-it-yourself' system means we are very practical people ready to adapt quickly, without undue panic or fuss, to situations as they arise. We have no greengrocers or butchers' shops. All vegetables are grown in our own gardens. Meat is delivered twice a week by the butcher – a quarter of a sheep at a time. Whether you want ribs or roast is up to you – you carve it up yourself.

To those folks living outside Stanley in the camp settlements, FIGAS (Falkland Islands Government Air Service) plays a major part in everyday life. Formerly made up of two De Havilland Beaver float planes and a Britten Norman Islander – running like a country bus service between the settlements with passengers, mail, freight, schoolchildren, cats, dogs and spare parts – there is not much that

FIGAS cannot fly. Among the more important passengers is the doctor. The medical services are centralised at the King Edward Memorial Hospital in Stanley where there is a good operating theatre, X-Ray department and dental surgery. Cases requiring specialist medical attention have to be evacuated overseas (before the conflict usually to Argentina, now to England). Each weekday morning at 9.30 one of the three doctors at the hospital holds a surgery over the air from the Radio Telephone Office in Stanley. Any settlements having medical problems chat them over with the doctor who decides what to send out, whether to arrange a visit or bring the patient into town. It's rather a chummy sort of system as most people tune in, so that everyone knows what's wrong with everyone else. To those with more intimate problems it's better to endure the discomfort a little longer and write a letter! All settlements use the R/T daily and Ileen Vidal, the Stanley operator, shows immense patience in juggling the settlements about as they come up with weather reports for FIGAS, emergencies for the doctor or the vet, or a complicated list of spare parts urgently required to get a tractor going again.

Besides the government R/T many people have their own two-metre sets – a sort of citizens' waveband. There are also a good number of Ham Radio operators, resulting in almost constant communication and chat throughout the Islands. Radio broadcasting is taken care of very effectively by the FI Broadcasting Station. News from the BBC is regularly relayed directly from London, which means that, generally, people here are as aware of world events as folk in England.

Education is good. Teachers are usually here on two- or three-year contracts from the United Kingdom and, with our small classes, attention can be almost individual. Academic achievement is remarkably high. 'O' levels are taken here and if a child shows promise, there's a scheme whereby he or she can attend the Thomas Peacock School at Rye in Sussex to study for 'A' levels. A hostel is currently being built in Stanley to enable children from the settlements to attend schools during term time, which will replace the earlier system of a teacher travelling between settlements on a regular beat.

Municipal services are taken care of by the Public Works Department who are responsible for the power, electricity and water supply, as well as the upkeep and maintenance of Stanley.

Law and order is kept by a Senior Magistrate, a Chief Constable, one policewoman and several constables.

Besides the garrison of some 40 Royal Marines based at Moody Brook, known as Naval Party 8901, and HMS *Endurance* which was on station between the Falklands and the Antarctic during the months of the southern summer, our own contribution to security was the Falkland Islands Defence Force (FIDF) composed of volunteers from Stanley and the Camp trained by the Royal Marines. When the occasion required they could provide a good turnout for a ceremonial parade, but they were much more at home in the hills. Skill with a rifle comes almost as second nature to many Islanders: this asset, along with local knowledge, the ability to understand and to withstand the sometimes rather sharp weather and an almost mischievous attitude and enthusiasm towards things military, results in an interesting and highly dangerous combination.

Such was the state of play in the opening months of 1982. As for ourselves, we had recently set up business as a guesthouse, having always been interested in that sort of thing. Rather than wait until I retired at 65, it seemed to be much more sensible to retire from my position with the FIC at 43, which would leave me free to do something else later on. Business was extremely good. There have always been three main types of visitor to the Falklands: the wildlife enthusiasts, those interested in the maritime history and the journalists. There is one other category of visitor who comes here for a bit of oneupmanship – they have been everywhere else in the world, so arrive, get their passports stamped and leave immediately. We have had several instances of people staying overnight in order to get the FI stamp in their passports.

Our new house had formerly been a guesthouse but we had lots of ideas of our own which we wanted to try out, so there was a full programme ahead of redecorating, and some rebuilding as well as looking after the guests. After several months it became obvious that we were attempting to do too much at once and Ileen's health went downhill rapidly as a result.

This was about the time that the South Georgia business blew up. I think that it was on 19 March that a friend telephoned from London to ask how we felt about the Argentines hoisting their flag on South Georgia. It was very frustrating that we had to rely on a casual call from England to learn what was going on virtually in our backyard – later to be confirmed by the BBC and our Governor. The gravity of the situation began to dawn on us, but none of us expected what was shortly to follow.

It has been suggested that a lot of nonsense has been talked about life under Occupation. An easy statement – seventy-four days dismissed without further thought. Admittedly things could have been a lot worse, but it was not an easy or a pleasant time for the 500 or so folk left in Stanley, nor a time which any of us would ever wish to repeat. At the same time it was an experience which none of us would have missed. Like all contingencies of this kind it was a great leveller. We were all reduced to the same standards, the same discomforts, the same fears, the same risks. After reading this account, my hope is that people will be able to understand why certain things did not take place in the same sequence as they do on television or at the cinema. Here in the Falklands neither side was putting on an act. This was the real thing.

John Smith
Sparrow Hawk House,
Port Stanley,
Falkland Islands.
June 1983

Thursday 1 April

Bright, sunny, mild day with very little wind.

Usual routine with our guests Ian and Phyllis Butler, in Stanley on business from their farm at Port North, Roy Cove, and John and Pamela Dixon, representing the *Daily Mirror* and *Woman's Own*, who have been with us for a few days now. Tyssen is a bit disappointed as he was looking forward to a visit on board HMS *Endurance* for the schoolchildren scheduled to take place tomorrow, but as she has gone off, we presume towards South Georgia to sort out the troubles there with the Argentine scrap merchants, the visit is off. Anya is finding school a bit of a bind, and is waiting for the end of term so that she can leave, hopefully to take up nursing at the King Edward Memorial Hospital here. I think, though, that she may have to wait another year until she is sixteen. Ileen has spent most of the day in bed as advised by the doctor; she really has been attempting to do far too much lately. Fortunately, whatever it is that they have given her to take is starting to become effective, but it's going to be some time before she is completely well again.

After work this afternoon Martyn and Jeremy took advantage of the glorious weather to go on their motor bikes down to Eliza Cove, then back to town via Sapper Hill. They said they had seen armed Royal Marines on Sapper Hill and that the marines were taking coils of barbed wire in lorries down towards the airport. The road down there has now been closed off to everyone.

From this point it will be best if events are recorded under the time they took place, as things began to get a bit hectic towards the end of the day.

1900 Hours

As we were preparing dinner for the guests, the Islander aircraft flew low up past the house to land on the racecourse. Very odd. Tony Hunt, the Governor's son, was with us, as he usually is during his holidays here, helping Anya to make a trifle which was going desperately wrong – turning out like thick custard.

2015 Hours

Still attempting to get the trifle under control when it was announced on local radio that the Governor was about to make an important announcement. This solved the trifle problem as Governor Hunt said that he had evidence that the Argentines were preparing to take the Falklands. An invasion was imminent – possibly at dawn tomorrow. He might have to declare a state of emergency. The radio station would remain open all night and the Falkland Island Defence Force were to report to the Drill Hall immediately for duty . . .

The enormity of this news left everyone absolutely stunned. How could an invasion force be assembled, put to sea, then be off the Falklands for some ten hours before it was discovered? It is absolutely incredible and appalling, that in the last quarter of the twentieth century this has been allowed to happen. Like our trifle – which has been completely forgotten about – something has gone desperately wrong somewhere.

The duty radio announcer, Mike Smallwood, behaved commendably after such a dramatic announcement by saying, 'Don't panic folks – we will now continue with "Record Requests" . . .' The show must go on.

Jeremy and Martyn looked at each other and said, 'This is it.' Tony said he had better get off home to Government House – if he had had any knowledge that anything was going on he did not show it; he seemed as shocked as we were. Now it is all suddenly, brilliantly clear why during the past week we have had overflying of the Falklands by Argentine aircraft. I think the last one was on Martyn's eighteenth birthday a couple of days ago on 29 March. At about 8.30 that evening when we were down at the 'Globe' with him for a drink, what sounded like a C-130 Hercules flew very low over Stanley after being reported over the settlements at Johnson Harbour, Green Patch and Port Louis. The Royal Research Ship *John Biscoe* was also buzzed by a very low-flying C-130 a few days ago while bringing the new Naval Party 8901 of Royal Marines down from Montevideo to Stanley. Apparently the marines' response was to line the afterdeck with backs towards the aircraft, then on the appropriate command they all bent forward and lowered their trousers in salute.

The boys got rapidly into their combat gear and away to the Drill Hall.

2130 Hours

Boys home for rations to last them for the night. Tea and sandwiches. The terrible reality of the situation has now hit us – they are going off to fight alongside the Royal Marines of NP 8901. A very swift farewell; God Bless and Good Luck said with a depth of sincerity which we hope we will never have to use again. Neither we nor they have any idea of what is about to happen. Ileen found it very heavy going but held out well. After they had gone Phyllis summed up the situation by saying that we were all now in the hands of God, and suggested that we all said a little prayer, which we did in the sitting-room. It was a spontaneous idea which took care of the situation most admirably.

2230 Hours

Ian announced that, Argies or no Argies, he was going to bed, and asked Phyllis to put out the light when she went downstairs – absolutely unflappable. Pam and John thought they would lie down for a while. Ileen, Anya and Tyssen also went off to bed; they were, I think, almost too dazed to grasp the full reality of what is happening.

Dave Emsley took over from Mike Smallwood on the radio and continued playing records as if all was normal – he has a most reassuring voice. There are occasional short notices from Government House to say that the position remains unchanged. The invasion will begin at dawn.

I decided to doze on the settee in the sitting-room.

Friday 2 April – Day One

0000 Hours

Stood on the steps outside the front porch having a cigarette. Magnificent night; no wind; completely cloudless; everything perfectly still; thousands of stars; complete tranquillity. This terrible situation seems all so unreal. Phyllis and Pamela pop down occasionally for cups of tea; there is absolutely nothing we can do, so we sit and talk. Towards 1 o'clock we had a bit of excitement when we thought we heard an aircraft overhead, so all went outside to look, but it turned out to be John's powerful snores from the bedroom above – remarkably like the drone of a C-130.

0315 Hours

Terry (Ileen's brother) arrived in full uniform. Because of events he has been reinstated as Superintendent of Police from which he has not long been retired. He was a bit muddy about the feet and trouser legs as he had been burying documents with Ronnie Lamb, the present Chief of Police. It must have been quite an amusing sight – Terry and Ronnie digging while Mrs Lamb stood by, holding a candle. Rather like a scene from *The Bodysnatchers*. After some tea and a clean-up Terry went off back to the station.

0430 Hours

The Governor, Rex Hunt, reports on the radio that an invasion at dawn is inevitable. The President of the United States has spoken on the telephone to the President of Argentina offering the services of Vice-President Bush to visit Buenos Aires for talks on finding a peaceful way of settling the dispute, but the offer has been refused. The United Nations Security Council is to meet. The Governor has no option but to declare an official state of emergency. In no way can anyone prevent what is about to happen. Government House is now permanently linked up to the broadcasting studio so that we can have first-hand information.

0540 Hours

The Governor reports that Argentine landing craft are entering the Narrows.

0545 Hours

First explosions and firing are heard just as dawn is breaking. Very, very loud in the still morning air – very close as well.

0600 Hours

Heavy firing from both ends of town. Besides the rifle and machine-guns there is some much heavier rapid stuff; sounds like cannons – the modern automatic sort, not the old-fashioned ones. Also some loud crumps which must be mortars.

0630 Hours

Everyone up and at the front bedroom windows to see what is going on. A patrol of Royal Marines has just passed along opposite the house, keeping low on the ground past the Fire Station, then – joined by another group a few yards up the road who appeared from the end of King Street at high speed – vaulted the fence into St Mary's Paddock and opened fire up King Street, a pitched battle which lasted for quite a few minutes. It was just like watching a film. We could not believe that there it was happening in front of us just on the other side of the road.

0700 Hours

It's now light enough to make out a Type 42 destroyer steaming up and down off the lighthouse, and an aircraft carrier is in Port William. Still heavy firing from most parts of town.

0800 Hours

Breakfast as usual, though somewhat hurried as we are getting more than a little worried about all this firing; if someone puts a burst through the house it could be devastating. We are also dreadfully worried about the boys, though no one is actually saying so. An awful lot of fighting seems to be going on all around us.

0830 Hours

Patrick Watts is holding out over at the broadcasting studio, doing a superb job. People are now phoning in from various parts of the town with reports of what is happening, which Patrick is putting straight through the radio. Alistair Greeves is just on the line to say that although he and his family are now having to spend most of the time lying on the floor, they can see tracked armoured personnel carriers coming up the road from the airport, six or seven of them.

0840 Hours

Ally Greeves still reporting from beneath his table says that APCs have opened fire; something big has just gone through the roof of the Ionospheric Station. Helicopters are overhead; the airport appears to have been taken. Other reports from folk in that area say that houses are being hit by shrapnel and cannon fire. Tom Davies has just come on to say a shell through his roof has burst the water supply tank making things rather messy as the water is pouring through his ceiling.

0900 Hours

Governor Hunt phones in to say that Government House is under heavy fire from all sides. We can hear it from here as it's only just up the road. There sounds to be a right old scrap going on. The Royal Marines and FIDF must still be holding out. Things are now very noisy indeed.

0930 Hours

Speaking again on the radio directly from Government House the governor says that they are now under increasingly heavy fire. He will never surrender to any bloody Argies! Whatever the outcome of this lot he seems to be going to conclude things in the proper manner and with dignity.

0945 Hours

The huge armoured personnel carriers have reached Government House; in no way can the Royal Marines and FIDF hold out against their cannons; they would blast the place off the face of the earth in a few minutes. The Governor says he will shortly have to call for truce and discussion with the Argentines. Calls up Vice-Comodoro Hector Gilobert of the Argentine Air Force who manages the LADE airline in Stanley, who goes to Government House; then after a short while walks up road towards Town Hall with Dick Baker, our Chief Secretary, carrying a white flag. A few shots from the Argentines at them, but soon stopped. Meanwhile efforts are being made to contact the senior officer of the invaders via the radio. This is dramatic and absolutely fantastic, as we can hear all that is taking place over the radio. Orders in Spanish and heavily accented English coming through, so they must now be in the broadcasting studio.

1000 Hours

Confirmed that the APCs are in the town, some at Government House. Estimated 200 troops surrounding the place with hundreds more on the roads leading up to town. It is incredible that they have to bring their army and navy to take a town of only 1,200 people – this includes babies, schoolchildren and the old folk. It's like using a sledgehammer to crack a walnut. Ridiculous, callous and inhuman.

The Governor has now met the commander of the Argentines and refused to shake hands with him, which the commander said was discourteous, to which Rex Hunt replied that it was discourteous of him to invade his country.

The broadcasting studio is now in Argentine hands; Patrick Watts has just said, 'No, I don't do anything until you take that gun out of my back.' He deserves a medal. Throughout the night and this morning he has kept up a running commentary from the studio until now being forced away from his microphone at gunpoint.

1017 Hours

The Argentine national anthem has been played over the radio. It now seems final. The Argentines have got us. The boys have just arrived back at the house under armed escort of Argentine commandos – the Buzos Tácticos – who have blackened faces and woollen hats, and are carrying silenced sub-machine-guns. The thankfulness is hard to express; all we can do is to let out a long sigh of relief, and light up a cigarette. Thank God they are safe.

1030 Hours

The Argentine flag is flying over Government House. Constant Argentine military band music being played over the radio; then within half an hour four edicts or communiqués broadcast, each preceded by a barrage of Spanish and their national anthem, which seems to go on for ever – each time we think it has stopped they start up again with a few more verses (the pause seems to be for the musicians to regain their breath). The edicts are read first in Spanish then in English, each one complete with full titles and address. Very time-consuming; the frills are the same on each so will only use them on the first one.

ARGENTINE REPUBLIC

MALVINAS OPERATION THEATRE COMMAND
COMMUNIQUE No. 1

The Commander of the MALVINAS OPERATION THEATRE, performing his duties as ordered by the Argentine Government, materialises heretofore the historic continuity of Argentine Sovereignty over the Islas Malvinas.

At this highly important moment for all of us, it is my pleasure to greet the people of the Malvinas and exhort you to co-operate with the new authorities by complying with all of the instructions that will be given through oral and written communiqués, in order to facilitate the normal life of the entire population.

ISLAS MALVINAS 02 Abril 1982

OSVALDO JORGE GARCIA

General de División.

Comandante del Teatro de Operaciones

MALVINAS

Copy: ESTEBAN ALBERTO SOLIS
Coronel
Jefe Departamento Asuntos Civiles
Cd. TOM.

COMMUNIQUE No. 2
RELIEF OF AUTHORITIES

As of now, the colonial and military authorities of the British Government are effectively relieved of their charges, and shall be sent back to their country today, with their families and personal effects.

Furthermore, it is hereby made known that General of División OSVALDO JORGE GARCIA, on behalf of the Argentine Government, is taking power of the Government of the ISLAS MALVINAS, GEORGIAS del SUR and SANDWICH del SUR.

COMMUNIQUE No. 3
INSTRUCTIONS FOR THE POPULATION

As a consequence of all the necessary actions taken, and in order to ensure the safety of the population, all people are to remain at their homes until further notice. New instructions will be issued.

The population must bear in mind that, in order to ensure the fulfilment of these instructions, military troops shall arrest all people found outside their homes.

To avoid inconvenience and personal misfortunes, people are to abide by the following:

1. Should some serious problem arise and people wish to make it known to the Military Authorities, a white piece of cloth is to be placed outside the door. Military patrols will visit the house so as to be informed and provide a solution.
2. All schools, shops, stores, banks, pubs and Clubs are to remain closed until further notice.
3. All infringements shall be treated according to what is stated in EDICT No. 1
4. All further instructions shall be released through the local broadcasting station which shall remain in permanent operation.

COMMUNIQUE No. 4
GUARANTEES

The Governor of the ISLAS MALVINAS, GEORGIAS del SUR, and SANDWICH del SUR, General of División OSVALDO JORGE GARCIA, notifies the population that –

Faithfully upholding the principles stated in the National Constitution and in accordance with the customs and traditions of the Argentine people, he guarantees:

1. The continuity of the way of life of the people of the Islands.
2. Freedom of worship.
3. Respect for private property.
4. Freedom of labour.
5. Freedom to enter, leave, or remain in the Islands.
6. Improvement of the population's standard of living.
7. Normal supply situation.
8. Health assistance.
9. Normal functioning of essential public services.

Furthermore, the population is exhorted to continue normally with their activities, as part of the moment in which this will be stated, with the support of the Argentine Government, in an atmosphere of peace, order, and harmony.

Our immediate comment is, what a load of horse manure, but we are now under a military regime. The Union Jack, the Falkland Islands Government, along with everything of which we were so proud an hour ago, have now been heaved out of the window. When the new government says jump we have to jump – but not too quickly . . .

1130 Hours

Outside on the streets armoured personnel carriers, armoured cars and DUKWs (amphibious landing vehicles) are rushing and roaring about all over the place, knocking down fences, breaking up the roads; troops and guns are everywhere. It's like a living nightmare. From the BBC in London we hear that they think the Falklands may have been invaded. Words fail us – this is the age of the train, rockets to the moon, computers and microchips and they only *think* that the Falklands *may* have been invaded. God help us all.

1200 Hours

Decided to try out the white-flag routine as instructed in Communiqué No 3, as someone has to go outside to get some more fuel and to collect the bread. Placing the cloth outside the door had no effect at all, so we waved it, the only response being that the Argentine soldiers waved back, smiled and went on their way. We then ventured out on to the road in order to speak with some of them, which we eventually did, but they had no idea of what the white-cloth business was all about. No one had told them; they assumed that we were just being friendly. So, we tied a tea towel to a bit of stick, then – holding it high – set off among the enemy to the Upland Goose Hotel for the bread. Quite a number of other people had met with the same white-cloth ignorance problem among the soldiers, so they were now doing the same as us. It provided a welcome bit of light relief to wave to each other with the improvised flags. The soldiers looked on curiously, wondering what it was all about. There seems to be a distinct lack of passing on information in their army. The day remains fine; the troops sit along the roadsides smoking and eating from sort of ration packs. They all seem a bit deflated; they have taken Port Stanley – now what next? No one within their set-up seems to know.

There appear to be two distinct types of troops. One group, who seem to be Special Forces known as Buzos Tácticos, are well trained, efficient and tough. The other lot are much younger, just plain soldiers. Their officers seem very important and pleased with themselves – strutting along taking photographs, shouting orders and waving their hands about . . . (perhaps if we were to tie their hands up they would be unable to speak). Their equipment is impressive, most of it fairly new. Tyssen is having a great time identifying it all: Land-Rover-type vehicles made by Mercedes; Panhard armoured cars from Belgium; FAL rifles also from Belgium; the APCs and helicopters from the USA; some other sort of helicopters which I think are French; the Type 42 destroyers from England; and, somewhat ironically, their aircraft carrier which was formerly HMS *Venerable* of the Royal Navy. They don't seem to have much, if any, home produce at all. They have done their military shopping carefully and wisely from England and a number of our old friends. Surely someone must have seen this invasion being built up. It's not a small snatch-and-run raid – they have thrown their entire military might against the Falklands. Troops and equipment now streaming ashore. Aircraft are landing and taking off every few minutes. Again it's ironic: American C-130s; Dutch F-28s and F-27s with Rolls-Royce engines. No home-grown stuff.

1300 Hours

There may be a dusk curfew; details later. News from the BBC will no longer be broadcast from the radio station. Some of the Falkland Government vehicles have been taken over by the Argentines. Our government vehicles are easily identifiable by the letters PATA (Plant and Transport Authority) painted on the doors in black on a yellow background. Young Robert Macaskill has arrived very quickly with his government Land Rover and Anya is helping him to do a swift repaint job on the doors as discreetly as possible.

1330 Hours

Tried to get some sleep or rest, but kept awake by constant air activity, then by shouting and crashing as two APCs tried to pass one another in front of the house, tearing up the kerbstone and knocking down the playing-field fence. Absolutely ridiculous of them to have tried; our road is not even wide enough for two Land Rovers to pass. They gave up trying, backed off, dragged the telephone wires down with their aerials and went on their way. The commanders of these APCs seem to consider themselves an élite unit as some have colourful pennants flying from the aerials. Others – I have seen two – have a sort of legionnaires' standard, topped with what looks like a silver eagle, from which hangs a banner in their national colours of blue and white. All very dashing and splendid but they spoil the effect by allowing their drivers to behave in a most irresponsible manner.

I am jotting down these notes as things occur during the day, but it is all so bewildering that it is a job to think straight. It must be the tension combined with lack of sleep. All of us must snatch an hour whatever happens.

1600 Hours

We have managed a doze and feel a bit better. Tony Hunt has arrived to make a very quick farewell as he is off in a few minutes to the airport with his parents. Farewells are normally unpleasant affairs but this one seemed even more difficult, so we all got it over with as swiftly as possible.

1615 Hours

An event which we may never see again – Don Bonner driving the GH car with flag flying, taking HE and Mrs Hunt to the airport. The Governor is leaving his colony with dignity, dressed in full uniform with plumed hat and medals (how he has managed to get away with that and flying the Union Jack on the front of the car is hard to imagine). It will remind the Argentines that there are certain things which an Englishman does, no matter what the circumstances.

They stopped at the Governor's Assistant Mike Growcott's house for a few moments to say farewell to them and to a number of local people who happened to be there at the time; then off to the airport where, we have since heard, the Argentines removed the Governor's medals. It was the final insult on their part – a spiteful gesture but presumably all that they could do to show their anger at him having made his departure from Stanley with credit and dignity.

1700 Hours

An announcement by the military government that all wives of Royal Marines of Naval Party 8901 are to assemble outside the Secretariat with their luggage ready to be transported to the airport. They make it sound as if they are shifting cattle. We carried Cheryl Black's bags across for her, as we are uncertain if we are allowed to drive or not – no one seems to know the rules now. Felt dreadfully sad for poor Cheryl and the other wives, herded together alongside their luggage like refugees, outside the Secretariat, with armed soldiers ordering them about. They last saw their husbands earlier in the day being held under arrest in the paddock at Government House. It is still not entirely clear if they will be travelling together or flown out on separate aircraft.

It was here for the first time that I turned and saw in the pale evening sunlight the Argentine flag flying from the mast at Government House. I really felt physically sick and emotionally drained; the cold light of awful reality set in.

The evening passed in a daze; we are all too stunned with shock and lack of sleep to do anything worthwhile.

Saturday 3 April – Day Two

A dull, cold, grey day with low cloud; very little wind but occasional misty showers.

This has all been too much for Ileen to take; we went along to the hospital this morning where it was suggested that she should be admitted for a while. We both agreed that this was the most obvious and sensible thing to do as conditions during the next few days are hardly likely to be very pleasant. Thankfully Phyllis and Ian are with us. During the past forty-eight hours – which now seem like weeks – they have become very much part of our family, and have happily agreed to give us a hand in running the house.

John and Pamela, being regarded as foreign journalists, were hurriedly flown out this afternoon. A super couple, really great people to share an invasion with. No panic or fuss, although we did admit over breakfast this morning how absolutely stupid we had all been yesterday in watching events from the bedroom windows, but felt a bit better after finding that most of the town had been doing the same thing.

Claudette Mozley told me the most lovely story about her part in the activities of last night. She was in her front porch watching at dawn when she saw a Royal Marine crawling about in the garden, so she called out, 'Is that you, Figgy? Would you like some coffee?' To which he replied, 'Get on the bloody floor you silly bitch, there's an invasion on.' That, I think, sums up the situation perfectly.

The foreign Press, mainly Latin American, were flown in at about lunchtime for a great propaganda exercise. There must have been forty or fifty of them all eager for reaction and stories, but I don't think that they got much out of the locals. The Argentine troops don't look quite so enchanted today, now that there has been a change in the weather. As the Press were wandering about all over the place taking photographs it seemed too good an opportunity to miss, so Tyssen and I joined in with them. It was exceedingly unpleasant taking photographs of jubilant Argentines, but as this is history in the making it is important to record as much of it as possible. Some incredible sights: armoured vehicles from one end of John Street to the other; St Mary's Walk packed full with amphibious landing vehicles; everywhere else cluttered with the impedimenta of the invader.

From the BBC news, which we now have to find on our own radios instead of having it relayed via the FI broadcasting station, we learn that Britain now has definite confirmation of the Argentine invasion. The first indications of it were apparently passed on from a ham radio operator who had been in touch with someone yesterday in one of the settlements near Stanley. We think that it may have been Bobby McLeod at Goose Green.

Early this evening the APCs and the DUKWs were driven into the sea from the slipway at the Falkland Islands Government Air Service Beaver Seaplane Hangar, a mile or so westwards from the centre of Stanley, from where they drove down the harbour to the Falkland Islands Company's East Jetty where the Argentine naval landing ship, *Cabo San Antonio*, has come alongside with her bow doors open. They drove into the ship, presumably to be taken back to Argentina. Attempts had been made during the day to take the APCs around to the naval fuel depot on the opposite side of the harbour, but they ran into trouble on the soft ground near Fairy Cove, sinking right into the peat, resulting in some very complicated recovery operations. They are really far too heavy and unsuitable for the terrain of the Falklands.

Went along to see Ileen at the hospital in the evening, with the boys and Anya. It seemed so unreal on the way home walking across the children's playing field with armed troops patrolling the streets and many camped alongside their lorries, huddled round their little fires for the night. No one attempted to stop us. The situation is very confused. So are we.

Some of the older folk in the town are just unable to grasp what is happening. Yesterday morning Ronnie Lamb, the police chief, had to get his officers to rescue old Henry Halliday from the front road, as he had set off for work as usual, through the main part of the invasion, just after seven.

Dear old Mabel Neilson went along to the post office as she normally does on Fridays to collect her old age pension, and elbowed the rather bewildered troops out of the way as they tried to prevent her going in. The Governor only said there was going to be an invasion; he didn't say anything about pensions not being paid out.

All sections of the Falkland Islands Defence Force had been deployed at 2130 hours, 1 April, armed with SLR rifles, and SMG and .762 GPM guns, with instructions to return to headquarters at 0530 hours next morning (excluding the machine-gun units and the Islander aircraft guard, who were to remain in position).

Lack of radios seriously impeded communication between the FIDF and the Royal Marines. At times there was the grave risk of the two forces opening fire on each other.

By 1100 hours on 2 April nearly all FIDF members had returned to the headquarters under their own steam or with Argentine military escort. At that time a captain of the Argentine Army arrived with Lt Pat Peck. The captain wished everyone Good Morning and congratulated them on a good fight. Members were then taken to their homes under Argentine military escort. Jim Fairfield, an ex-Royal Marine on the reserve list, had reported directly to Government House for duty with NP 8901 the previous day. He was very lucky not to have been held and shipped out with the rest of the marines – fortunately during the fighting he had lost his beret and so was not identifiable and was taken to be an FIDF member.

Sunday 4 April – Day Three

Another coldish, overcast, grey day with hardly any wind.

This is not really much of an entry in the diary as I am too tired to write. I also find it difficult to recall events to set them down in their proper order. It's been a quiet day wondering what is going to happen next. The whole world seems to be up in arms about Argentina's completely unwarranted military invasion, while here in Stanley after seventy-two hours of shock and disruption everyone is still absolutely stunned by events. Our entire world, life-style – everything – has been completely capsized.

There are still some press and television people wandering about the streets. Constant air activity bringing in many more troops. I tried to phone England but the military say it is not possible. We went to Mass in the morning; terrible air of unrest; lots of Argentine troops present. Many people are leaving town by Land Rover for the Camp settlements. There are those who say that they shouldn't, but who can blame them? This is a time when everyone reacts in their own different way to what is happening.

I spent part of the day burning up papers and documents which I had collected during my service as an elected member of the Falkland Islands Executive and Legislative Councils – nothing really incriminating but certainly not the sort of thing which should be allowed to fall into Argentine hands. I also put our large Union Jacks in a place of safety where hopefully they will not be found. With things as they are at the moment, though, it seems a bit doubtful if we will ever need them again here. The British Government is outraged at the invasion, but will it respond positively to getting the Argentines out of here? The political ball is now firmly back in their court.

The situation now seems to be sufficiently grave to justify the forceful removal of the padlock on our electricity meter in the house so that we can recycle a single 50p piece. If they issue any more silly edicts about having to stay indoors it may become difficult to obtain more 50p pieces should we run out.

The congregation at the evening service in the cathedral sang 'Auld Lang Syne' at the close, which was very, very moving according to those who were there.

Monday 5 April – Day Four

Started the day with another edict broadcast by our new military government; with immediate effect all vehicles will drive on the right – so much for preserving our way of life. Water supplies restored to the town during the morning. The post office has now been closed until further notice. Cable & Wireless open for distress cables only – this is a bit ironic as we are all in distress. However managed to send off – or hand in – a cable for home assuring them that we are at least alive and healthy. Two armed guards on duty at the counter aged about eighteen, very dirty and fed up; gave one a cigarette. The two girls on duty, Julia and Suzie, were as efficient and cheerful as ever, which seemed to puzzle the guards a bit – but it was sad to see them at work facing two rifle barrels. Julie is only fifteen.

The intensity of military activity seems to be lessening slightly in the town. Now they have got here they are not entirely certain what to do. The majority of the troops look cold, hungry, dejected and somewhat bewildered. The Type 42 frigate, presumably the *Hercules*, has moved round into Port William, anchoring off Yorke Bay. At midday five Mirage fighters with drop tanks made a spectacular display over the town for ten minutes, after which they headed off west home again. Fortunately we must be almost at the extreme limit of their range.

Our only source of news is the BBC, so we now all cluster every hour around the radio on the kitchen table. Conditions are a bit crackly but we were able to hear that the first ships of the Prime Minister's Task Force have sailed for the Falklands; thank God someone has stirred off their backsides at last in a positive response to the invasion. The speed with which this force has been assembled is absolutely incredible. We also heard that Lord Carrington has resigned, along with Richard Luce and someone else. It was also reported that Governor Hunt and the members of NP 8901 arrived at Brize Norton from Montevideo by VC-10.

All the BBC news programmes are now devoted to the Falklands.

Yet another edict issued later in the day. Stanley is now to be known as Puerto Rivero. This is named after one Antonio Rivero who was the ringleader of the Port Louis Murderers in 1833, a gaucho who murdered the senior British resident, Capt Matthew Brisbane, along with several others at the then principal settlement of the Falklands.

Made a couple of visits to the hospital during the day to see Ileen. She seems a little brighter but the large numbers of Argentine soldiers milling about in the building do not help matters. Everywhere there are now armed men. Dozens of vehicles. Even the air smells different, with exhaust fumes and the smoke of foreign cigarettes. The town has been raped brutally and without warning, leaving everyone in a deep state of shock. It's going to be a long time before the awful reality of what has happened sinks in with some people. Many are utterly confused by this sudden transition from tranquillity to military occupation. Still, we must be thankful that we are all still alive.

Tuesday 6 April – Day Five

Grey, cold day with low cloud. Weather really broke after lunch, Force 5 wind from north-east with rain, continuing into night which was wet and windy. All very unpleasant for the Argentines, especially as they have had some magnificent weather since their arrival, which has given them a completely false idea of what the weather is generally like at this time of the year. It has surprised us as well. The high wind is causing some splendid problems among the Argentines who are issued with voluminous waterproof capes or ponchos which the wind gets under, causing them to blow up over their heads, rendering them temporarily blind and completely out of control – so much so that a couple of them have accidently fired their rifles while trying to disentangle themselves. (It would be safer for us and for them if they were to put their weapons down before attempting their unwrapping operations.) Living in the wet is taking some of the shine off the recovery of their beloved Malvinas. Serves them right.

During last night a frigate and supply ship moved into the harbour. The supply ship – of about 7,000 tons – is moored alongside the Camber fuel depot for the Royal Navy on the north side of Stanley Harbour. It is not possible to get her name yet. One has to be very careful about using binoculars for such things, or in fact anything nowadays. We have an excellent view across the harbour from the upstairs front-bedroom windows. By standing fairly well back in the room and looking with binoculars through the lace curtains it is possible to get a pretty good general picture of what is going on, but the curtains make it impossible to get any great detail. With so many Argentine troops on the streets now it pays to be very wary about doing things, as we are all obviously being kept under careful watch. The frigate is anchored well down the harbour opposite the Narrows – the harbour entrance. I think she is either the *Drummond* or *Granville* – French-built, and armed with Exocets and a single gun in a turret on the foredeck.

Announcement on radio at 10 o'clock this morning that owing to lack of space there would be no mail for the inhabitants (that's presumably us) on today's incoming LADE flight. Patrick Watts thoughtfully followed this announcement by playing 'When the Circus Came to Town'. We are now informed that the post office is again open for business. Rosettes in the Argentine colours are nailed up outside. Mail will be accepted for overseas bearing the usual Falkland Islands stamps, which are crossed through with a ball-point pen and a special Malvinas handstamp applied.

Today's lunch-time fly-past was at 12.15. Two Skyhawks did a couple of quick circuits of the town and harbour.

Very difficult to receive BBC lunch-time news; it seems to be being jammed.

Walked round town with Tyssen and the dog during the afternoon. Among a large crowd of Argentine senior officers coming out of the Upland Goose Hotel, all in splendid uniforms, was Vice-Comodoro Carlos Bloomer-Reeve – we had previously known him and his family during the time they were based in Stanley a few years ago when he was in charge of the LADE airline office. He recognised us, left the party and came over. It was a somewhat embarrassing meeting. In the uniformed circumstances I said, 'Hello, sir.' He replied, 'It was "Carlos" before, John. I'd like to keep it that way.' That broke the ice somewhat. To have adopted an aggressive or defiant attitude at this time would be asking for trouble. He then enquired how Ileen was, which caused more embarrassment, as I had to explain that the events of the last few days had done nothing to improve her condition. He then suggested that perhaps a visit by him might do some good. It was both a kind thought and Christian gesture but we declined the offer. Carlos seemed genuine enough: in fact I think he found the whole incident as embarrassing as I did. He said that only a few days beforehand he had been in Germany as the Argentine Defence Attaché in Bonn, then had been recalled quickly to Buenos Aires and told of his appointment in the Falklands. His family still remain in Germany. His position in the Falklands seems to be that of Chief Secretary in the new administration, where he will act as liaison officer between the civilian population and the military government. He has been promoted since his last stay here and is now a *Comodoro*, which I think is the Argentine Air Force equivalent of a full captain in our Royal Navy. His official title in the Falklands is *Secretario General.*

Tyssen and I continued our walk up towards Davis Street East to look at the damage caused by the shelling from the invading operation on Friday. There were a lot of bullet holes through the houses in that area. Big bullets – 30mm cannon by the look of it. The Radio and Space Ionospheric Observatory Station seems to have received a rocket through the east end of the roof, a big black hole surrounded by splatter marks. On the other side of the road in the 'White City'* most houses are like pepper pots with bullet holes everywhere, along with larger bits ripped out, presumably by cannon fire. The people up there must have had a very rough time of it.

There were quite a number of small two-man tents pitched in the paddocks alongside the Ionospheric Observatory; the wind had increased a fair bit by this time, causing the troops to have to fight hard to keep them pitched on the ground. This, combined with their waterproof capes blowing about over their heads, really was quite amusing, though we both thought it would be best if we didn't laugh. I took a couple of photographs discreetly, but was stopped by guards who told us that taking photographs was not permitted, so had to continue to take them with my camera sheltered under my shooting jacket as we walked along; not ideal conditions or weather but hope they come out. A smaller camera might be a better idea if there is another event of this kind, as this large Zenith I have at the moment gives me rather an ample-bosomed effect. There are now quite a lot of white-helmeted military police patrolling the town, who fortunately did not notice my unusual shape.

Home in time for tea about 4. Phyllis had cooked some scones, so after tea took some along to Ileen and gave her details of our afternoon's adventures. We left out some of the more military details. She seems to be fairly well sedated but unable to sleep properly. I am surprised they have not put her in a ward of her own for peace and quiet. The disturbance rate in this particular ward is very high, with lots of enthusiastic visitors full of good intentions, but they are really the last thing which Ileen wants.

At 7.20 this evening there was a special broadcast to the Falklands from London, with lots of reassuring messages and superb recordings of the departure from Portsmouth of the ships of the

* 'White City' is the name given to a row of white-painted prefabricated bungalows recently built to accommodate government and technical assistance personnel with their families employed on contract from the United Kingdom.

Task Force. Nothing like this has taken place since World War II. All England seems to have suddenly united with a common aim to free the Falklands; it brought tears to the eyes to listen to it.

Shortly afterwards on our local announcements there was a savage edict from the military government announcing that all ham radios and 2-metre transmissions were to cease forthwith. All such equipment owned by people in Stanley is to be handed in to the military, while people in the Camp are to dismantle their equipment, divide it into two lots, one of which is to be stored or buried 2 miles distant from the other. Any persons not complying absolutely with this edict will be liable to severe penalties under military law. This is a bad situation as it means that now all communication between Camp settlements is cut off, resulting in complete isolation from each other and from Stanley.

There was also an instruction that, as from now, all persons must carry identification documents.

Wednesday 7 April – Day Six

Last night's wind suddenly dropped away at about seven this morning, leaving a blood-red sky in the east. By 10 o'clock the wind had got up again to 30–35 knots from the north-west, increasing during the afternoon to something over 50 knots. This fine wind caused some serious disturbance among the military. The tents up at the Ionospheric Observatory blew down; then the huge Argentine flag hoisted on the pole outside the Secretariat flapped itself out of control, snapped the pole and flew off in great confusion down Ross Road, chased by anguished soldiers and watched by delighted locals. A large radar installation which the Argentines had set up on Canopus Hill near the airport also blew down. Out in Port William an Argentine supply vessel dragged its anchors, which then got tangled up with those of a Polish trawler anchored there. The wind is very much on our side.

Lots of air activity – C-130 Hercules and F-28s started to fly in at about a quarter to nine and continued throughout the day. They seem to be bringing in more infantry battalions, who are being tented up by the old army camp* near the FIGAS (Falkland Islands Government Air Service) hangar.

Went down to the police station this morning to renew 'white cards' in view of last night's announcement about carrying identity documents. There was a large notice on the inside door saying 'Keep Out' but the military policeman asked me to go in while he consulted his superiors. He was quite unaware of any instruction about identification documents and surprised to find it had been announced over the radio. He went off into the inner office of his chief, who moments later came out like a dose of salts and asked why I was in his outer office. When I said that I'd been asked to go in by the MP, he then had a go at him. The result was that I was told to

* The site used by the West Yorks Regiment, who were stationed at Stanley during the 1939–45 war.

go away and that they knew nothing about any such documents. Strange people.

The local gang in the Public Works Department are today employed painting white lines and arrows on the streets in an effort to assist us in driving on the other side of the road. The control of all public works is now under an Argentine colonel. Our lads in the dockyard seem quite enthusiastic about this painting idea as it provides great opportunities for creating traffic problems among the military vehicles, which go where directed in order not to upset the good work. I don't think the Argentine intention will be entirely successful as the local response is to drive in the middle of the road, causing confusion and pleading ignorance.

At 2 o'clock this afternoon the new Argentine governor was sworn in in the council chamber of the town hall. His title is Gen Mario B. Menendez, General de Brigada, Gobernador Militar. A large party of high-ranking military arrived during the morning for the occasion, after which they held a celebratory froth-up at the Upland Goose; fifteen military vehicles parked outside – record-breaking for Stanley. Some very elegant uniforms with gold braid, red tabs and hair cream. Mainly army and air force with very few naval officers present. One army bloke carried a fine stick with a great silver affair on one end; he must have been a sort of field marshal I suppose. Later in the afternoon a large group of them walked about the town surveying their capture. Ex-President Videla was among them, accompanied by Capt Goffoglio of the Argentine Navy, who looked the other way as they passed me. Perhaps he was a bit embarrassed after having stayed with us as a guest not long ago. He seems to be one of the main figures in the invasion arrangements. I remember that he had a most contented smile on his face at a dance in the town hall a couple of weeks ago on the evening that word first came through of the trouble with the scrap merchants on South Georgia. At that time he was in Stanley supposedly awaiting the arrival of one of the Argentine naval auxiliary supply vessels. He spent most of that evening dancing with a large blonde Argentine woman who had arrived to teach Spanish in the schools. By her attitude and manner she was also in on the South Georgia business.

About 4.30 this afternoon the masts of a large merchant ship were visible in Port William behind the Camber; about 12,000 tons.

At 5 o'clock Cable & Wireless opened a telephone link with England for two hours for personal calls – no press messages.

Lucky to get a brief call into Mrs Burden at Hamble to let Mum know all is as well as can be expected with us.

On the BBC news at 6 this evening we heard that as from 0400 hours on Monday 12 April a 200-mile zone would be established around the Falklands. Any Argentine ships found within this zone would be sunk.

The six Royal Marines who had evaded capture by the invasion forces and escaped out into the Camp have been found and were flown out last night. They had been kept at the police station and their guards collected their food from the hospital. This evening the guards turned up to collect the prisoners' supper as usual, plus four extra lots for themselves, and didn't mind having the pudding put on top of the dinners in the container, in their anxiety to get away quickly before anyone realised that the prisoners are no longer here. One interesting story going about today is that the marines were captured by an Argentine helicopter at the house of the Neil Watsons at Long Island, and as they departed one of the Argentine officers left his machine gun on the sofa in the house, so Neil had to go outside and wave the helicopter down to give it back.

The troops are very hungry and dispirited; one young Argentine soldier was picked up by the MPs off the street last night dragging his rifle along the road and howling his eyes out.

Went along to see Ileen this evening; she is still desperately in need of sleep and peace and quiet, so didn't stay overlong. It was while we were there that we picked up the story about the prisoners' food.

Today the chief of the Argentine Air Force medical section signed the following document at the hospital.

> I, BRIGADIER ENRIQUE IRRGANG, Director General de Sanidad Fuerza Aérea, hereby declare that I and all my Medical Staff will work under the terms of the GENEVA CONVENTION governing medical treatment and care.
>
> I note that war has not formally been declared, but nevertheless accept these conventions.
>
> 7 April 1982 Signed ......
> King Edward Memorial Hospital

Handwritten at the bottom of the document was the statement, 'I also accept the above declaration', signed by Dr D. Haynes, the Senior Medical Officer.

The town street lights were put off for the early part of the evening but came on again later. C-130 Hercules were still flying in and out when we turned into bed at 10 o'clock.

Thursday 8 April – Day Seven

Windy but warm and sunny.

Maundy Thursday. I never thought that we would see one under such circumstances – invaded and occupied by a foreign power, shot at and under military rule, a British Task Force sailing to our assistance and Ileen in hospital. Still, we are all, thank God, alive and our home is undamaged; things could have been a lot more unpleasant. And I suppose that there are many people worse off than we are.

Not a particularly exciting or eventful day. A lot of troops about in the streets, some still asking for food. The remains of the broken flag-pole still lie forlornly outside the Secretariat; hopefully they will not bother to replace it, but it would be nice if they cleared up their wreckage.

Plenty of heavy aircraft coming and going all day, mainly Hercules and F-28s, but this afternoon I noticed one four-engined, turbo-prop airliner finished in blue, silver and white – possibly some sort of transport for senior officers; may have been a Lockheed Electra.

Went to Holy Thursday Service of Watching in the chapel; a time for thought and reflection. Several Argentine soldiers there; one asked for Monsignor's blessing. I suppose that now when writing up this diary there is no longer any need to specify Argentine soldiers or forces; they are all bloody Argentines – we haven't got any others . . . yet.

Friday 9 April – Day Eight

Although it is now well into our autumn we have had a superb summer's day, which unfortunately collapsed into a strong north-west wind with rain at nightfall; by 10.30 this evening we were in for a really rough night.

Like the weather the military activity during the day started in a tranquil manner but increased rapidly. About 9 o'clock this morning an F-28 aircraft flew in and was off again three-quarters of an hour later. During its stay a Chinook helicopter flew very low up the harbour from Moody Brook – where we presume the Argentine headquarters are – to the airport. It's said that one of their senior generals returned to Buenos Aires on the F-28 for talks with the US Ambassador, Haig, who we understand from the BBC is on his way to Buenos Aires for talks with the Argentine Government.

At 11 o'clock a frigate of the Drummond type anchored in the harbour. No troops in sight anywhere; the town is absolutely still. Our lunchtime fly-pasts resumed today: three Mirages at 12.15 and two at 12.30. Another cargo ship in Port William in the early afternoon, and a ship with tall mast steaming north at about 20 knots some 3 miles off the lighthouse. This I think was the Argentine ice-breaker *Almirante Irizar*, as she anchored in Port William between 3 and 4 o'clock, after which there was constant air activity by helicopters flying with stores between her and Moody Brook. Two Chinooks flew from the airfield to Moody Brook at 2.20. Then two F-28s and a Lockheed Electra took off between 2.30 and 2.40. From 3 o'clock onwards F-28s and C-130s were arriving and departing very frequently. This has been the heaviest air activity since the invasion day. They were still coming and going at 10.30 this evening. The approach of the Task Force seems to have livened them up a bit. A lot more troops arriving accompanied by Panhard armoured cars which sound as though they have two-stroke engines, very tinny and noisy. They also have long radio aerials which get caught up with the telephone wires. The Argentine navy personnel are driving about in some new British Land Rover long-wheel-base vehicles, while the army are getting in large numbers of superb Mercedes Benz Land-Rover-type vehicles, all apparently brand new. The weakness of the Argentine forces seems to lie in the men, not their equipment. The majority of the troops still appear bewildered, cold and hungry, yet certain small sections seem to have far better standards and morale.

An Argentine cargo vessel which arrived last night sailed during the day, as did the *Isla del Estados* naval auxiliary supply ship which had been moored alongside the Camber all night. There is so much coming and going of shipping nowadays that it is a job to keep track of it all.

The BBC news at 5 o'clock this evening was interesting. Still reports of the Argentine aircraft carrier *Veinticinco de Mayo* being trapped in harbour by the presence of British nuclear submarines. Ambassador Haig is impressed by the firm attitude of Her Majesty's Government. Military reservists being called up in Argentina. President Galtieri says there may be a war!! Mention was also made of a letter received in London from the Falklands signed by several people, including the Chief Constable, saying that they wished for a ship to be sent to evacuate the civilian population. Governor Hunt has apparently stated that 90 per cent of the Islanders wish to stay, and it is noticeable that the letter did not include the signatures of any of the elected members of the government here. We have heard talk of this letter, but no one seems to have actually seen it or to know who has signed it. Hope the community is not going to split into sections acting independently for their own safety. Now is a time for unity not fragmentation.

On the local news was a call for volunteers to man the fire brigade, so we all joined up. From the military authorities we had instructions that tomorrow all 2-metre and ham radio equipment is to be handed into the military; anything capable of transmitting is to be given in. Again notice was given that persons outside Stanley should dismantle their sets, with the valves to be placed at least 1 mile from the set. I don't think that many people have valves nowadays, but it means, sadly, that we will have to part with our faithful old Eddystone set, which came from a whale-catcher at South Georgia years ago. When all else failed we could always rely on the Eddystone to keep us in touch.

Visited Ileen before the Good Friday service which as usual

commenced at 3 o'clock. She is really no better for her stay in hospital; she would have got more rest and peace and quiet at home. The hospital has unfortunately ended up like a railway station, with seemingly no attempt to control the number of visitors. Children are running about whooping and shouting; it's not unlike a social centre. Goodness knows what's happened to the organisation. They seem to have lost control of discipline and routine. The strong Argentine military presence in the hospital does not help Ileen, or any of the other patients for that matter.

We all made a special effort to dress properly for the service; in no way are we going to allow the present circumstances to interfere with our standards. We will carry on as normal and maintain our usual family way of life. The Argentines may be here in large numbers but they are not going to influence the conduct and way of life of the Smiths. Life at Sparrow Hawk House will continue as normally as possible.

When going home from church noticed that troops had pitched tents down in the garden of Gilbert House on the waterfront in the dockyard. I have no idea why it has its present name. It started out life at the turn of the century as the Victoria Cottage Hospital. I believe that Capt Goffoglio is now in residence.

Heard Pamela Reid in an interview on the radio speaking from Comodoro Rivadavia.* She seemed quiet and passive; possibly she regrets having taken Argentine nationality.

Lots of lights on at the new government school hostel again this evening. It was recently built to accommodate 80/100 children from the Camp settlements who were intended to come into Stanley for their education. The method and quality of its construction has been the cause of some lively comment during the past four months: it has never served its intended purpose. The Argentines seem to be moving in. There are machine-gun emplacements being set up on the roof. With any luck it will collapse, as the building was condemned by the Public Works Department as being unsafe a few weeks ago.

* Pamela, a Falkland Islander, married an Argentine who has lived in the Falklands for many years. She left with her family shortly after the invasion. Her husband, Reynold, is still here.

Saturday 10 April – Day Nine

Cold clear morning; wind from north, Force 4.

There has been lots of air activity throughout the night, almost non-stop. At 8 this morning the *Isla del Estados* arrived back in harbour to FIC jetty. No sign of the *Almirante Irizar* in Port William; only one lot of masts visible now. Considerable helicopter movements up and down harbour; mainly airport to Moody Brook, presumably ferrying equipment which is being flown in from the mainland.

Encouraging 9 o'clock news again this morning. All EEC countries to ban Argentine imports. They all also support the UN motion instructing Argentina to withdraw her forces from the Falklands. Russia says that Britain should not have sent the Task Force.

Just after breakfast saw a great number of newly arrived and terribly keen soldiers moving towards Ross Road from the Drill Hall. They were all very alert, but nothing was happening, which seemed a bit of a let-down for them.

Tyssen off to schoolteachers' John and Anne Peatfields' home for lessons, picked up by car. Anya off to work at the hospital again.

Aircraft arriving all day. Hundreds of troops being brought in along with more vehicles, armoured cars, pack howitzers and wombat guns. Goodness knows where they are putting everything; neither the equipment nor the troops can be accommodated under cover because there are just not enough buildings in Stanley to cope. Things will be all right until the weather breaks, then both men and equipment are in for a rough time.

Walked up the road with Reynold Reid who was very depressed. The great Argentine take-over and victory has not turned out as he would have wished it; the rejoicing and liberation of the people does not seem to have happened. I also think that now that they are here in force, Reynold finds himself a very small fish in a very large pond.

People must have been avoiding him as he thanked me for talking with him, which was rather embarrassing.

Took down the rifles and pistols from the study walls this morning, ready for handing in after lunch with the Eddystone radio transmitter. Rather a sad occasion as we have built the collection up over a long period of time; each one has its own particular story attached to it. Painted my name in large letters on the stocks in the hope that one day we may get them back. The study looks very bare now. We had an impressive display – seven rifles and two pistols plus assorted ammunition; hope they don't want to take in the bayonets and the swords.

Carted everything down to the town hall after lunch with the aid of the boys, only to find that they didn't want firearms today – only radios. Seems an odd sort of way to do things – I would have given priority to getting in the firearms. There are lots of enthusiastic and extremely good shots here in the town who would not need much encouragement to take advantage of the hundreds, if not thousands, of excellent targets now available. Fortunately the self-control of everyone is nothing short of remarkable. The collection of the radios is all very proper with receipts being given, and progress is slow as there are only a few Argentines who can speak English. These seem to be very young lads about seventeen or eighteen – enlisted straight from school I suppose. Everyone in Stanley seems to have responded with great vigour to the instruction about handing in radio gear. Great piles of old junk are being carted in by folks; some of it must have broken down years ago but the idea today is to keep the Argentines busy documenting and labelling each piece. It is very unfortunate, though, for the many who are forced to hand in some extremely expensive, sophisticated equipment which it's doubtful they will ever see again.

New announcement for the population from the military government. These are now greeted with hoots of derision and raspberries. Today's great news is that as from next week we will have real live television – broadcast from Stanley. To enable as many as possible of their fellow countrymen in the Malvinas to benefit from it, the people of Argentina have sent to us 100 TV sets which can be obtained by paying a deposit of £20, then ten monthly payments of £10. So for £120 we can have a TV – in colour as well. The immediate question from everyone is, 'Does it speak English?' We are assured that a certain amount of the broadcasting time will be specially put over in English. Great stuff. Hurrah.

The big Chinook helicopters have been really doing their work today, making their way up and down the harbour with their curious throp-thropping noise. The vibration set up by the double rotors really makes the houses shake. It's odd to think that while on holiday last year in England we watched several of them in a tight formation fly low over Ileen's sister Noreen and her husband Strom's house where we were staying at Ramsgate. I think it was Ileen who remarked then how sinister they looked and how terrible it would be to be caught up in a war in which they were involved. No comment! But full marks for foresight.

Day developed into a still, sunny evening, surprisingly mild for this time of the year. Went along to the hospital before the Easter Vigil service. Suspicious glances by the military at the hospital when I arrived looking respectable; I'm sure they thought I was engaged in some kind of subversive activity. Ileen's condition about the same and the civilian noise level even higher. You could get far more rest in Woolworths.

The Easter Vigil service went off very well with a good attendance. Not one Argentine was present. They did, however, make their contribution by drowning out parts of the service with the noise of their aircraft and helicopters. The altar looked very beautiful with its decoration of flowers. To me it was like a funeral, almost as if the flowers had been set up in mourning for the colony. I was very proud to see all three of our boys serving at the Mass. Tyssen quite untroubled by all of the outside noises, and although Jem and Martyn are eighteen and nineteen now, it still does not deter them from being altar boys when the occasion requires it. Wish Ileen could have been there with us. Poor Anya felt the sadness of the occasion and shed a few tears, but braved it out until the end. I gave her a Librium when we got home, which soon took effect.

Sunday 11 April – Day Ten

Fine but coldish with little wind; incredible for this time of year.

Aircraft have been flying all night long. If this goes on I will write to my MP, as it is taking the value off my property. Intensive flying continued through the day. They are now using civilian Aerolineas Argentinas 727s as well as their military F-28s, F-27s and C-130s. Troops are pouring in; we are told that 9,000 are here now. Hardly seems possible, but I think probably true. They are in tents as far out as Mount William, out along the Darwin Road and all over the Common towards Eliza Cove and Mullet Creek. God help them when the weather breaks.

Gen Menéndez was at Mass this morning – a short, squat bloke who kept his head down most of the time. Several other senior officers also in attendance.

Great news – Ileen home from hospital just before lunch. It will be a long time before she is really on her feet again, but at least she is back with us.

Argentine reporter came to the door just after lunch with photographer; wanted to know what we thought of the situation. Told him that it would be a good idea if his newspaper let the mothers of Argentina know that their glorious country had provided almost free television sets for the people of the Falklands while their sons in the army were rummaging in our dustbins for food. They didn't seem to think this was a very good idea and pushed off quite quickly. There are apparently several domestic cats missing up at the west end of town and a horse has been found up near the race-course with stab wounds in its body. Hunger is driving these troops to desperate measures. It has now been announced by the military that any soldier asking the civilian population for food will be shot. The civilian population may, however, give food if they wish.

Tyssen and I went on what has now become our daily walk around the town with the dog. News of the departure of the Task Force seems really to have got through to the Argentines. They are digging everywhere: in front of the town hall; on Victory Green; the Drill Hall is heavily sandbagged. Even the high-level water tank on Callaghan Road is fortified. Large convoys of Mercedes Benz military lorries packed with ammunition going in the direction of Moody Brook from the airport. Tyssen finds these walks very interesting as he is able to recognise most of the equipment and weaponry – the majority is of European manufacture.

As we were having tea about 4.30 a group of about sixty or a hundred troops passed the house, having come up from the airport on foot. I was about to write 'marched', but that would have been an entirely wrong word – they were young lads completely exhausted after only 4 miles, some dragging their equipment; four fell down on to the grass on the children's playing field, while another couple collapsed into the gutter. This is a completely amazing and somewhat tragic sight. It's like watching an army in retreat instead of supposed victors; a picture of utter dejection. Their uniforms and weapons appear to be brand new, as does their equipment, which includes steel helmet and goggles. By the look of things they have been swept up from the streets in a vast conscription exercise, given a rifle and uniform, packed into a transport plane, then dumped in the Falklands. There seems to be no *esprit de corps* with them; those who collapse are ignored; the remainder shamble on.

At 6 this evening the naval transport *Bahía Buen Suceso* arrived through The Narrows. Tyssen and I watched her sailing up the coast earlier this afternoon. We didn't know what she was then, so popped into old Mrs Mary Goodwin's front porch up on Davis Street to have a discreet look at her through her son Laurie's binoculars. She is now moored alongside the FIC jetty packed tight with cargo. The jetty has today been reinforced with sheets of aluminium matting which came from the temporary airstrip. More heavy equipment must be expected. She was lucky to get in this evening; tomorrow the British naval blockade comes into effect, so she would have been liable to be sunk. One presumes that the Royal Navy has some submarines on station in our waters to make the blockade effective.

The jetty and ship are under very heavy guard; absolutely impossible to get near. There is great speculation that on board are the Royal Marines and BAS (British Antarctic Survey) personnel from South Georgia being taken to the mainland of Argentina.

Mail was received today from UK dated about 29 March.

Monday 12 April – Day Eleven

Weather cold, clear and calm, remained so all day. Wind west Force 3-4.

From the BBC this morning we heard that the British naval blockade of the Falklands has begun. Effective from 0400 hours – the report continued that the entire Argentine fleet was in port with the exception of one destroyer and one frigate.

Haig has returned to London for talks with the British Prime Minister. Japan has joined the countries imposing economic sanctions against Argentina. Canada has banned imports from Argentina.

New instruction from the military government: all radio-telephone communication between farm settlements and with Stanley is to cease, except for medical emergencies, the doctor from Stanley being allowed half an hour on the air each morning, under military supervision, for radio consultations. All radio 2-metre aerials owned by people in Stanley are to be handed into the town hall.

Announcement from the military government: the civilian population are advised that a military exercise will be held in and around Puerto Rivero tomorrow – suppose that's us.

On the FIC jetty great heaps of frozen food unloaded from the *Bahía Buen Suceso* are lying rotting. The Argentines don't seem bothered about moving it. God knows how their minds work. Cats are still disappearing, troops are still scrounging cigarettes and food. Up on Davis Street last night eight soldiers were seen cooking two chickens on a bit of corrugated iron over a tin of diesel oil. Domestic chickens are beginning to disappear rapidly now. The ship also brought in more Alsatian guard dogs to back up those flown in a few days ago. There are about eighteen here now, all kept in the playground of the infant and junior schools.

Air activity increased towards midday, continuing well into the night, with both military and requisitioned civilian aircraft.

Tyssen and I took the dog around the town with us on our walk. We persuaded Ileen to come as it is essential that she gets out; the hundreds of troops on the streets naturally do not have a very reassuring effect on her, but she realises that she must get used to things as they are now. We had just got up past the Secretariat when a battalion of some 200 troops marched down towards us, completely filling the road. As it was our road we decided to keep walking right in the middle of it, causing them to open ranks to allow us to pass. It was rather like running the gauntlet. As some looked a bit hostile I deliberately said 'Good Afternoon' in a fairly loud voice to as many as possible of them, which seemed to create some uncertainty in their ranks. Once past them and up by the telephone exchange we noticed they had a sort of mobile trailer kitchen from which soup was being dished out. We popped into the post office in the hope of collecting some mail from England, but no luck. The place was very scruffy and full of troops. The Queen's portrait has been replaced by a painting of Argentine national hero Gen San Martín, who does not appear too happy about the state of things – miserable-looking old blighter. More troops are digging in on Ross Road, and anti-aircraft guns are being set up on the high ground at the back of the town.

In the town hall corridor all the photographs of former governors of the Falklands have been taken down, as well as the sword and scroll presented to the colony by the Royal Marines at the time of their being granted the Freedom of Stanley. Also missing is the patent of baronetcy, with its great seal, of Admiral Sturdee, Commander of the British Naval Fleet at the Battle of the Falklands in 1914. Plenty of broken glass on the floor. This is not good enough – I must see the military authorities about it. If they consider the Falklands to be theirs, then our heritage is theirs as well; irreplaceable parts of our history must be properly looked after.

Sent another cable home. Susie and young Julia are still holding the fort up at Cable & Wireless complete with guards. They said that they had given one guard a couple of buns, but a senior NCO came in, took them from him and stamped them into the ground. The conscripts are no more than dirt in the Argentine Army, only cannon fodder.

A new flagpole has been erected outside the Secretariat to replace the one blown down a few days ago. It was made by our locals in the dockyard, who have cleverly arranged the band supporting the stays so far up the pole that it is impossible to fly anything larger than a very small flag from it.

Mass at 5.30. Two senior officers there – someone said they were generals. Both appeared distressed. They had also been in chapel earlier on in the afternoon. Both had one star; the Argentine system of badges and things to denote rank is very confusing. It seems that the more stars one has the lower the rank in certain brackets of their army. Silver stars on a red circular cloth backing seem to be the very senior officers.

Have just heard the dreadful news that Bill Luxton and his wife and family are to be removed from the Falklands for subversive activities; apparently comments on the radio. They have been picked up by helicopter from their farm at Chartres and brought to town, and are to be deported to England tomorrow. We shall all have to watch our step a bit now, if this sort of thing is going to happen. It just goes to show what a pack of bloody lies their edicts were when they first arrived: 'The continuity of the way of life of the people of the Islands'; 'in an atmosphere of peace, order and harmony'.

From the BBC this evening we heard that Haig is now returning to Buenos Aires after twelve hours of talks in London. Time is running out; no hope yet of a settlement or withdrawal. No incidents are reported from either side in the naval blockade. They also reported that Bishop Cutts of the Anglican church in Buenos Aires has cabled the Prime Minister – but conditions got very bad so were unable to hear what it was all about. I wouldn't put much faith in it myself as he has always struck me as being very pro-Argentine.

Jem is duty fireman at the hospital tonight. There is now a system of having at least one member of our Volunteer Fire Brigade actually sleeping in the hospital each night to deal with the emergency fire fighting equipment there and to be on hand, should a fire occur, until the arrival of the rest of the brigade. With things as they are at the moment there could well be delays and problems in members getting to the Fire Station after dark.

Our Government Air Service Islander aircraft was seen flying this afternoon. Must be the Argies; no one in FIGAS knew about it.

All outgoing passengers for the LADE flight tomorrow are to assemble at the LADE office at 0900 hours.

The recently completed and condemned government school hostel has now been fully taken over for use as an Argentine military hospital.

Tuesday 13 April – Day Twelve

Another superb morning. Calm, clear and cold. Temperatures about 3°C last night. Remained fine all day.

Five Argentine jet fighters over at 11 o'clock, then more vapour trails above the town about 4 this afternoon. The air activity now seems to increase each night about 9 o'clock. Still much speculation that the British Antarctic Survey personnel and Royal Marines ex-South Georgia are on board the *Bahía Buen Suceso*. She is certainly very heavily guarded by troops and dogs. A party of Argentine troops has been today searching the beach down past the FIC offices for bodies from one of their landing craft which was sunk during the invasion. Some have already been washed up.

More of the expatriate staff flew out this morning, including Dick Baker, the Chief Secretary, and Ronnie Lamb, Chief Constable. Financial Secretary Harold Rowlands is the most senior member of our former government left here now. I suppose that technically he must be the acting Governor as far as we are concerned. All very confusing.

Announcement at lunch-time that petrol is to be rationed. Ten litres per week for a car or Land Rover and two litres for motor cycles. The fuel station will only be open twice a week from now on.

Troops are taking over the Globe Store. More and more of them arriving during the day, all very young. There seem to be very few older, professional soldiers among them. Those dug in on the harbour-front are washing themselves and their mess tins in the sea near the sewer pipe. Up at the meteorological station, now taken over by the Argentine Army, only the officers are allowed to use the toilets inside the building. The troops are washing themselves and their equipment in puddles outside. All very unhygienic. Two rather smart modern harbour patrol boats turned up in the harbour today. Painted white – manned by Argentine civilian crews. Think they may have been brought over as deck cargo on larger ship. They are about 60ft long and seem to do about 20 knots. The *Isla del*

Estados arrived back in harbour at 5.30 this evening, berthing alongside the *Bahía Buen Suceso*.

Mowed the lawn during the afternoon. Got some rather odd looks from patrolling military police; surely there can't be a law against doing that. Ileen packed away some of her china and ornaments for, with the situation as it is, it is not entirely clear how things are going to turn out. If the Argentines don't back down we could be in for one almighty scrap. I thought it prudent to take down from my study wall the scroll recording the Freedom of Stanley for the Royal Marines, partly because I am named as responsible for it being brought about – which may offend our new leaders, in which case they may confiscate it – and partly because it is also signed by Maj Gen Sir Steuart Pringle who had his leg blown off in the savage business with the IRA last year. He is a most likeable man who I am proud to have met. The scroll in the town hall has gone, so I suppose that mine must be the only one left in the colony now.

Terry (Ileen's brother) has been told to get out of his house, which is on the high ground at the back of the town, along with several of his neighbours, as the troops want to install anti-aircraft guns up there. All are very indignant about this, but there is little they can do under the military regime. More private vehicles are now being commandeered by the military; mainly diesel ones, as I suppose the Argentines fear a petrol shortage if the naval blockade remains in force.

The troops pinched Ileen Vidal's and her daughters' push bikes during last night. They must be getting really hard up for transport.

One bright bit of news was that Veronica, John Fowler's wife, gave birth to a son – Daniel – today. Both mother and child are well. Unique circumstances to be born in (or should it be 'under'?). The Fowlers have been associated with the Falklands for some years now in the educational field, firstly at Darwin School and now in Stanley where John is presently Superintendent of Education.

Gloomy news at 4 from the BBC; Haig leaves London for an undisclosed destination; giving up; solution lies with Buenos Aires; he apparently can do no more.

The Falklands Government Plant and Transport Authority (PATA) has been taken over by the military. All civilian staff sent home. 'Rag' (Robert Macaskill – no one knows how he got his nickname) is now out of a job!

The government Public Works Department in the dockyard is

still functioning, in difficult circumstances, under its new management.

Attended Mass with Ileen at 5.30. Argentine military priest there. They now hold a Mass for their forces at 6.30 each evening.

The day ended with a few rifle shots nearby at about 10 o'clock.

On 'Calling the Falklands', which is now broadcast each day to us from London, we had messages from Ileen's sister Noreen and family, and John and Tina Harradine – they were out here four or five years ago when John was doing research on the habits of the Falkland Upland Goose, during which time we became very close friends. We also had an encouraging message from another good friend, Bob Wade – Radio Officer of the Royal Research Ship *John Biscoe*. It's really great to get these messages as they do a tremendous amount to boost our morale.

Wednesday 14 April – Day Thirteen

Fine and clear in morning; not over-cold as far as we are concerned for this time of the year but the Argies look a bit cool this morning. At midday the weather broke. Started to rain, skies clouded over; temperature fell; getting very cold.

Flying continued through most of the night. Very noisy jet fighter low over the town just on dawn.

BBC 8 o'clock news reports Soviet surveillance ship in Ushuaia (Argentina). Argentina is learning the position of the British Task Force from information from Soviet satellites. Meeting of both Houses of Parliament in London.

Our overseas mail system still appears to be working after a fashion. Mail ex-Stanley last week has now arrived in England. Received letters today from Ev and Jim at Tickhill, Wendy Newbold at Hamble and George Guzzio in New York. Anya also heard from the education people (ours) that she has passed her 'O' level in English language. A most interesting letter arrived today, posted from Buenos Aires on the 12th according to the postmark. It is worth copying in full:

> Dear Sir,
> You don't know me and I don't think you ever will. I was given your address by two English boys which stayed with you this year; this letter is hard for me to write. I have lived in the Argentine for just over a year working in a low class job compared to the other British that live here. They all have fat Bank Accounts in England and Buenos Aires. I read in the newspapers today that the leaders in the British community are sending over the Arch Bishop to tell you (and the Kelpers) that living under the Argentine Government is quite good. Please I beg you don't believe them. They think only for themselves and their own interests here. They look upon the worker as shit and the Argentine Government treats them as shit. If the Falklands stay part of the Argentine there will be nothing left in five years.
>
> If or when you are freed I would like to come and live there. I leave

tomorrow for England and I'm sure that in England there are many young people who think like myself, so stay with hope.

I know England has let you down, but I pray that they can help you. I know what I'm talking about but I just can't write it.

All the best

During this afternoon went along to see Monsignor Spraggon and Padre Bagnall to discuss the letter with them. Both agreed and were as encouraged as we are that someone should have the kindness and forethought to at least try to warn us of events. Padre Bagnall, the senior representative of the Anglican Church here, has no idea when Bishop Cutts and his 100 followers are likely to arrive, even less idea where they are all going to stay.

Great excitement during the morning when the Argentines were descending Philomel Hill in one of the big Russian Bellars trucks which they had taken over from the PATA – the brakes failed. The hill has a gradient of something like 1 in 4. After a series of adventures, and presumably some rather disturbed stomachs, it was brought to a halt. Doubtful if the mystery of the malfunctioning brakes will ever be solved . . .

Apart from the Bellars truck incident, it has been a fairly unexciting day. Panhard armoured cars patrol the town, more for something to occupy themselves with than for any real purpose. Adrian Monk was allowed to get in touch on the radio with the farm settlement at Roy Cove to see if all was well. The reply was that things were OK but they were a bit low on the whisky. A true Kelper reaction to a grave and serious situation. Priorities absolutely right and no panic. Much less air activity today. There are reports that during last night seven persons were taken from the *Bahía Buen Suceso* in an unlit military van to the airport. The Argentines have now occupied both of our schools, the Globe Store and Waverley House.

Tyssen off to school at the teachers' house. They are doing a grand job in attempting to keep things going. It also has the more important advantage of keeping the children occupied; they possibly do not learn a great deal but are at least having a routine to adhere to. Went to the Secretariat in the morning to get a set of the Colony Estimates and Census before they get destroyed by the Argentines. Dressed properly. Stopped by armed guard on way into the building in very proper manner but all he wanted was a cigarette; that seemed to be the extent of his English. On the way home called at the Upland Goose Hotel with some wide sticky tape for Des King – the owner. This tape is very handy for placing in strips across the windows, which reduces bits flying about when damaged by blast. In another capacity Des is chairman of the Falkland Islands Anglican Church Council and is justifiably hostile towards the proposed Bishop Cutts visit.

Another anti-aircraft gun installed behind the town hall; all troops having a go on it; like a new toy to some of them; their keenness is commendable but their lack of skill is frightening as they may well end up doing more harm to themselves than to their enemy. On second thoughts – why should we worry?

Cleaned the silver during the afternoon; seems a bit pointless but one must keep up a routine. If standards start to drop then so does personal attitude, which can quickly turn to apathy. This is easy to write at the moment but none of us knows how long this affair is going to last, or how we are going to react under what looks like being a long term of anxiety, uncertainty and waiting.

Mass at 5.30. Not great attendance, probably due to the weather which is absolutely foul. Lots of wet, bedraggled troops assembled outside LADE office.

Evening news from England still very much on our side. Haig now on way to Buenos Aires from Washington. Strong unity in both Houses at Falklands Debate. No change in the Prime Minister's attitude; supported by the Opposition; prepared to go on for a long time if necessary. Great stuff. The quicker we can get the Argentines out of here the better. Britain also announced doubling of the number of Harriers being sent down with the Task Force. Requisitioned another container ship; HMS *Intrepid* now being fitted out for service along with the schools cruise liner *Uganda*.

The highlight of our evening was a broadcast by President Galtieri to the Falkland Islands at 9 o'clock. We all sat spellbound, listening for fifteen minutes, but were unable to understand a word as it was all in Spanish with no translation. We are thus none the wiser.

Weather forecast for the night – temperature down to 1°; south-west gale with rain. The troops on the hill won't be quite so enchanted about their beloved Malvinas by the morning.

Thursday 15 April – Day Fourteen

Watery sunshine; wind now dropped from full gale which blew most of the night from the south with temperatures down to zero. High cloud first thing this morning, but turned dull with rain and got very cold again later in the day.

From 8 o'clock news this morning learned that Dick Baker, etc have arrived safely in England. Also that the Argentine general commanding the Falklands has stated that the people here won't send their children to school. He apparently did not mention that the schools are full of his soldiers, but said that the delay in response would give the Argentine authorities time to prepare the new curriculum with Argentine history and traditions as part of it. Don't think I've mentioned yet that the Argentines are also in full occupation of the gymnasium, the town hall, Stanley House and the police station.

The tight guard on the *Bahía Buen Suceso* has eased off; people ex-South Georgia must have moved out. The *Islas del Estados* sailed during the afternoon. A mine or something similar went off about 3 this afternoon in the Dairy Paddock area up at the back of the town. Wombat guns being towed along Callaghan Road at the back of town towards the west, while 105mm pack howitzers are being towed along the seafront on Ross Road towards the east. There are now eight Panhard armoured cars based up at the disused European Space Research Organisation (ESRO) station (this is occupied by Argies as well). Learned at lunch-time that an aircraft crashed at the airport during the night. This accounts for no flying this morning. Things must have been cleared shortly after 3 this afternoon, as there has been intense flying from then onwards. An expatriate electrician and his young family flew out today to return to England. His wife has been very unwell and was flown in from Darwin by Argentine military helicopter.

Argentine troops seem to be everywhere. Two seventeen-year-olds told us that this time last week they were at school in Buenos

Aires; sent here because they knew English, very few want to fight. Things must be getting a bit desperate with both men and equipment, as I passed one chap on guard today looking very efficient and warlike, but he had forgotten to put the magazine in his rifle. In the east part of the town, down towards YPF (the Argentine Fuel Plant – Yacimientos Petrolíferos Fiscales) and the rubbish dump, real anti-aircraft guns and heavy weapons are alternated with fabrications of vehicle wheels, gas cylinders and 6-in diameter fuel pipe, covered in camouflage netting to look like real guns. I suppose that it may look convincing from the air. Troops are well dug in down there, with some very professional-looking roofed-in trenches, complete with chimneys, which tend to give them away a bit. From what I've seen so far, the Argentine Army seems to do some excellent soldierly things but then immediately goes and spoils the effort by doing something stupid. We are most grateful as this is all in our favour.

Took dog for walk as usual. She imagines this war is entirely for her increase in daily exercise. We find it very useful for seeing what is going on about the town. Tyssen adds to the effect as he insists on still wearing his shorts, which puzzles the troops. They often stop and ask him why he does not feel the cold. This is useful as it gives a bit more time for a look around. A schoolboy's interest in military equipment and goings-on is, almost every time, encouraged by the soldiers, which is very handy.

Changed last United Kingdom cheque at the FIC today. Terry Spruce, the manager, was really great in assisting, as the Company have stopped accepting cheques owing to the uncertainty of things. We can now hold out for a little longer. The guest-house business is getting a bit thin nowadays, and we cannot possibly consider Phyllis and Ian as guests; they are now part of the family, after all they are doing for us in helping out with the running of the house and family. They are a really superb couple, completely unflappable no matter what the situation, though they have their worries too, as their daughter Brenda had intended to come out from New Zealand to join them and there is no way for them to find out if she is on her way or not.

The Argentines now want to take over the annexe of St Mary's Church to house troops, so went along this afternoon to clear out the valuable things and lock up everything else, such as the cutlery and crockery. Afterwards went to Ileen's brother Pat and his wife

Maureen's house for tea. They were incredibly lucky during the morning of the invasion as there are a good number of bullet holes in their house, not rifle bullets but big jobs from the .5-in cannons on the armoured personnel carriers. One had shot off the leg of their bed after passing through the outside wall and the dressing table. Their front porch was badly damaged as well by bullets.

Went to Benediction at 5.30. Lots of young soldiers in and out during the service. About 300 newly arrived troops lined up in the road when the service was over. Absolutely pathetic. It looked like a youth club outing. Very few were over eighteen. Many looked towards the Monsignor standing on the church steps – some asked for his blessing. Terribly sad and depressing sight.

Received telegrams from Jim and Evie at Doncaster. Listened to 'Calling the Falklands' on radio in evening. Francis Pym broadcast to us saying that they are doing everything they can to aid us. Haig is on his way back to Buenos Aires. Russians accusing the US of supplying intelligence to Britain. Also accused Britain of armed aggression by sending of the Task Force. The British attitude still remains as firm as ever, but the situation is very grave.

The civilian population of the town is dwindling rapidly as many people are heading off to the Camp settlements. We will stay put.

Friday 16 April – Day Fifteen

Another superb morning, brilliant and still; harbour flat calm. I cannot recall ever having weather like this at this time of the year before. At 8 o'clock the bugles rang out clearly as the military regime commenced another day of their occupation by hoisting their blue and white flag over our islands. Under different circumstances the sound of the bugles against such a serene background would have created feelings of strong emotion. Today, however, I could have quite happily pushed their bugles down their ruddy throats.

Another night of intense air activity. Some time during the hours of darkness the *Isla del Estados* returned to the harbour. The BBC at breakfast time reported that Galtieri telephoned Haig asking him to return to Buenos Aires in an attempt to look for a peaceful solution. The Malvinas recovery operation has so far cost Argentina $500 million. The country faces severe economic difficulties, with no credit in most countries. Part of the Argentine fleet sailed during the night, leaving women crying in the streets of the naval garrison town of Puerto Belgrano. Chile is on a Grade 2 alert.

At about 10.30 this morning the military arrived to take away my collection of rifles and the boys' Defence Force uniforms. Two military police stationed outside the gate with their Mercedes vehicle, another MP in the front porch, with a captain, a lieutenant and a sergeant to do the actual work. They were extremely polite, explaining that the reason for the gathering in of weapons was that in the case of theft during these difficult days the owner could not be held responsible if any incidents happened involving these weapons. All very plausible. They showed their papers authorising them to carry out the operation. This did not help me a great deal as I couldn't understand a word of it.

In the study I offered them coffee explaining that in this country it was usual to offer visitors to the house such courtesy. We then all sat down and had a discourse on the merits of and otherwise of the

Ouzi handgun against the Ingram which the captain had. He very kindly took it to pieces in order to explain how it worked. When it was reassembled I suggested that he placed it on the table pointing towards the window in case of any accidents, as he had just said that it had a rate of fire of 300 rounds per minute. We then discussed a model of a De Havilland Rapide which I had recently completed building, and by coincidence the lieutenant, I think it was, had also just completed the same kit.

It was at this point that two Mirages went past the window at rooftop level at very high speed, waking Ileen who came downstairs, to see the MPs and me in the study with the fully armed Argentines. The shock was a disaster and she broke down again. Her sobbing from the next room did have some effect on the military, as they got their formalities over fairly rapidly and had the decency to apologise. Proper receipts were given to me for the weapons and the uniforms. But the job could so easily have been carried out by two of them without the accompanying military dramatics. This whole business is sickening. It was, however, a most useful exercise in meeting the enemy face to face and learning a bit about their attitude and what they are up to. It seems, also, to unsteady them slightly when they are faced with a firm but courteous reception. Good manners cost nothing and the results gained from their judicious use can be most useful.

Usual amount of air activity today. Two Canberras flew low up the harbour at 2 o'clock this afternoon. Little did I ever think, when I watched Roly Beaumont flying the prototypes at Farnborough in the 1950s, that I would see them being used against us. It must be all of ten years since I last saw one flying. A new helicopter has appeared on the scene today, a Puma I think, finished in blue and white with an odd sort of finish on the fuselage sides which resembles corrugated iron. Two more Mirages gave a low fly-past at 4.30. I think that these high-speed displays must be calculated to unsettle the public. It must be extremely expensive on fuel, though it does acquaint the pilots with the Falklands terrain, which may prove handy for them if it comes to a battle with the Task Force.

Eight members of the British Community in Buenos Aires arrived for the day. No sign of the Anglican Bishop and his mates. The eight got a very cool reception from the locals. They were accompanied by some press and TV people, said to be Italian. Victory Green on the harbour's edge opposite the Upland Goose

Hotel was full of newly arrived troops, as was Davis Street; possibly for the benefit of the visiting press and TV, who seemed very disappointed at so little reaction to the military by the local people. They are bewildered and unsure when we treat them without physical hostility. It is, I suppose, what is termed passive resistance. It is perfectly clear and obvious that we do not want them here, yet no one can be charged with insolence of any kind, which must be extremely frustrating for them. If we were to give them the fingers, throw bricks at them, even poke out our tongues, it would give them something positive to react against. As it is, there is nothing that they can accuse us of doing to upset them. Serves them right; they shouldn't have come here.

All in all a rather unsuccessful day for the Argentine Army. One soldier had his foot amputated at the hospital after an accident with a hand grenade, and was later moved to the hostel hospital. Another group seemed to have run into transport problems, as they were seen pushing a great field gun up the Darwin Road. Some locals eventually gave them a tow with a Land Rover and under the umbrella of human kindness were able to find out what sort of gun it was and where it was going to be positioned.

People travelling into town on the Darwin Road during the past couple of days have passed several heaps of dead soldiers – the total varies between thirty and fifty – stacked up on the side of the road up near Sapper Hill. There are also a large number of soldiers on stretchers. Our climate is not agreeing with them; exposure seems to be the problem. Not surprising, as many of the troops come from the northern provinces of Argentina where the climate is tropical. To plunge them suddenly into the environment of the South Atlantic is both stupid and criminal.

Two soldiers at Mass this evening. From the evening BBC news we learn that a big troop build-up still continues at airports in southern Argentina. Passengers arriving at Comodoro Rivadavia have to draw the aircraft window blinds while landing and on the ground; the windows of the terminals there are blacked out. The attitude of those at the talks in Buenos Aires seems to be more flexible. Our two FIGAS air mechanics who were here, seconded from the RAF and deported by the Argentines, have arrived in England where they gave what is described as most important information on the Falklands situation to the MOD. Haig may now return to London after his talks in Buenos Aires. Poor man can't know whether he is coming or going these days. I sincerely hope that his valiant efforts are rewarded by a peaceful and sensible solution.

On 'Calling the Falklands' tonight there was a message from our former police chief, Ronnie Lamb, who left Stanley earlier this week and has just arrived in London. In the hurry and confusion of his departure arrangements, he completely forgot that there was still a prisoner in the cells at the police station, so would someone here please go down and have a look, and let him out if necessary.

Saturday 17 April – Day Sixteen

Day started with low cloud and drizzle; wind west, Force 4. Conditions rapidly improved. By lunch-time we had brilliant sunshine with absolutely no cloud or wind. Closed with superb evening.

No aircraft yet this morning; most unusual. Only one helicopter just before 8. Anya off to the hospital for work. All nursing staff now wear large white capes with big red cross on the back, a sensible precaution. BBC news this morning says Haig still having meetings in Buenos Aires with view to diplomatic solution. Various unconfirmed reports suggest dual government with neutral country and United Nations peace-keeping force based here – they can stuff that idea. Three British journalists held at Ushuaia for spying. Withdrawal of Argentine troops still possible. Britain has requisitioned another twenty-five ships for the Task Force. Mrs Thatcher certainly means business.

In view of the fine weather, decided to paint some of the front of the house with Jem, Martyn and Rag. Music outside with the amplifier, along with lots of larking about and laughter. This mystified the troops and the drivers of six armoured cars which were patrolling the streets. It gave us an excellent and valid opportunity to see what was going on in the town, especially from the roof, from where one can see the airport. Pity that there is so little flying today. There was, however, a military exercise this afternoon; supposed to be held outside the town but included Victory Green and Callaghan Road. Lots of shooting and banging. Sounded like mortars and field guns.

Great heaps of ammunition boxes stacked high in the junior school playground. The senior school is now some sort of important military post, as it is fortified along the front with 40 gall. fuel drums filled with peat, with armed sentries at either entrance. Stanley House is now apparently a command post, with hundreds of telephone wires leading out of it across Ross Road, then along the ground towards Moody Brook. These wires are constantly and carefully inspected by at least six soldiers. The two recently arrived fast patrol boats were painted in camouflage during the night. One refuelled at the Camber this morning. The *Forrest*, also under military control, is at the public jetty, loading brightly painted orange 40 gall. drums. A very large tent with red crosses painted on it has been erected at the north-west corner of the school hostel. One of the ex-Royal Marine three-tonners packed with bags of onions was heading for Moody Brook this afternoon. Plenty of vitamins for the troops.

Some new troops have arrived; obviously professionals; much older and more experienced; much the same standard as we had on Invasion Day. They wear very dark maroon berets with a large badge over the right ear.

A bombing exercise by the air force with Pucaras is going on in York Bay/Tussac Island area. One of the islands was well alight by mid-afternoon, with the smoke and flames rising hundreds of feet into the air. An enormous dense plume of smoke hangs over Port William. The diving Pucaras sound just like Stukas. Very sinister.

No fast fly-pasts today. Ian Butler, who is desperately trying to return to the farm at Roy Cove to attend to his stock, went to see the military authorities this morning about getting a flight out there, but was told that the Islander aircraft is not being flown because of contaminated fuel. It then flew over the town about lunch-time. Ian's patience is being stretched a little, to put it mildly.

Some families from town who had moved out to the farmhouse at Port Harriet were today ordered to return to town. It seems to be in a military zone – the whole place seems to be one vast military zone to us. Dysentery is now affecting the troops.

On our Argentine local news this evening we hear the captain of HMS *Invincible* has requested to put into a neutral country as there is some indiscipline among the troops on board, who do not want to take part in the Falkland Islands operations. We were also informed that the Argentine soldier who had his foot blown off yesterday trod on a mine left by the Royal Marines – so there.

The fire engine was called out to Cable Cottage this afternoon. Nothing very exciting; it turned out to be only the dustbin on fire. The Argentine senior officers live there.

Ileen walked with Anya up to her sister Joan's this afternoon on Ross Road West near the racecourse. She says that she must regain her confidence and get among people again. The troops are going to be here for a while yet by the look of things, and she must get used to them. It is taking a lot of effort on her part to go out; she realises that it must be done. I think that the tablets from the hospital are doing a lot to get her back to her old self again. I went up to meet them at about 5 this afternoon as the noise from the military exercise was a bit hectic and was even louder up where Joan and James live. The troops seem to be exercising along the ridge at the back of their house. It was very unpleasant to walk down the road towards town again with the Tussac Island blazing in the distance; almost unreal; the aircraft are still bombing. Stopped by Government House gate for a chat with our vet, Steve Whitley, and his wife, Sue. They are determined to stay and stick things out, even though – being expatriate staff – they have the opportunity to return to England. Steve has his castrating scissors in his pocket at all times now to carry out operations on the Argentine telephone wires when the occasion arises.

Sunday 18 April – Day Seventeen

Dull and cloudy. Wind west, Force 3. Cloud lifted mid-morning; rest of day dry and cold, ending up with rain in evening.

A quiet day in all respects. One loud explosion last night about 3.30; various others during the day. At 11.30 what appeared to be a Lockheed Starfighter passed overhead very high – 10,000 ft, maybe a bit less. Long fuselage with short, stubby wings. Saw a lorry-load of potatoes go up the road in the morning towards Moody Brook.

Went to Mass at 11. Few troops and several senior officers there. It is said that Bloomer-Reeve is ill. Perhaps he is finding the strain a bit much. He is obviously doing his best to keep relations between the civilian and military population at a good level, but naturally finding it difficult. He is a very clever man, one of the kingpins in this whole operation, but I have the feeling that he may have been manipulated into the situation and is finding it tough going.

We are all wondering where the Task Force is, so spent much of the afternoon with the atlas, pencils and dividers. The rubber came in handy afterwards as our map of the Atlantic Ocean looked like the London Underground, with lines over it from the great navigational exercise. The following conclusions were reached. At 12 knots, would take approx 28 days – should be here in a couple of weeks. At 18 knots, would take approx 21 days – will be here next Monday. At 24 knots, would take approx 13 days – they will either turn up about supper time, or have already gone past.

The entire family are placing their bets on high speeds. By 11 o'clock this evening nothing had arrived, so we all went to bed.

Monday 19 April – Day Eighteen

Another superb day; sunny and clear but coldish.

Very tired, as got very little sleep last night. There were several loud explosions and I heard seventeen aircraft pass over.

It appears that two other soldiers were killed when the one had his foot blown off a couple of days ago. Another twenty have died from exposure on the Darwin road; this is not surprising. They are not adapting well to conditions down here, though the present weather is great to us. The temperature during the last few weeks has been between 6° and 8°C, with occasional bursts of 10° for very short periods. Telephone calls by the troops to their families in Argentina have been stopped as it upsets their morale.

Went with Ileen to the hospital in the morning for routine visit. Had an extremely good talk with young Dr Mary Elphinstone. She really offered some of the most understanding and sensible advice yet to Ileen. Lots of military at the hospital, gradually attempting to take over by the look of it. There is an armed guard at the door who looks about seventeen. He does not appear to be entirely sure what he is supposed to be there for, but I suppose in a military regime there must be guards on all important buildings. It does little to reassure us.

Lots of explosions during the afternoon; sounds like blasting in progress or over-enthusiastic mine-laying.

Another instruction from the military government: as from today all town water will be turned off from 8pm to 6pm. We are therefore advised not to pull the plug out of the bath, but to keep the water for operations such as flushing the toilets. Another step backwards. There must be a severe strain on our water supply, which was designed to cope with the requirements of a town with a population of 1,200. Now we have an additional 10,000 troops at least, so the poor system must be on its last legs.

Brought in some bulk stores, such as extra bags of flour and sugar. Supplies are lasting out very well; there has been no panic buying. The pressure has been eased considerably by the large number of town folk who have moved off to Camp settlements, but on the other hand we have not had our re-supply of stores which normally occurs at this time of the year, on the FIC charter vessel from England. The military authorities must be aware of this, as their troops are forbidden to enter the local shops. They obviously do not want to have to be responsible for feeding the civilian population should the troops buy everything up.

Very often soldiers will come up to us in the street and ask us to get them cigarettes, biscuits or chocolate. This places one in a very difficult position morally, especially when confronted with a very young, very fed up and hungry conscript. I think it is fair to say that a good number of us have been guilty of making the odd purchase now and again. This can perhaps be justified by seeing the different standards between the officers and the conscripts. The officers can be spotted a mile away by their sleek, well-fed and – in most cases – arrogant appearance. The conscripts are treated like dirt, regarded as no more than animals; no bond of loyalty or trust exists between them at all. The basic glue which holds an army together is totally lacking. The professional soldiers seem to be a law unto themselves.

School, such as it was, finishes today. Most of the expatriate teachers have decided to return to England tomorrow. (John Fowler, the Superintendent of Education, has decided to stick it out here.) Tyssen and the other pupils are pleased, but it does leave us rather on our own. A great pity, but in fairness to the teachers, they did not sign a contract to be caught up in a war situation. One of them, Richard Cain, gave us the custody of his Land Rover until, or if, he returns. What an odd situation – to suddenly end up with a not-very-old, petrol-engined, truck-cab Land Rover, with instructions to use it as we think fit. I went home in a daze to announce the news to the family, who were delighted. Admittedly we are somewhat restricted as to how and when we use it, but nevertheless we have it, and it hasn't cost us a penny. Richard had little choice, as no one here would actually buy anything in that line at the moment.

As the military are still rather keen on getting hold of good vehicles, we set about immediate preparations to ensure its safety. In the garage we have our elderly, broken-down Land Rover, which one day we had hoped to resurrect, but with today's windfall we threw aside all plans in a great effort to get the old one out and the new one in – and out of sight. The old one only had three wheels on and our jack had been stolen, so the boys and I attempted to lift the thing while one of us got the wheel in place. Despite heaving, straining and a bit of rope tied to the roof beams, we just could not lift the thing high enough. Then, in the middle of all this, disaster struck – a lorry-load of troops stopped outside the garage door. There was only one course open to us to prevent awkward questions, that was to ask them to give us a hand, which they kindly and willingly did. It was truly incredible – seven fully armed troops in the garage with us and the job was done. They were all delighted with their efforts, so we edged them outside and gave them some cigarettes and a roll of 35mm film and they went on their way. Never has such relief been expressed more graphically. I cannot possibly record the words here; sufficient to say that we were all ecstatic. The ancient Rover was towed quickly away to Richard's back garden, and his new one installed in the garage in record-breaking time. What a cock-eyed army they have – they had completely forgotten the purpose of their visit.

Tuesday 20 April – Day Nineteen

Cold, dull, windy and wet. Real April weather. Reports of more Argentine deaths from exposure during the night; numbers vary from three to ten.

Took Richard Cain with his wife and teacher Jem Baylis with his wife, Marie, along with their young family to the airport this morning. About ten Land Rovers with outgoing passengers for today's flight assembled outside LADE office to travel in convoy, escorted by three vehicles full of guards. Some doubts at first as to whether an aircraft was going to be available. Eventually moved off at 10.30, a sad procession.

This was the first opportunity to get to the airport since the invasion, it now being a high-security military zone. The windows of the terminal were blacked out with old newspapers pasted over them. Passengers hustled inside very rapidly, then we were escorted back to Stanley. Masses of troops everywhere. Hercules C-130s and civilian Boeing 727s on the runway and apron. There seemed to be far more ammunition than food stacked up in great heaps at the airport. Hundreds of small tents housing troops all over the entire area, with many Wombats and anti-aircraft guns surrounding the airfield and approach road. The Canache* has been mined on both sides of the road, with barbed wire entanglements and heavy wooden stakes driven into the ground at close intervals to prevent any possible landing from the seaward side. It was a very unnerving experience to drive along a narrow road with a minefield on either side. Very relieved to get back to town. This war business does not appeal to me at all. It's all right for the films and the television, but in reality it's bloody awful. The Falklands have been raped, there is no other word for it. We heard later in the day that the passengers eventually took off at 11.30, after having to wait for young Angus

* The narrow neck of land at the east end of the harbour which connects Cape Pembroke to the mainland of East Falkland and separates Stanley Harbour from the Atlantic Ocean.

Macaskill, Robert's brother, to arrive in from Darwin in an Argentine Chinook. He is going to stay with relatives in Scotland.

Got the Land Rover into our garage and out of sight very quickly on returning from the airport. Spoke with the Monsignor and offered its services for the parish to use getting old people to and from church, to the hospital, shopping or anything else. We must put it to as good a use as possible. Monsignor was most agreeable; almost went as far as to say that it would come under the protection of Rome. He did say, though, that should there be any sign of it being commandeered by the military then we should contact him immediately in order that he might sort things out. The occupation has given him a new outlook on life; his people are being disturbed by intruders and he is having none of it. He is not going to be pushed about or sat on by anyone. The Argentines do have a great respect for the clergy and tend to treat him with a certain amount of caution.

Not a great deal of air movement today. Very large vessel put into Port William at 4.30 this afternoon. It's rumoured that the ship is Russian, arriving to land a sick man. She was flying the pilot flag and one other which was very small; impossible to make out any detail on it. Her bridge is aft, with a large gantry forward. The hull seems to be buff and white. The funnel is square, painted white with a black badge on it; two thin, black lines around the funnel above the badge. There are what seem to be buff-painted cranes in the stowed position between the forward gantry and the bridge. Impossible to pick out her name as the observation has to be carried out through the lace curtain in one of the guest bedrooms upstairs. One of the patrol boats went out to meet her after she had eventually anchored well up almost behind the Camber House. She must be about 10,000 tons. There is no unusual or great excitement apparent over her arrival.

The food situation for the troops seems to be slightly improved judging by the lorries carrying onions and potatoes. The mobile kitchens with their smoking chimneys are being towed about the town, stopping to dish out the pasta or soup at key points. The quantities do not appear to be over-generous.

Another announcement for the civilian population: all houses in Stanley are to be blacked out in case of air raids. All citizens are advised to put out the lights and get under the table if one happens – gosh. It was not made clear who was going to carry out these wicked air raids. We are also instructed that all vehicle lights are to be masked out, leaving only a 2-in wide strip through which the light can shine. The speed limit is to be 20 km per hour. During an air raid everyone is to be off the streets except the fire brigade. This seems to be a move to alarm the population. Our table is barely strong enough to support the crockery, let alone withstand the effects of a bomb. It's also not very big; we would never all fit underneath it.

Wednesday 21 April – Day Twenty

Brilliant day; calm and cloudless but quite chilly.

The birthday of Her Majesty the Queen. Special notice from the military government: all workers are to be allowed the day off on pay if they so wish. In addition, the name of the town is to be changed from Puerto Rivero to Puerto Argentino forthwith. Do wish they would make up their minds.

The telephone exchange has now been fully taken over by the military, who speak only Spanish, which makes telephoning almost impossible. Calls are being taped. The intention of the Argentines when they arrived was to improve our standards, but we now seem to be going steadily backwards. The troops also seem to be a bit bewildered by it all, as they came to liberate us from the wicked British and take us out of our poverty and squalor, but it is quite obvious to them now that we were doing quite nicely as we were.

The Task Force is now only 2,500 miles off the Falklands. It has been circled by an Argentine Boeing 707, in military colours, which was chased off by Harriers.

The vessel which arrived in Port William yesterday turns out to be an Argentine container ship, *Formosa*. Vast amounts of gear being ferried into Stanley in containers by the *Isla del Estados*, which seems to be acting as a sort of tender. It's a great pity that such a large ship should have slipped through the naval blockade.

Sent off telegrams to Mum and the family at home through Cable & Wireless. It's comforting to know that they are still allowed to operate, though one can't really say much, except that we are all still safe and well, but even this must be reassuring when so little news seems to be coming out of the Falklands.

This afternoon the Pucaras again bombed the Tussac Islands in Port William. Savage flames cover the ground while a huge pall of dense smoke rises hundreds of feet into the air. God knows what all this is doing to the wildlife out there. It is being said, though it is difficult to find evidence to support it, that the Argentine dead still being recovered from the invasion, and the deaths from exposure, are being put on the islands so that no trace remains of their losses, which during the invasion period were far heavier than admitted.

There is a lot of air activity again which seems to coincide with ground exercises; very heavy explosions during most of the day.

In view of the increasing build-up of preparations by the Argentines to defend Stanley at all costs, we have thought seriously about our own defence precautions. A secure shelter of some kind is the principal need if there is to be street fighting or attacks from the air. So we built one under our front porch – conservatory would be a better description. There is a reasonable space – the shelter is some 18 ft long, just under 6 ft wide, and 4 ft high. The floor is earth and smells of damp and cats, but it has the advantage of being protected on one side by the house, with the front and ends being constructed from rock and concrete blocks. Most fortunate of all is that the roof – the porch floor – is of cement, laid on sheets of corrugated tin and supported by iron joists. It almost seems that whoever built the house had this sort of circumstance in mind. The tin and the corrugated iron are rusting and flaking, but it does at least give some degree of protection against blast and bullets. Entry is through a trap hatch in the floor just inside the front door. In the event of the conservatory collapsing the floor seems sufficiently strong to take the weight of the wreckage. The gravity of our present situation seems to have increased my ability as a carpenter considerably, though all that I have really done is to lay a wooden floor on joists resting on the earth. Not the proper way of doing things but it will keep us from being too damp. On top of this we have laid polysomething or other sheet to act as insulation, then some lino. We will at least be fairly warm and hopefully out of harm's way should the need arise.

Today about thirty of the West Store staff have started to sleep in the store at night, which does safeguard the stores as well as themselves. The store is probably one of the strongest buildings in town.

Some time during today, Terry moved quietly out of town into the hills. No one saw him leave, no one knows where he is going – although several of us have our own ideas. People wisely do not commit themselves to saying much on certain subjects these days.

Thursday 22 April – Day Twenty-one

Dull at first, then another splendid day.

My birthday. Have now managed to survive forty-four years. This one seems to be a bit dodgier than the other forty-three, with the way things have been going lately. Awoke early, about 4 this morning, to a salute of landmines. There has been quite a bit of this lately, causing several deaths among the Argentine troops when they get out from their tents for early morning piddles. They seem to wander about among their mines, still dazed and fuddled with sleep, then step on them. I do wish they would be more careful. Not only is it causing problems for them, but it is disturbing our routine to be woken at such an early hour. Also had a fly-past of five Mirages during the morning, but I don't think this was purely for my benefit. The heavy military banging has continued all day with occasional firing; they must be exercising.

After lunch our new volunteer fire brigade had its first practice. Tremendous enthusiasm as the Land Rover fire engines were manned to the brim, then off to various points around the town at which pumps were set going, and hoses coupled up, sending water everywhere, mostly over spectating Argentine soldiers who stood fascinated, watching their new fellow countrymen going into action with hose and pump. One of the best scores of the afternoon was to partly fill up the back of one of their lorries with water before they realised what was happening. Many of the new firemen seized the wonderful opportunity to cut as many Argentine telephone cables as possible during the afternoon. All great stuff; goodness knows what would happen if we had a fire as well.

Jem and Martyn are signed on as drivers, while I am a sort of assistant. The riding about in the back of the engine is very exciting – just like the pictures – but smoke does tend to make me cough and wheeze a bit, so it has been suggested that I do not remain too long at the blaze but return to the headquarters in order to put the kettle on ready for the lads' tea when they have extinguished the fire.

This arrangement enables me to take part in a few heroics without coughing. Thoroughly enjoyed the whole thing. Hope we have another one soon. Most of the regular brigade members have gone off to the Camp, so we hope we novices can cope if the need arises.

President Galtieri visited Stanley today. He passed by Tyssen and me while we were taking the dog for a walk; we didn't realise who it was till later in the day. We exchanged waves but would have blown a raspberry had we known who it was. Troops all tidied up for the occasion. He obviously did not see the hungry ones.

Built ladder into shelter. Ileen lined the floor with an old carpet, while Tyssen installed a few empty boxes for shelves. Anya says that she would rather stay up top with the bombs instead of going down under cover with the possibility of earwigs and spiders. I notice that the boys have been referring to me as Joseph since I started my carpentry; actually they are doing most of the work while I issue the instructions and design things as we go along. Young Robert Macaskill is coming out with some most sensible suggestions, such as knocking odd outcrops of rock out of the way with a sledge hammer instead of trying to build around them. Martyn also has some useful ideas, but poor Jem and I share the same practical disability where wood and tools are concerned. His school reports for woodwork regularly showed the concern of the educational authorities for the vast amount of timber which he managed to consume for even the most simple piece of work. Damage to tools also caused them a certain amount of anguish. I remember similar circumstances when I was at school.

Not much in the way of news from the BBC today, except that the MOD have announced that the nuclear submarine HMS *Superb* has been at her base in Scotland for the past five days. This will no doubt aggrieve the Argentines even more, as they have believed her to be patrolling their eastern Atlantic coast since the naval blockade. We got 'Calling the Falklands' from the BBC on which we heard that the Cains, Baylises and Townsends have arrived safely in UK. Also fairly clearly were messages to us from Evie, Jim and Philippa who are our oldest and closest friends – we always think of them as part of the family. Ileen went to school in Stanley with Evie who later married Jim Elliott when he was out here for four years with the Meteorological Office in the late 1960s. Philippa, their daughter, must be about 15 now – how time flies by. They presently live just outside Doncaster at Tickhill. We also had another message from John and Tina Harradine in Wales. It was really great to receive them, but it all seems so impossible that this is really happening. They are worried stiff about us back in England, while we out here are worrying more every day how this situation is going to end. It was not very encouraging this morning to see some sort of missiles being taken up Philomel Hill in the back of Land Rovers, four at a time. They seemed to be of grey plastic with a red nose and white pipes or handles down the sides. They stand about 5 ft high. I think it is the outer cover we can see rather than the missile itself, as the fins look far too thick to be any use. There were several loads of them. It does not pay to linger on the road and have a good look as they are accompanied by plenty of troops.

The military government announce that as from tomorrow our inter-island air service will operate again, using the Islander aircraft with an Argentine Air Force pilot. We are also informed that the special Argentine television sets can be obtained from the post office tomorrow.

Went along to Benediction. Not a very large congregation, but we all did well, responding loudly against the background of explosions and machine-gun fire as the military exercise continued. Madge seemed somehow to get a lot more volume out of the organ, which urged us all to sing louder. The *Tantum ergo* was particularly good; don't suppose it was really composed for organ and gunfire. Madge did really magnificently to keep playing under such conditions. I suppose she must be well into her seventies now.

Started letter to Jim at Tickhill, but unable to say too much as it is highly likely that outgoing mail will be opened.

Several people arrived back in town today from the Camp settlements for more supplies. If this situation keeps up, with no coastal shipping service and extra people on the farms, things will start to get a bit tight.

The invasion was three weeks ago this evening; how time flies.

New aircraft flying about today. Looks like a Miles Skyvan, very square and box-like.

Friday 23 April – Day Twenty-two

St George's Day. Fine, clear, sunny, windless day. Temperature about 9° or 10°. Incredible for so late in the year. It got very foggy towards evening.

Ian and Phyllis are on their way home to Roy Cove at last. Tyssen and I drove them down to the airport at 9 this morning. Through the minefield, then up to the terminal past mountains of military stores and equipment; lots of missiles, which have apparently just arrived, awaiting transport to their various sites. We drove slowly and were able to get a good look at them. They are in their outer protective covers, with instructions such as 'Do not lift here', printed in English. I think they may be Tiger Cats.

While we were waiting for the aircraft to take off we saw Vice-Comodoro Hector Gilobert in uniform, with pistol in belt. He waved, hesitated, then came across to us, noticeably embarrassed. We exchanged greetings, politely avoiding the current situation. His wife and family are in Buenos Aires. He hasn't seen them since before the beginning of the occupation; they must have left Stanley a couple of weeks previously when Vice-Comodoro Gammen took over from him. He is worried about the effect this is having on his wife as she is about to have another child, very soon. She enjoyed the two years or so when they lived here and seemed almost a kelper at heart, as did their two young boys, Javier and Gustavo. They fitted in so well at our schools, as have the children of the previous vice-comodoros who have lived here in charge of LADE. The last time we heard anything about Hector was on the morning of the invasion, when he carried a white flag up Ross Road to arrange a meeting between our Governor and Admiral García, who commanded the invasion force. His concern and good wishes today for our future were, I am sure, genuine and sincere.

The Butlers got away safely with Vice-Comodoro Gammen as pilot in the Islander. What a hassle they have had in trying to get this flight. They must be very relieved. Ileen had the opportunity to go with them for a break, but she is now fit enough to stay with us in Stanley and responding to treatment very well. It was so kind of Phyllis and Ian to suggest her going out to the farm with them, but the return journey could present problems. We are going to miss them about the house with their cheerfulness. I honestly don't know what we would have done through this difficult period without their help. The house is very quiet without them.

So ends another day. The air service has started again, but for how long? No radio communication with the farms in any form; water turned off at night; no schools; driving on the right; private vehicles requisitioned; no local coastal shipping service to the farms; what a hell of a state to be in.

Picked up this morning on the radio a sort of Argentine 'Tokio Rose' broadcasting in English to the British Task Force, the theme being, 'Why don't you give up and go home, British soldiers? You stand no chance of winning, your loved ones and families are missing you, etc. etc.' The approach of the Task Force is obviously having an unsettling effect on the Argentines when they have to resort to using this kind of psychological warfare.

Ileen and I went to the library this evening and it gave us a great fright, as we opened the town-hall door, to have a soldier pointing his gun at us. I think we may have given him a bit of a fright as well, as he looked as if he hadn't heard us approaching. It's a bit much when we have to have an armed guard on the public library. Stuart Booth, the librarian, says he didn't realise he was that important. We deliberately made a bit of a clatter as we were going out so as not to alarm the guard again; he really did look awfully young and nervous.

Saturday 24 April – Day Twenty-three

A cold, crisp and clear day with little wind. Under normal conditions it would have been the sort of day to take the dog on a good free run up over Sapper Hill or among the sand dunes at Yorke Bay. Good ideas but non-starters at the moment. Both places are thick with troops and out of bounds. Now to make a trip anywhere outside the town one has to have a very good reason, in order to obtain a permit to do so from the military authorities. We are all confined to Stanley. It is not until we are prevented from going where we want that we realise how great a thing freedom to do as you please is, and how often we used to do it. This time last month, we all had the entire Falklands at our disposal. Now we are prevented sometimes from even looking to see what is going on on the opposite side of the road.

The news from the BBC at 9 this morning was interesting. Argentina has reported British warships, which they describe as two frigates and a troop carrier, about 54 miles north of South Georgia. No landing has taken place, but according to them there is a British intention of a possible attack. BBC went on to say that a helicopter from the *Hermes* was forced to ditch in the night and one man was lost. The Argentine Foreign Minister is to fly to New York later today. Britain's Mr Pym has returned from Washington with new plans on the Falklands crisis; has had a two-hour meeting with the Prime Minister. The South American Terrorist organisation, the Monteneros, have decided to support the Argentines. The South Georgia news is extremely encouraging. If the Argentine report is true then we have British forces only some three days' steaming time away from us, less if they are in a hurry.

So bucked up by this news that I telephoned Vice-Comodoro Bloomer-Reeve for an appointment to see him at 10 o'clock to make a protest over the taking down of and lack of care being shown to the pictures of the former Governors which hang in the town hall. Put on tweed jacket with collar and tie for the occasion; also made sure my boots were shining brightly. Was stopped at the Secretariat by one of the sentries, who only wanted a cigarette, so gave him one; and one for his mate as well in view of the splendid South Georgia news. Hope the Brits do have a go at them or I will have wasted two good cigarettes on the enemy. Discussion with Bloomer-Reeve were extremely cordial and successful. Capt Hussey of the Argentine Navy and Capt Vinelli, a legal officer also from the navy, were present too. I put it to them that if the Islands were theirs, then all the history and the heritage were theirs also and should be looked after accordingly. This worked – someone was telephoned to put the pictures of the Governors in a safe place immediately, along with the other items taken down from the town hall. Bloomer-Reeve went on to apologise for overlooking such an important thing, and said that it was their intention to leave Government House as it was, so that a museum could be established there as soon as things had settled down. How nicely he put it – by the sound of the news this morning there is a bloody great scrap brewing up. However, back to the meeting.

Things went so agreeably that it was possible to point out the importance of the shipwrecks and hulks in the harbour. A permanent reminder of the maritime heritage of the Islands, their importance was being now recognised on a world-wide scale. We were, up until twenty-three days ago, using a set of special commemorative postage stamps depicting some of them. It was of the utmost urgency that the troops did not saw them up for firewood now that the days are getting colder, or damage them in any way. Capt Hussey backed me fully on this. Being a mariner he recognised how unique it was that here in Stanley we have the last surviving examples in the world of an East Indiaman, an American packet ship, an American clipper, a British trading barque, and a British iron three-masted barque. A living essay in nineteenth-century shipbuilding. I pointed out that once every couple of weeks I used to go on board the hulks to look for any signs of breaking up and generally keep an eye on them, so that remedial action could be taken if necessary. Could I continue to do this? They agreed – a special pass would be drawn up for me, and would be ready for collection at the legal department on Monday morning. It's really quite amazing that once 'history', 'culture', or 'heritage' is mentioned, then the Argentines support it. For them I suppose it is a way of helping to improve the Islanders' understanding of culture.

For me it is a great personal achievement to have secured the protection of these old ships.

The news on South Georgia this morning seems to have had a powerful effect on both the Argentines and the civilian population. The Argentines are digging in on Victory Green, in the paddock behind the West Store, in the open space behind the FIC office block – everywhere in fact. They practised sounding the air-raid sirens at 11 o'clock this morning, which coincided with a fly-past of Mirages. There has been a fair amount of air activity for the rest of the day. The Argentines must have great faith in their early warning system for approaching aircraft, as they announced on the radio that two sirens would be sounded. The first would be to indicate that an air raid may be imminent. On hearing it, the population should proceed to the safe houses or shelters. Then, twenty minutes later, another siren would sound, at which time everyone should take cover. We in the population do not share their confidence in having twenty minutes' warning. The need for the establishment of a civil defence committee is paramount. Mike Bleaney, Dr Alison Bleaney's husband and Works Manager of the FIC, discussed this with Ron Buckett (Mechanical Superintendent in the Plant and Transport Authority). Both are ex-servicemen – Mike Royal Navy and Ron Army – who, having served in the Falklands, returned with their families to settle. Mike is also a partner in the farm at Bluff Cove. They put it to Vice-Comodoro Bloomer-Reeve, who agreed, but with the proviso that an Argentine representative should be present when the arrangements were being made, so that they would be in the picture. Francesco Moro, a member of the Argentine Civilian Staff recently brought in to work in the Administration department, was delegated and attended the first meeting, which was held at the Bleaneys' home in Stanley Cottage.

Stanley has now been split into sections, each under the supervision of a person selected for the responsibility of that area.

Under the co-ordination of Ron Buckett, a head count has been carried out today which shows that there are 545 persons presently in Stanley. This includes 50 children. Terry Spruce is passing this vital information on to FIC's London office, by telex. Every householder in Stanley has been contacted and given the civil defence leaflet and the allocation of a 'safe house' if required. A map has been prepared, showing the location of safe houses, stone houses and houses where people don't want to move. This information is being passed to England with the people leaving the colony, some of whom are being briefed on the whereabouts of Argentine military installations in Stanley.

The butchery has been taken over under protest from the FIC, who don't really have much option. By still remaining at the butchery they have to kill cattle for the Argentines but are able to safeguard the stocks of mutton for Stanley, which has been killed and deep-frozen to ensure that there is enough meat for the immediate future. The staff are on a 'go slow' routine, and when the Argentines want cattle killed they are able to try to safeguard the dairy cattle by letting them go and kill privately owned cattle, which ensures a supply of fresh milk for the town. With all outside communication cut, it is impossible to get fresh supplies in from the farm settlements.

I spent most of the afternoon putting some more finishing touches to our shelter, which has become known as the 'bunker'. We stowed down there containers of water, biscuits, blankets, pillows and candles. Also painted the DAP signs on the four outside walls of the house, in bright red, as advised by the military government – no one seems to be entirely clear within their organisation what exactly DAP stands for – so as an extra precaution painted 'CIVIL DEFENCE' in big letters as well. The sign is a diagonal cross inside a circle, with the letters DAP along the top and a white background. This has mystified most of the troops, who haven't a clue what it's all about. Their senior officers don't seem to have told them of it. In fact some troops viewed the painting operations on the various houses with great suspicion, apparently thinking that it indicated some sort of underground or subversive movement. We also thought it a good idea to paint red crosses on the Land Rover – on each door, the radiator grille, tail-board and truck cab roof. Several other people have done the same, especially those of us who take old people shopping or to the hospital; this last item does in a small way justify the use of the red cross. Things are getting a bit tense these days, so it pays to take every precaution. The troops do seem to realise the significance of the red cross, which is helpful. At the hospital and Admiralty Cottage – the nurses' home – local volunteers are painting huge red crosses on the roof and walls. The boys are filling sandbags, which are being stacked up outside the large glass windows of the operating theatre as blast protection. All windows are criss-crossed with adhesive tape.

The Monsignor came up at 4 to have tea with us and to inspect the new bunker. We were lucky to have had some water on hand for the tea, as it had been turned off all afternoon, for some unknown reason. Young Rag has also been inspired by the bunker, so much so that he asked if he could move in with us for the duration. He is welcome, as I feel that the more people we have around at a time like this the better it is. He lives with his parents up on Davis Street, which is rather exposed, and they are going to spend the nights sleeping down at the FIC West Store, along with others whose houses are in the same situation. Our friends Duffy and Jeannie Sheridan also had a quick inspection of the bunker, so we advised them to book early if they required space!

Conditions very poor for receiving the BBC, so we are a bit out of touch with the latest news. At about 9.30 this evening, I was asked if I could take Xenia Barnes, a young nurse, along in the Land Rover for night duty at the hospital. This almost turned out to be a disaster, as we suddenly ran into a military road-block down by the public jetty. The whole area had been sealed off and was crawling with armed troops. We were stopped by guards who poked their rifles into the cab, demanding to know why we were in that part of the town. The red crosses on the Land Rover got us out of it, as they seemed to imagine that I was a doctor with a patient, so we played it that way and got out fast.

The language difficulty is appalling sometimes. The cause of the intense security seemed to be that they were bringing in military equipment from the *Formosa*, which was being off-loaded at the public jetty, and we were obviously not supposed to see what it was. It was a dodgy few minutes; I really thought that we were going to be arrested for spying.

I later read the air-raid precautions distributed today from the Stanley Civil Defence Committee:

Air-raid Precautions

It is most unlikely that the town of Stanley or its inhabitants will be affected by any potential hostilities. Nevertheless it is common sense to be prudent in times like these and the following information is presented for your guidance in the event of an air-raid warning being sounded.

The information in Appendix 'A' is for those who wish to stay in their own homes. Those who would like to go to a place of shelter other than their own homes are requested to give their names to the person delivering this leaflet.

When all names have been collected, shelter rations will be allocated. Further information is contained in Appendix 'B'.

APPENDIX 'A' – *For those happy at home*

a If your house has a central lobby, use it as your shelter.
b Move furniture to outside of shelter area.
c Stick heavy paper to windows and panel glass using treacle/syrup/jam.
d Cover doors with mattresses.
e Provide water container and simple high-energy rations (glucose, chocolates, biscuits).
f If possible fill the window embrasures with sandbags.
g Provide emergency toilet facilities (you may not be able to get to the WC) ie buckets, disinfectant, toilet paper.
h Provide mattress to lie on + blankets and/or cushions.
i Provide radio for local station and spare batteries.
j Provide torch(es) and spare batteries and/or candles.
k Cut off any fuel supply to house.
l Cut off water supply, drain tank.
m Provide books/toys/cards as required.
n FIRST AID. There is no need for elaborate first aid kits. In fact the most useful item to have at hand is a clean linen sheet which can be torn into strips if required for compression pads and bandages. If cuts are sustained, bind a pad of linen to the area and secure with plastic strips. Do not interfere with the wound or attempt to remove any material. Calm and reassure the injured person and obtain qualified assistance as soon as possible. Do not administer alcohol, food or drink, until medical advice has been taken.

It should be understood that the above notes are not instructions, they are simply notes for your guidance to be acted on if you see fit.

Finally, if possible contact the hospital as soon as you can after assembly in your house to help them account for the population.

APPENDIX 'B' – *Those going to a shelter station.*

Have bag packed ready containing:

a A flask containing water.
b A few simple rations (chocolates, sweets, biscuits).
c Torch and spare batteries.

d Toilet paper/tissues.
e Diversion for any children (books/toys).

NB Carry a cushion and wear warm clothing.

The boys called on old Syd Lyse to enquire if he wished to be evacuated to a safe house but he declined, assuring them that he was quite well prepared where he was, with his two cats and his sword. The war does not mean a great deal of difference in Sydney's life-style, other than interfering with his drinking hours at the Rose Hotel. If you happen to pass his house early in the morning he still pops his head out of the bathroom window to enquire what day it is.

Sunday 25 April – Day Twenty-four

A cold, dull and watery day. Snow showers in the afternoon. Wind south-west, Force 4–5, increasing to Force 7 plus, with heavy sleet later in the evening.

The weather might be lousy but the news is superb. South Georgia has been retaken. We got wind of something big going on during the morning, when there were reports of an Argentine submarine being attacked at Grytviken (South Georgia) just after dawn, and that a Royal Marine SBS (Special Boat Squadron) unit had been on South Georgia since last Thursday. Then on the 5 o'clock news this evening we got the great news of the victory. The surrender came after an assault by helicopters, backed up by HMS *Exeter** and a Royal Fleet Auxiliary which was not named. There was a two-hour battle, after which the white flags are flying. At 5.30 the BBC announced the news that Her Majesty the Queen has been informed that the Union Jack now flies alongside the white ensign at South Georgia. No wonder the Argentines here were a bit touchy yesterday and today.

It's been a very busy day. I tidied up the garden a bit this morning. It is essential that we do not slacken off our standards and get apathetic in these grim times. At 2 o'clock there was an announcement that a group of Anglo-Argentines have arrived to talk with the Islanders about the benefits of co-operating with Argentina in an effort to bring a peaceful solution to the current problem. They described themselves as being ordinary working-class people who enjoyed many blessings and advantages under their Argentine military regime.

It was proposed that if we accepted their suggestions a new town would be built specially for us, some distance away from Stanley, in which we could all live happily ever after, with a sports complex, swimming pool, and other untold delights. What a load of old

* It later transpired that it was HMS *Antrim*.

rubbish it was. They didn't mention the size of their own bank books. They had either been pressured into coming here, brainwashed, or were just plain bloody stupid. It was most obvious that they were very much afraid of the approaching Task Force. The underlying theme of their message was to persuade us to ask Mrs Thatcher to turn back her Task Force. Having had their say on the radio, the military government arranged for the radio-telegraphy office to be specially opened up for one hour to enable them to get reaction from the Camp settlements on their proposals, which they were prepared to discuss in greater detail if necessary. It was not necessary. An unequivocal 'No' to any of their proposals came from all settlements.

A public meeting was then arranged in the post office, so that they could meet the people of Stanley. This turned out to be a very fiery affair, resulting in a complete disaster as far as their cause was concerned. The boys attended to find out how things went. I thought it would be unwise to make an appearance at this stage of events as those present were bound to be noted by the military. Several of their senior officers including Bloomer-Reeve were among the crowd. Their presence did not stop some very forceful speaking from a large number of Stanley people. The military soon got the message that in no way are we prepared to back down or give in, so the Anglo-Argies could only put their visit down as a dismal failure, returning to their community in Buenos Aires later in the evening. Serves them bloody well right. They want to enjoy the best of both sides. Although most frightfully British, they are completely in the grip of the Argentines. They don't appear to have any real loyalty; only a noxious mixture of greed and snobbery, probably more dangerous than the Argentines themselves. The news of the progress at South Georgia has not really helped their day here; slimy creatures; hope they find their financial assets frozen when they get back to Buenos Aires.

Intense military activity during the afternoon. Between 3.30 and 3.45, three Hercules C-130s and one F-28 took off from the airfield. The weather is worsening rapidly. Hundreds of troops marching in their flapping waterproof capes from the Drill Hall up to Davis Street. They were still going strong at 6 o'clock, by which time the wind had increased to almost gale force, with continual rain and sleet. There have been convoys of lorries full of troops, all heading east towards the airfield. It's difficult to know quite what they are up to – are they pulling some troops out, or are they expecting a landing by the British in the Cape Pembroke area?

Collected some of the elderly ladies in the Rover for Mass this evening. Our service from St Mary's was broadcast on the local radio. Unfortunately I got caught for the reading of the Introduction and commentary. It was rather interesting, however, that while introducing the Bidding Prayers I was able to get away with praying 'for the Queen and to guide our government and council'. I wonder how many people noticed. There were about thirty high-ranking officers in church. All had their weapons with them, which made a lot of clattering as they moved about; they could have left them outside with a sentry. We had a powerful sermon on peace by the Monsignor. Delivered all the ladies safely home again afterwards, which provided an opportunity to watch the troop movements. It's impossible to say, with the weather as it is, whether the aircraft are taking off or landing, but there is a continual stream of them. The red crosses on the Rover are proving most useful in getting waved on by the military through their convoys. Was very relieved, though, to get home and off the streets; there are too many guns poking about tonight for my liking.

Reception conditions on 'Calling the Falklands' very poor tonight, but did manage to hear Noreen speaking to us from Ramsgate. This programme is a great relief during these days. It's being jammed by the Argentines, but just to know that our families and friends are daily sending us messages is a great morale booster.

Jem is on fire duty at the hospital tonight. All firemen now have to wear an armband, on which is painted 'BOMBERO – FIREMAN'. This enables them to be on the streets after dark without question from the military. Hope Jem has remembered to put his on.

Monday 26 April – Day Twenty-five

Fine, clear and dry; last night's wind has dropped away, leaving a pleasant, bright day. Wind west, Force 3, dropping to 2 later in day. Very warm for this time of year; again must be all of 9° or 10°. This alternating weather must be having a most unfortunate effect on the troops living in tents and trenches.

At 7.30 this morning hundreds of troops were marching towards the west down Ross Road. Perhaps they are those who were taken up to the airport in the convoys of lorries yesterday; maybe they are new ones; it's hard to tell. About 11 o'clock there was a convoy of fourteen lorries full of troops heading out along the Darwin road.

Picked up an interesting programme on the radio this morning while trying for the news. It's apparently a request programme for the Task Force from London; certainly very handy as we can find out what ships are on the way.

This is one criticism of the BBC: they assume that we know what is going on. For instance, England and the rest of the world know what ships have sailed as part of the Task Force for the Falklands; we haven't got a clue. It is very frustrating to say the least. Surely someone in England must realise that we have a total lack of communication with the outside world. It was the same yesterday with the most important military success in South Georgia, yet because it was a Sunday the news bulletins were chopped out in favour of stupid plays. At the BBC, wars seem to stop for the weekend. Sporting-cum-cultural programmes take over till Monday morning, then it's on with the war again. Those in control of the BBC should have a go at being on the receiving end in a war situation occasionally, from which position they would see the importance of accurate and, above all, regular news bulletins. After all that, we hear on the 9 o'clock news that 180 prisoners have been taken at South Georgia; Leith Harbour was taken at daybreak. The Argentine radio news broadcasts still insist that fierce resistance is being put up by their troops.

Went along to the legal department as arranged on Saturday to see Capt Vinelli, who was very polite. Under his orders, some soldiers put carefully away in the strong-room the pictures of the Governors, along with the Admiral Sturdee's patent of baronetcy, and the sword presented to the colony by Royal Marines on their being given the Freedom of Stanley. I suggested that it was important to ensure the safety of the land documents kept on the shelves of the legal department. These date from the formation of Stanley in 1843; absolutely irreplaceable. Capt Vinelli agreed and gave me leave to put whatever I thought fit in the strong-room, and would provide soldiers to assist in the lifting and shifting. A kind offer but I managed with the assistance of Frances Biggs who was still working in the office. She is coping wonderfully with things, despite the fact that her first baby is only a few weeks away. Between us we got everything possible into the strong-room. Capt Vinelli then gave me a document prepared and signed by him which, translated, reads:

> By order of the Military Governor of the national territory of the Islas Malvinas, South Georgia and South Sandwich islands. I declare this Authorisation by means of which Mr John Smith, Historian of these Islands, may visit all the Wrecks and Hulks existing in Port Stanley and the vicinity with the sole purpose of conserving and assisting in their conservation, preserving them from all harm which could affect their historical value. To this aim he will be given access to these remains of seagoing vessels, adopting however the means of vigilance necessary to prevent all violation of the Military Security.

Not a great deal of air activity today, apart from lots of helicopters flying between the airport and Moody Brook. Our own two Beaver aircraft of the FIGAS are both outside the hangar parked on the slipway, very neglected; the Argentines are seemingly not going to bother about them. Some people say that the Islander aircraft has been camouflaged.

The *Bahía Buen Suceso* moved from the FIC jetty out to Port William, alongside the *Formosa*, during the day. At the public jetty, the *Monsunen*, now taken over by the Argentines, is loading what appears to be boxes of ammunition, thousands of them. Well over 200 troops are waiting around the jetty, ready to go on board as soon as the loading is completed. Obviously bound for one of the Camp settlements, but have no idea which one.

Towards 4 o'clock this afternoon, there were a lot of heavy explosions out towards the west of the town. Anya found these a bit frightening, so I walked with her up to the Sheridans to return young Maxwell home. The troops are digging in well up near their house.

We actually got some mail in from England today. Everyone is well, but naturally very worried indeed about our situation out here.

Very surprised about 6.30 this evening to see two Mustang fighters fly over. The Argentines must have borrowed them from some museum or other. They were accompanied by two other jet fighters with straight wings and small circular air intakes at the wing roots; they are familiar but can't remember the name of them.

It is Argentine Army Day, which was celebrated on the radio with a great speech to the troops by Gen Menéndez, preceded by lots of inspiring music. The theme seemed to be that they are to fight like lions for their fatherland. He obviously has not seen some of his lions lately. A vet might come in useful.

Tuesday 27 April – Day Twenty-six

A dull, cold, watery sort of day. Very off-putting for the troops, most of whom look as if they wish they were back home.

The news from Buenos Aires this morning is still of fierce resistance by their troops at Leith Harbour. Having sampled the information bulletins given out by the Argentine military regime, we are inclined to believe the BBC, even if they are a bit slap-happy about news at the weekends.

There was some sporadic firing during the night, with lots of vehicles moving out along the Darwin road. Very few aircraft about. One F-28 at around 20,000 ft at breakfast-time.

Jem and I went off to the FIC jetty to look at some of the hulks there. The pass worked. We were accompanied by an officer, who although most interested and helpful, was a bit of a nuisance as far as we were concerned. The military clearly did not want us to wander unaccompanied on the jetty where they were unloading equipment. Reasonable enough, I suppose; we would have done the same. In fact we were jolly lucky to have got as far as we did. The old *Snowsquall* is hanging together but won't last a great deal longer. The troops seem willing to help us later on in getting some ropes across her deck in an attempt to brace it together. Might as well make use of their assistance while they are still here.

In view of our restricted circumstances nowadays, we decided to get one of the Argentine television sets, so we paid the £20 down and brought home a splendid American Colorama 22-in screen model.

After lunch events took a new turn which developed rapidly throughout the afternoon. When coming out of the post office, we saw large numbers of fresh troops, who had clearly just arrived on some of the C-130s which came in during the latter part of the morning. They seem to be a sort of commando unit, very professional in appearance and somewhat older than the majority of those already here; about mid-twenties to early thirties. Dressed in full camouflage gear, with green berets, armed with sub-machine-guns, and bristling with grenades and spare magazines. Hard-looking men. They have set up their headquarters in the gymnasium.

We were just having tea in the front room when I happened to look out of the window in time to see Martyn being taken into a military vehicle by the new troops. Shortly afterwards one of his workmates rang to say that he had been arrested and taken to the police station, so rushed down there to see what was going on. He was with about twenty other local people in the station front yard, surrounded by the new troops, fully armed. From the captain in charge, I learned that they had all been arrested for not having any identification documents, so rushed back home for his passport and 'white card'. People were being arrested left, right and centre; it was just on 4.30, when they were on their way home from work. Bill Curtis was sat on the pavement with his hands on his head, held at gunpoint by one of the new troops. Bill, a Canadian, has recently come to the Falklands to settle with his family. Until this lot started he was well along with building his new house up on Brandon Road, but like the rest of us, his plans have been severely disrupted. Back at the police station, the presentation of the documents had no effect. Capt Ramanov said that they were Special Forces whose authority superseded all other military, that those detained were about to be taken away to a nearby settlement and that I was to join them. This was not on; the only thing to do was to call their bluff, so said that I was off home, turned my back and walked away. This honestly was the longest walk of my life; only 20 yd until the shelter of buildings, but it seemed like miles. No one opened fire. Once in the shelter I went like the clappers up through the garden of St Mary's Church, expecting any moment to be fired on. I think they had lost me as I'd dodged in through the church and out through the vestry.

Once home, phoned Bloomer-Reeve, who confirmed that the Special Forces overruled all others, but promised to do what he could. Within half an hour, Martyn and several others were released and home. The effect on Ileen was not good, but she bore out that hour wonderfully well. Several people were taken away in an aircraft to what the military describe as a nearby settlement.

We have a strong feeling that life is going to be a trifle different from now on.

Poor Nancy Poole, our 22-year-old niece, was in a terrible state, as she had been told that Raymond, her husband, had been arrested, so she left their nine-month-old daughter Andrea and headed for Bloomer-Reeve where she had a great argument. Her knowledge of Spanish came in useful, although she said later that most of what she used was the worst language imaginable. Tonight we are instructed that all houses are to be blacked out completely, and that a curfew has been imposed from 5 o'clock in the evening until 7 o'clock in the morning. This is a full curfew; no one allowed on the streets between 5 o'clock in the evening and daylight next morning. All the population are to go inside their houses and remain there. Any person ignoring or breaking these instructions will be dealt with under military law.

Identification documents are to be carried at all times. New ones will be issued by the military government very shortly. These announcements sound even more sinister, as they now always end with, 'Signed by the Military Governor of the Malvinas, Georgias del Sur y Sandwich del Sur'. After the events of the weekend the Military Governor must have written the bit about Georgias del Sur with his tongue in cheek.

Wednesday 28 April – Day Twenty-seven

A fine, bright, calm, cloudless day. Quite perfect for this time of the year. Temperature about 3°C. Wind west, Force 2.

Jem and I again tried out our military permit to go on board more wrecks this morning. We thought that we had better make the most of it before these new 'heavies' crack down on us. The slipway opposite the *Charles Cooper* is thick with dug-in troops, who summoned their officer to look at the pass, after which we were allowed to launch the dinghy, row out and go on board. The same happened up at the *Jhelum*; no problems at all.

It's an odd life these days, with plenty of jobs about the house which need doing but the inclination to get on with them has gone. It is even more difficult to try reading a book or making a model. Painting is right out of the question. A feeling of constant uncertainty prevails. It's fair to say that everyone left in town is absolutely confident that we will come out of this OK in the end, but we are all wondering what is going to happen in the meantime. We are trapped; the getting out is not going to be too easy, unless Argentina has enough common sense to withdraw her forces.

After the somewhat exciting events of yesterday afternoon, the new television provided a welcome bit of distraction. We got it going last evening after supper. Despite the rather shaky aerial set-up the reception is quite good. Patrick Watts does the announcing in English, while a smooth-looking Argentine does a Spanish translation. The weather forecast seems quite genuine enough, but the news is cooked up by the Argentines in an attempt to give them a bit of self-confidence, and us a few laughs. We watched some 'Tom and Jerry' cartoons, followed by a sort of '24 hours' programme presented from Buenos Aires in English by a lurky sort of Anglo-Argentine. Not the sort of thing which we would normally waste our time on, but it does help to relieve the boredom.

Thursday 29 April – Day Twenty-eight

Another fine day, after a dodgy start.

Blacking out the house last night kept us busy for a while; we seem to have twice as many windows as anybody else. We used blankets, cardboard and anything we could lay hands on. It was very difficult to let the dog out for her nightly tiddle; the method is to get into the scullery after telling everyone else not to open the door which leads into the kitchen, then put out that light, open the back door carefully, and push the dog out, hoping that no troops have noticed the door opening and that the dog will quickly get through whatever she wishes to do and return to the back door, hopefully not racing off around the garden as she usually does. Fortunately she came straight back, as she was a bit bewildered by there being no street lights on. It's very very eerie indeed.

Duffy called this afternoon to ask if he and Jeannie, along with Eli and young Maxwell, could take us up on our offer of sharing our bunker, as troops are digging in in their back garden, and just a little to the west of the front of them is what appears to be a very large ammunition dump. Jeannie openly admits she is terrified – so are we – so we may as well sit this lot out together. It will also have the advantage of filling the house up. With no spare room we are unable to take in guests, which is fortunate as the Argentines are looking for accommodation for their officers. They pay cash down in advance, but in no way do we wish to have any of them living here. The Sheridans arrived with their bags and provisions this afternoon, so we quickly arranged them in the guest bedrooms so that all beds were in use; now there are eleven of us in the house.

During the morning our telephone didn't seem to be working, so made enquiries resulting in the news that on the orders of the military government it had been disconnected, along with all other houses in which members of the former Falkland Islands Defence Force lived. This seemed to be another move to the part of the Argentine Heavy Brigade who arrived on Tuesday. This is definitely not on, so got in touch with Bloomer-Reeve's office, explaining that as this was designated a safe house and now accommodating eleven people including young children, it was essential that we had the use of a telephone, particularly for emergency medical calls after curfew. It was reconnected during the afternoon.

There is a wonderful atmosphere in the house, rather like a railway station with people and luggage everywhere. It's great.

The Heavies brought in their own motor bikes with them yesterday. They are kept in the gymnasium. Twenty or thirty Kawasakis, all brand new, which they are now learning to ride. Some manage quite well, but others are quite desperate as they patrol the town, done up in combat gear with sub-machine-guns slung across their backs. The silencers not really suitable for Special Forces operations, as the bikes can be heard approaching for some time before they actually arrive; most convenient as far as we are concerned. They have even brought their own padre with them, complete with combat bike. They appear to be an absolutely self-contained unit.

There is also a major with another brigade here who has a personal motor bike, a thing called a Red Rocket which his fellow officers are learning to ride. It's an incredibly noisy affair, quite unpredictable in its habits as they often go wildly off into unexpected wheelies, losing all dignity and control.

This motor bike craze is catching on among the troops, with the strong possibility that civilian bikes may be commandeered by the military, so the boys have taken the precaution of dismantling parts of their bikes which are now safely out of the way in our garage. The removed parts are now in the shed at St Mary's. The Monsignor seems to have somehow found justification in taking them into the protection and custody of the Church, lest they should fall into the wrong hands. When the Day of Reckoning comes, he is going to have a lot of explaining to do, but I think that he will be allowed in.

Friday 30 April – Day Twenty-nine

A bright day with not much wind, warm and mildish.

A pretty routine sort of day in these times. Duffy and Jeannie bringing down bits and pieces from their house – food, sleeping bags, etc. Duffy, as well as being an artist, is a fine carpenter and has modified several bits of my woodwork in the bunker. He has the most thoughtful way of suggesting possible improvements – so tactful, in fact, that I am now thinking that I might have been intending to have done things that way anyway.

We let Tyssen and Eli take young Maxwell down into the bunker to get him used to it. He is one year old today – what a way to spend one's first birthday. Still, I suppose that in years to come he will be able to enthral his grandchildren with epic tales of the occupation. Today he also walked for the first time, a few steps across the sitting-room.

Several callers during the day to look at the bunker, mainly the boys' mates whose chief concern is whether it will be safe enough to store the beer in. It does seem, though, that a number of people have similar ideas about using the space beneath their houses as a place of safety. Rudy and Camilla Clarke next door have also got a refuge under their house.

On 'Calling the Falklands' from London this evening, there was a very interesting message to us here that, should any of us wish to leave the Falklands because of the occupation and somewhat uncertain near future, the British Government would pay expenses, etc. All one has to do is to get from here – by, presumably, the Argentine Air Force – to Buenos Aires, where the Swiss Embassy can be contacted, who will assist in arranging onward travel to the United Kingdom via Uruguay. Conditions are a bit bad, but I think they went on to say that some sort of subsistence allowance would be paid once in the UK. A very generous offer and one which deserves some thought in view of Ileen's health. She is coping well at the present, but if things should get tougher then it may well cause her to lose the progress she has recently made.

The idea is good, but fraught with very difficult decisions which we would have to make, and, in making them we would have to weigh up most carefully what effect they would have on Ileen. The biggest and certainly the most painful would be having to have the animals put down; the two cats and the dog are very much and very deeply part of the family. It would be unthinkable in the present circumstances to leave the responsibility of their welfare to someone else. Other things to be considered are what would be done with the house, along with all our possessions. This is an emergency situation where departure would have to be made with only the minimum of luggage. Again, we could never leave the huge responsibility of house and home to anyone here. The chances of losing the whole lot, by either pillage or destruction, seem very high. We are, too, such a close family that if one goes we all go; this would be the only way in which Ileen would even consider leaving. A crushing decision to have to make, but one which will have to be made in a realistic and logical manner in the long-term interests of us as a family.

At the moment I don't feel either logical or realistic, so will discuss it with Jem and Martyn in the morning. Anya is bearing up so well that it would be totally unfair to mention anything to her yet, although I can see that she is very much aware of the present problems. Being head of a family in times like these imposes some very heavy responsibilities.

How strange it seems to have television here in Stanley. We watched the news this evening, live from the broadcasting studio in English and Spanish. What a load of old rubbish it was again, cooked up by the Argentines for our benefit. How Patrick Watts can read it out without laughing I do not know. It must be a great strain on him having to read such claptrap, surrounded by Argentines. We are fortunate indeed that he has had the tenacity to keep going. With him still within the broadcasting service we have not surrendered it entirely to the Argentines; even though we all know the news is rubbish, it is at least being brought to us by one of our own, who will not abandon his post.

The main content of tonight's '24 Hours' programme was the visit of President Galtieri to Stanley, and we learned that he was present at the passing-out parade of some of the young conscripts. I am surprised they admitted that sort of thing, as it shows just how new and untrained some of their troops are – I suppose he told them where they were? We met some the other day who thought they were on exercise in Southern Argentina, near the Chilean border. They were very surprised to find that they had ended up in their beloved Malvinas, but not over-enchanted as they were a bit cold and damp. Nor were they over-enthusiastic about their splendid new rifles and uniforms; they were also hungry. Galtieri also wickedly twisted the Catholic faith a great deal, making a big show of passing his rosary beads about among his young soldiers and assuring them that the Blessed Virgin Mary was on their side. One very young lad offered the General his rosary beads, but he waved them away saying, 'You will need them more than I do my son.' It was sickening to watch. The television closes down each evening with a fifteen-minute broadcast by an army chaplain, wearing dark glasses, who compares some part of the Bible with the Falklands situation; pumping away at the religious side of things in what is an effort to boost the morale of the troops. I'm sure he will never get to heaven.

Saturday 1 May – Day Thirty

Superb day – clear, crisp and windless. Sunny this morning, but got dull in the afternoon.

What a day it's been. At 4.37 this morning we were literally thrown out of our beds by the most fearful explosions. The house seemed to lift off its foundations. All of us sleeping upstairs arrived on the landing at the same time, in a big heap, wondering what the hell had happened. By the time we had got to the bottom of the stairs, a tremendous barrage of anti-aircraft and machine-gun fire opened up from all over the town. It was a very still night, so that the sound seemed to be coming from outside in the garden; very noisy indeed. This woke the boys, who have their bedroom downstairs. The ensuing chaos is hard to describe. Robert fell out of the door still in his sleeping bag, trying to hop towards the bunker entrance; Jeremy and Martyn were rushing about in the nude trying to find some clothes to put on, while we were in the porch attempting to get down into the bunker, all at the same time. Ileen tried to get out of the loo with the door still locked; Jeannie threw herself flat on the guests' bathroom floor. All of these things took place almost simultaneously, but eventually we were all settled inside the bunker, debating just what had taken place.

The firing stopped after a while, causing someone to suggest it was about time we had a cup of tea, so we all trooped back up to the kitchen. We tuned into the BBC to see if they could offer an explanation, but all we could get from England was a most interesting but rather unhelpful programme on birth control for overseas listeners. At last the news came on, from which we learned that our airfield had been bombed by a Vulcan of the RAF. This wonderful news was celebrated with another brew of tea, with which we sat waiting for daylight, which came in dramatically with a bunch of Harriers streaking in through the harbour entrance almost at sea-level at a truly incredible speed. The water and earth boiled with their cannon-fire; then they let go their bombs on the airfield.

It was all over in seconds; just one long, mighty blast and roar of sound, then absolute silence with a great pall of smoke and flame rising up hundreds of feet into the sky above the airfield. The most fantastic sight I have ever seen. Goodness only knows what the casualty rate was in the area among the thousands of Argentines camped and dug in down there. Immediately afterwards the anti-aircraft guns opened up again; great panic among the troops; they just didn't know what had hit them. Then, in what seemed to be a move to confuse the Argentines even further, one Harrier came in low from the east, streaking up the harbour, then made off among the mountains. As she went over the *Formosa*, which had pulled out from the jetty to anchor in the harbour last evening, the ship suddenly opened fire with guns from the bows and stern. We had thought that she was unarmed. There was lots of black smoke, but her gunners missed completely.

Things remained fairly quiet, but very tense as far as the Argentines were concerned, until quite late in the afternoon. Just before 3 o'clock, the Argentines once more opened up with anti-aircraft fire. Something or other had given them a fright. Duffy, with the boys and I, turned to building a barricade around the front of the porch with all of the old timber we could find, on top of which we piled my collection of ploughs, cart-wheels, and flower tubs. It was a worthwhile exercise as the Argentines seem liable to open fire indiscriminately in all directions at the thought of Harriers arriving. If only they would point their weapons up in the air it would be to some advantage. During the morning's performance they were even doing their bit with rifles and pistols, which was a trifle hair-raising. On the corner, just over the road by the Co-op, they are reinforcing their dug-outs and machine-gun pits, creating a sense of competition in which they frequently gave us friendly but noticeably nervous waves. We returned with new-found confidence.

Between 4 and 4.30 the Royal Navy arrived on the scene to bombard the airport from seawards, with what we think were three frigates. Then the Argentine Air Force turned up with some Mirages and Canberras. A great barrage of anti-aircraft fire was sent up by the Argentines on the ground, who obviously had no idea that their own planes were up there. Their enthusiasm was so great that they managed to bring down one of their own Mirages, over the hill towards Port William, while our Harriers got a Mirage and a Canberra. A very noisy and hectic afternoon.

At 6 o'clock we switched on the television to see how the day's events would be presented, Argentinian-fashion, but were prevented from doing so as a very intense burst of machine-gun and small-arms fire opened up somewhere close by – so close, in fact, that we all dashed into the bunker and left the television to itself. The firing only lasted a short while; have no idea what it was all about, but as it was just on dark it's possible that the troops took fright at some movement or other in the half-light.

Sunday 2 May – Day Thirty-one

A dull, cold day with very little wind.

Well, our first night in the bunker was really quite comfortable. The eleven of us just fitted in without an inch of spare space. For extra comfort we had taken the foam-rubber cushions from the furniture in the sitting-room and front porch, and laid them on the bunker floor. We then put our sleeping bags on top, arranging ourselves in head-to-tail fashion, with the ladies and Maxwell at the far end and the boys in the middle, and Duffy and I near the ladder up to the hatch. Lighting was no problem as we had rigged up a wander-lead, which was suspended from an old poker stuck into one of the cracks in the concrete wall. As a precaution we also had candles and matches at each end of the bunker.

Shortly after settling in there was a lively debate on ventilation and our prospects of suffocation if the hatch was closed. This was soon resolved, at 11 o'clock, when what seemed to be a naval bombardment opened up. The decision to shut the hatch was swift. The bombardment lasted for about three and a half hours. It is difficult to say if there were one or more ships. They seemed to be steaming up and down the coast from Cape Pembroke to Port Harriet, then back again, as the sound of the crumps and bangs seemed to gradually increase in volume then die away. The firing was very regular: about twelve or fifteen rounds at three-second intervals, then a pause for a few minutes – which we put down to either the gunners having a cigarette, or allowing the barrel to cool off a bit – then off they would go again.

The idea seemed to be, according to the military strategists among us, to saturate the Argentine troop encampments with gunfire as a morale-breaking and softening-up process; whatever the object it must have been very, very frightening out there. Return fire from the Argentines seemed sporadic but very definite, as we could hear the much sharper, biting crack of their artillery going off, whereas the navy shells coming in from the sea were more of a crump. I suppose what we are hearing is one lot of shells coming and the other lot going. Verdict on last night's performance was that a lot more arrived than went out.

In view of yesterday's air attacks and daylight bombardment, the Monsignor decided that it would not be very prudent to hold Mass. We spent a fairly quiet day. Anya was on duty at the hospital. Being Sunday, the news from London was sparse, but comforting. The news from the Argentines was grim, and, we hope, wishful thinking on their part. They reported HMS *Hermes* had been badly damaged, with five of her Harriers lost. The BBC reported that there was no damage and that all her aircraft had returned safely.

At dusk this evening, the Argentine helicopters carried out what appeared to be a low-level search up the shores of the harbour. Perhaps they fear the possibility of Special Forces arriving.

So ends the most encouraging day since this whole affair began. The spectacular events of the past few hours brought about a unanimous decision to sleep the night in the bunker; all signs of bravery and heroics had disappeared. As Duffy so graphically put it, 'This is for *real*, boy.'

Monday 3 May – Day Thirty-two

Dull and rainy with low cloud. Typical May day.

Another good night in the bunker; all very quiet; if there was a naval bombardment I didn't hear it. Anya woke me at 7.30 to go up to the loo. The main disadvantage of sleeping alongside the ladder is that anyone wanting to go up top has to clamber over you. We find that by closing the hatch about three-quarters of the way, it is possible to have a good flow of air through the bunker, which keeps everyone fresh. If firing starts, we close it fully. We also do this when we have the light on, as the black-outs in the front porch are not over-great (the roof is of glass which is difficult to black out properly). It is important to remember, when entering or leaving the bunker, that it is vital to have all lights out.

On the news front we have just heard from the BBC that the *General Belgrano* has been sunk by torpedoes. Details are still very sketchy, but it is reported that she had about 1,000 men on board. Militarily this is in our favour, but what a terrible tragedy.

The *QE2* has been requisitioned by the Government to join the Task Force – words fail me. Her voyage time is estimated to be about ten days; plus two other unnamed ships requisitioned. I find it incredible to think back to 1977, when I was at the rehearsal for the Silver Jubilee Fleet Review, and that many of the ships we passed, including the *QE2*, should now be approaching the Falklands in a war situation.

There was also news of some small Argentine craft being attacked, but conditions were so bad that it is impossible to receive accurately what was said. It seemed to be that two patrol vessels – a smaller vessel and a gunboat – had been attacked, presumably by aircraft from the Task Force.

Reception conditions may have been poor due to the Argentines, who are most definitely jamming the 'Atlántico del Sur' broadcasts in Spanish from London to the Argentine troops here. Have managed to pick it up fairly clearly on a couple of occasions – it's most odd to hear the chimes of Big Ben followed by a broadcast in Spanish.

Tuesday 4 May – Day Thirty-three

A dull, windless day; not over-cold (as far as we are concerned). Still most unusual weather for this time of the year.

Slept fairly well in the bunker until about 4.30 when we were woken by a very loud explosion which shook the house, followed by several less loud ones. On the BBC news this afternoon, we learned that there has been another Vulcan raid on the airfield, which presumably was the bangs we heard and the crashes we felt. This morning on BBC news we heard that survivors are being picked up from the *General Belgrano*. It is not entirely clear the exact number of persons on board; it seems to range between 700 and 1,000. She is now presumed to have sunk.

Jeremy arrived home from work on his dumper truck this morning for breakfast. As the Public Works Department is under new management these days, work on the construction of the new Darwin road has ceased, and certain changes have taken place. Work now begins at 8.30 each morning and finishes at 1 pm. The power station is also under the new management, so Martyn is having to abide by the new rules as well. Jeremy has just spent two years at school in England – the Thomas Peacocke at Rye – for his 'A' levels, and according to the advertisements in the Sunday supplements has the necessary qualifications to fly a Phantom or command a frigate. His achievements so far under the Argentine military regime in the dockyard amount to the command of a dumper truck collecting the town refuse each day. Martyn has a fairly interesting time at the power house, as they have installed a missile site at the back of it, which tends to make life a little more exciting at times. It's highly dangerous anywhere outside nowadays, as during bombardments or air raids the Argentines open up with everything they have, including their rifles. How they avoid shooting each other is a mystery to us all. We lead a curious existence now, from one BBC news to the next, hopping down the bunker if firing sounds a bit too close, then up again to prepare meals.

The new Government announces that our clocks will not be moved from Summer Time to Winter Time this year. This news has not created any noticeable excitement among the population. Some nights the street lights are switched off. It's all very eerie, and one has to be careful to take in the washing as the Argentines open fire on anything that moves after dark.

Because of the curfew and curious new working hours, the Monsignor has decided that Mass will be at 3 o'clock each afternoon. Only a very small congregation today.

We all spent most of the afternoon cutting the tops out of 45 gall. oil drums, and filling them with earth, to further reinforce the front porch defences.

On 'Calling the Falklands' this evening we heard Robbie speaking to us; it was great to hear his voice again. Then at 6.20 they announced that the *Sheffield* had been abandoned and sunk after having been hit by a missile. It is thought that all her crew except twelve have escaped. We have also lost a Harrier and pilot during the day. This news has left me terribly depressed. The full reality of what we are in comes right home hard. I do hope that someone somewhere will cause this terrible conflict to come to an end. Why don't they ask the people of the Falklands? Is this a defeatist attitude on my part?

Wednesday 5 May – Day Thirty-four

Very foggy and damp day.

Poor old Mrs Perry's house was shot up by the Argentines during the night. Why they opened fire is a mystery, but they made a terrible mess of old Howard Johnson's suits, which were hanging in the wardrobe; all riddled with bullet holes.

The oil stove in the kitchen is playing up, so spent most of the morning with Robert attempting to sort it out. Then shopped with Ileen and Anya at the West Store.

Went to Mass at 3 this afternoon. The annexe at St Mary's is being made ready for use as a temporary school by John Fowler and Steve Whitley for the few children who remain in town. Although no one said as much, I personally think this is an attempt to put the building to a good use which will prevent the Argentines from moving troops in there to live. The Monsignor says nothing, but has a satisfied look about him.

Good reception, or at least better than usual, for 'Calling the Falklands'. Received messages from Viola, and John and Tina Harradine, and Noreen spoke. All good stuff which gives us a tremendous boost. If only they could see us listening, huddled around the wireless on the kitchen table, with the windows blacked out with blankets; all dressed in what has become our standard garb nowadays, more practical than elegant – jeans, jerseys, bodywarmers and training shoes, with our rubber boots placed handy, along with torches, matches and candles. When the need arises, we can all get into the bunker with remarkable speed in the darkness. Also placed handy is a plastic food container which is our family first-aid box, containing everyone's particular things from Librium to asthma cure. In the event of a general scramble for the bunker, the first priority is split between grabbing young Maxwell and the first-aid box. In a totally unconscious way we have recently all developed an awareness of the need to have the essentials of life near at hand at all times.

Reasonably good evening on the television: an elderly American film about a violinist, followed by a superb English comedy about a family and bees. It reminded me so very much of Rye; felt extremely nostalgic, especially with the bird-song in the country lanes. Really felt better after watching it.

Information via the local broadcasting station is difficult to get hold of these days. Hardly any information is given out on the announcements by the military. Some houses in town are connected up to the rediffusion system – the 'Box' – over which Pat Watts gives out such local information as he is allowed to – weather forecasts, etc – but these can only be received within the rediffusion system. It was installed years ago and is being phased out. Our receiver has packed up, so we – like many others – are unable to listen in.

Thursday 6 May – Day Thirty-five

Dull and still again, with fogbanks rolling in throughout the day.

Very comfy and quiet night until about 5.30 when we were woken by nearby small-arms fire from the direction of the hospital. Later this morning found that it was caused when an elderly patient from Stanley was taken into hospital in the ambulance. Being a traffic movement before the end of curfew, the military opened fire on it. There seems to be little or no liaison between the various units of the military in the town. Total enthusiasm for opening fire at every opportunity seems to be the only cohesive factor among the Argentine forces. The military must have known about the departure of the ambulance, as the hospital is under their control, complete with guards. In fact one of them must have accompanied the ambulance on its mission.

The 8 o'clock news seemed a bit brighter this morning, with more efforts on peace talks. This was a rather false booster to morale for the day, as the later news bulletins became more sombre. By 4 this afternoon, Argentina had rejected new peace proposals. Britain still requires complete withdrawal of Argentine forces before any further negotiations. It's now back to the United Nations. Two Harriers have been lost while on patrol in the Maritime Exclusion Zone. They are presumed to have crashed and not been shot down. The MOD announce that there are about twenty persons missing from the *Sheffield*. There was only two seconds' warning of the missile attack on her. The fire was fought for five hours before they were forced to abandon hope of saving her. It is so difficult to grasp that this is happening just off our coast – people are being burned to death, drowned. A Type 42 destroyer, to my mind the most elegant warship for years, has been destroyed by a single missile. For some reason I had built up over the years the idea of the 42s being almost infallible – I suppose that the Admiralty thought they were pretty good as well.

Lots of troops about the streets today. We are now used to several hundreds sculling about the place as a matter of course, but today more seem to have turned up from somewhere or other. Had a yarn at the gate with the Ashworths when they delivered the milk this morning. As usual the entire family in the Rover, quite oblivious to shot, shell and bombs as they go about their delivery. Malcolm is a bit worried about the safety of his dairy cattle as the Argentines are rather short of food down in his part of town. Fodder is also causing him considerable concern as there is no way of bringing hay in from the settlement farms now. Down at the dairy they are virtually surrounded by troops dug in and camped around the YPF fuel depot area, the rubbish dump and the cemetery.

Went along with Duffy in the Mini van to shop at the West Store during the morning. Duffy has a number of elderly folk under his care as part of the town civil-defence plan, whom he shops for and visits daily. This, besides being most Christian and charitable, gives him the opportunity of getting about the town far more freely than many of us. It's quite surprising how one can gauge the tenseness or otherwise of the military atmosphere in various parts of the town during these runs.

It is impossible to actually pinpoint what conveys the mood, but I know that on some days one can actually feel whatever it is in the air. I try to get along on these trips fairly frequently as it gives us a picture of what and who is where in the military field. I would go more often and perhaps do more, but I don't like leaving Ileen too long. The results of being caught out in a raid or being swept up in a snap arrest by the military would not be good. The attitude among some of the older troops and some of the officers seems to be hardening, though the conscripts are as bewildered and fed up as ever. We notice this especially after Mass each afternoon when we make a point of taking the dog for a walk for half an hour, finding out who and what is where, as they tend to move things such as guns and a mobile radar unit around the town from day to day.

A bit of air activity this afternoon. About 2 o'clock the Skyvan took off from the airfield with the intention of landing on the racecourse, but things went a trifle wrong during the landing, causing it to end up in the ditch against the north rails. From eye witness accounts it is bent rather badly, which has given a little boost to the morale of the townsfolk – it is really quite surprising how news travels, especially good news. At 3.30 a Hercules C-130 landed at the airport, which means that it must still be usable. It took off again at 5 o'clock to great cheers from the troops down in front of the town hall as it flew past. There was even a *feu de joie* from some soldiers.

Jeremy went off at 4.15 to the hospital on fire duty, while Duffy, Martyn and I filled everything we could with fresh water as the supply seems to be somewhat sporadic these days. Apart from the increased population of the town, I do not think that the nightly naval bombardments help a great deal either, as some of the shells land spectacularly close to the plant, causing the aged equipment – including the tanks themselves – to creak and groan a bit. In fact a few days ago one of the water-department people told us that one of the main holding tanks had shifted some 4 in out of line, which gives some idea of what being on the receiving end of a naval bombardment feels like. I've noticed that since the first Vulcan bombing of the airport our front gate will not close properly, and a chunk of cement has fallen out from the inside of the front doorstep.

Tonight's Argentine television gave us a most interesting programme by David Attenborough called 'World About Us', which was filmed in Brazil. I remember meeting him while he was staying in Stanley not long ago; very pleasant chap. This was followed by a sort of recycling of Argentine propaganda junk on the heroics of their countrymen in the Malvinas. There is a marked difference between the confidence of the bloke on the television and the actual conditions outside. Someone is not telling the truth. They are claiming that the airport is undamaged, but the film being shown looks remarkably similar to that which was screened just after the invasion. News was followed by an Argentine comedy which we turned off. The news, I think, was the better comedy of the two.

Friday 7 May – Day Thirty-six

Superb start to the day – fine, sunny, fresh, but very chilly and tingling. The harbour was absolutely still, like a mirror; so still that it was possible to see the logger ducks over at the other side as they swam close inshore. Later in the day there were some misty, foggy patches, and it got quite a bit colder, but still no wind.

Excellent night in the bunker. Heard no firing so presume that there was none, but having said that I must confess that the steady rhythmic crash of the naval bombardments does have a soporific effect on me, in fact on all of us. It is only when the Argentines return the fire that the rhythm is disturbed, which unfortunately tends to wake us up.

This sudden drop in temperature has caused great starting problems with the military vehicles; lots of activity, shouting and crashing as they have to bump start their lorries. There was also a lot of early morning helicoptering. The troops seem in a cheery enough mood.

This occupation or situation, or whatever people may wish to call it, has made us all very much aware of the somewhat frightening business of just living from day to day, creating an almost careless attitude towards certain things. When we put up the black-outs, we go around with a couple of hammers along with a jar of nails, happily banging away with no thought of the future, when we will have no black-outs but will be faced with window-frames riddled with holes. They are beginning to look a terrible mess, but I just don't worry about it. Yet on the other hand, in order to keep up some semblance of normality, I spent a couple of hours outside in the garden tidying up. It was particularly nice this morning to watch Aunt Mally on her bicycle pedal quite unconcerned through a squad of marching troops. I wonder what they really think of their so-called fellow countrymen of the Malvinas? I also saw Robin Pitaluga going to the R/T with his guard. I don't quite know what has happened to him, but it seems that he used his radio, thus breaching the military instructions, causing him to be arrested, brought into Stanley and kept under sort of house arrest at the 'Upland Goose'. He looks very well, almost as if he is doing the guards a favour by accompanying them on their walk.

BBC news is still encouraging: twenty more Harriers are to be flown out to join up with the Task Force, along with some Nimrods. Britain has now announced that the Exclusion Zone extends to within 12 miles of the Argentine mainland. The search for the two missing Harriers has been given up. Two more young lives lost because of Galtieri's madness. We had an encouraging message to us from Phil Warne on 'Calling the Falklands' this evening. I imagine that he is taking an especially keen interest in our goings on, as he has had a taste of the Argentine Navy when he was captain of the *Shackleton* a few years ago, when they actually fired on her while on passage to Stanley. A very brave man and a good friend.

Did a bit of shopping in the West Store. Shelves are becoming noticeably emptier, but the management have things very carefully under control, so that essential things such as butter, sugar, tinned milk and the like are kept out at the back or under the counter. There is no rationing as such, but Ynonne Turner and Isobel Castle on the tills keep a sharp eye on who has what in their shopping baskets. Any sign of luck-pushing in the way of stores is quickly and effectively dealt with, but it is really commendable for those of us who remain in town not to have started hoarding essential supplies.

A most noticeable and really quite amazing change has occurred in Stanley now. There is an air of much greater companionship among everyone; we all seem to have a lot more trust and a lot more faith in one another – war is a great leveller. It's also interesting to see different character changes taking place. Some of the John Wayne hero types of the town have quietly slipped from the front row, and their places are taken by the most unexpected people. I know that's not the right word, but what I'm trying to say is that there are now people in town who one would never have dreamed of taking charge of situations and now they are emerging as absolute leaders as well as creating tremendous confidence among us all. The flamboyant ones have collapsed like pricked balloons, while the quite quiet, unobtrusive ones are coping and taking charge of the situation.

The area down towards the FIC offices, jetty and workshops, etc, is now a restricted military zone under heavy guard. The managers, along with all their staff, now have to have a pass to go to work.

The air blockade by Britain must have a few holes in it, as two C-130 Hercules arrived and departed during the day. They fly noticeably lower now, just skimming the hilltops as they take off, then keeping close to the mountains, using the valleys as shelter.

Went to Mass, as is now our routine, at 3 in the afternoon. The Argentines can't quite make this out, as we go off in a bunch, mustering outside the front gate, all six of us; then off down the road, passing the time of day loudly in English to the watching soldiers. It's interesting to note that we are observed each day by some sort of a duty look-out posted in one of the windows of the town hall. Perhaps he sets his watch by our movements. We occasionally give him a wave, so that he has either to ignore us or respond, which all helps to confuse and undermine them.

After Mass we make a point of standing on the chapel steps having a cigarette with Monsignor and Father, which gives us a good opportunity to see what is going on over on the other side of the road at the gymnasium, where the Special Forces are billeted; also at the town hall and the police station. They can't very well order us to move on, and it's surprising just how long one can make a cigarette last out if something interesting is happening. This also has a somewhat disturbing effect within the Argentine troops, as many, as they pass by, acknowledge the presence of the Monsignor, who obliges with a wave and blessing. It is quite apparent that some of their officers do not like this procedure, but being good Catholics there is little they can do about it.

After Mass we take the dog for a walk. She is rather fed up with this occupation business, as she is so used to being free and able to run long distances. Now, because of the heavy military traffic, we have to keep her on a short lead and are confined to the town. She is an extremely powerful dog and noticeably impresses the troops as she lunges along on her chain-lead, which we have to keep short, causing her to pant loudly and froth at the mouth. To those who do not know her she must look like a killer, but actually she is quite daft. The fact that she is totally deaf helps a lot too, as we control her by taps and hand movements which give the mistaken impression of total obedience and strict training. Actually it's all very much pot luck what happens, but it does create the right image.

I forgot to mention the other day that, on one of our walks, a rather cocky soldier loosed off a couple of rounds from his rifle into

rom left to right: Martyn, Tyssen, Ileen and I in the bunker, with
scape opening behind.

nya, Rag and I in the bunker during a naval bombardment. The
in bottle contains some of the emergency supply water, and I
appened to be lighting a cigarette for someone else at the
ame time as my own. Without this explanation, the effects of
tress may be somewhat misleading!

Argentine armoured personnel carriers enter Stanley.

The rocket-damaged Ionespheric Research Station at the east end of Davis Street, occupied by Argentine forces.

'he Argentine flag flying at Government House with Mount
'umbledown in the background.

ırgentine Aeromacchi aircraft at Stanley airfield.

We're sorry, but we're hungry. Please buy only
for me ([redacted]), Micky and Ivan.
When you see a man with stars or red lines
you can't speak with us.
Please if you can, buy us these things

2 Tootbrash
3 Wafer Cadbury's
4 Mars
3 Regal Cadbury's
3 Orange sandwich o L'orange Cadbury's
8 Whole Nut Cadbury's
4 Piece of Ham

And if you can, buy other things
for eating.

Thank you

Note passed by hungry Argentine troops to civilians in Stanley.

Esta ración fue embalada
por voluntarios, hombres
y mujeres de todas las
edades.
Estamos con ustedes

¡VIVA LA PATRIA!

Card included in Argentine ration packs – 'These rations were packed by volunteers, men and women of all ages. *We are with you.* Long live the Fatherland!'

Argentine 155mm gun in Davis Street.

Argentine Panhard armoured cars.

After the surrender, hungry Argentine POWs discover that their army had many tons of food stacked in containers throughout Stanley.

Some of the first Royal Marines entering Stanley after the surrender.

Stanley, 14 June: An hour before Argentine white flags of surrender begin to appear, fierce fighting is still taking place, with the nearby mountains to the west completely obscured by smoke and flames.

Public jetty, Stanley, 16 June: British troops rounding up Argentine prisoners. The LSL *Sir Bedivere* is about to come alongside the FIC jetty, just out of the picture to the right. The small camouflaged vessel is the Argentine patrol craft *Islas Malvinas,* later to be renamed HMS *Falkland Sound.*

Liberation: Eli and Tyssen happy to be alongside a British tank.

the air as we passed, in what was a distinct attempt to frighten the dog. It did not work, but had a considerable effect on Ileen and me, although we tried not to show it. Another advantage in having a dog is that it prevents troops snooping about our garden during the night foraging for food, shelter, or whatever they may be able to make off with from the sheds and outhouses.

During the afternoon, Duffy got to work with the sledgehammer and knocked out another large outcrop of rock in the bunker, which provides a bit more space. It's getting really quite luxurious down there now, as we have all more or less got our own little spaces, filled with personal bits of junk, etc. The children – Tyssen and Eli – are absolutely marvellous during quick descents, with no fuss or panic. That usually starts afterwards when the lid is closed and the electric lead lamp is on. It's more fighting than anything else, when someone has pinched someone else's comics or book; then Maxwell invariably wakes up, full of enthusiasm, crawling about over everyone in their sleeping bags, doing general acrobatics and refusing to go back to sleep.

Martyn is duty fireman at the hospital tonight. The Argentine casualties have been moved out during the day. No one seems to know where they have gone; possibly evacuated to the mainland on one of the Hercules which came in. The hospital is rather full now at nights, as most of the old folk have been moved from their homes into more or less permanent beds, while other staff spend the nights there in case of an emergency. The Argentines also have their medical staff and military guards, which tends to make things a bit crowded, so that people have to sleep on mattresses in the corridors. The boys say the guards are friendly enough. There are now even occasional competitions between them and the local ex-FIDF lads in stripping and reassembling their weapons. The local boys always win. Some of the guards also give away rounds of ammunition as souvenirs which are enthusiastically received, as it all helps to reduce their stocks – only fractionally, but every little helps.

Saturday 8 May – Day Thirty-seven

A grey, misty day. Rather cool, though not at all like it should be for this time of year. Wind west, Force 2–3.

Big event: spent all last night upstairs in bed with no firing heard by any of us. Woke about 8 o'clock with hay fever; perhaps should remain sleeping in the bunker. Found Duffy and Rag already up, sitting in the kitchen supping tea and listening to the news: much the same; the UN taking up our cause with little success. Spent the morning cleaning the stove which is a very messy business. It's quite a modern oil-fired affair but tends to clog up badly with soot and allied deposits in the place where the flame burns, around the bottom of the hot plates and down the sides of the oven. As we got so dirty, we decided to sweep the chimneys as well, which is done from the pots downwards. This gave us an excellent reason to be on the roof much longer than really we needed, but it's not often now that the chance occurs to get an uninterrupted view over the town as far as Port William and the airport. Heard a jet aircraft high overhead but too misty to see anything. The airfield looks a bit tangled; they say that the terminal building is now just a ruined shell. A C-130 Hercules came in and seemed to land on the grass at the side of the runway.

The boys connected up one of the domestic heating gas cylinders so that we had a good supply of hot water. During the past weeks we have had them disconnected and stowed well up the garden, because the effect is quite spectacular when they are hit by bits of shrapnel. It means that the hot water and heating system is reduced to only the oil firing, but that is vastly preferable to having the front of the house blown off.

Had a generally relaxed day. The night in a proper bed has had a beneficial effect on everyone. (For clarification, we were not all in the same bed.) The boys and children watched the television during the afternoon while Ileen, Jeannie and I walked around the town with our Hound of the Baskervilles. Everywhere looks scruffy and dirty. Troops still wave, and I do think many would like to talk if the language barrier could be overcome.

Cousin Nancy brought us some eggs, the first we have had for weeks; young Andrea is as lovely as ever and growing rapidly. They are coping well under the circumstances, which are not entirely pleasant up in their part of town opposite the senior school, which is now converted into a sort of fortress, with guns poking out everywhere. Raymond says they have installed an anti-aircraft gun round the back, in the playground, which is a bit noisy at times. Like most people here, he is a master of understatement – to have a twin-barrelled 35-mm Oerlikon gun pumping out about 500 rounds per minute only 50 yd away can be a trifle disturbing. The front of the school is barricaded with drums of earth, sandbags and concrete blocks. I think they may have some kind of communications centre there. Whatever it is, they are looking after it most carefully.

After Mass the Monsignor came up to have tea with us; looking remarkably well and complaining bitterly about having to chase a bunch of Argentine troops out of his peat shed last night. Going in to peat sheds for shelter is all very well, but they will insist on lighting up their little stoves, which is highly dangerous and likely to set the whole shed on fire.

Hilarious supper time with young Maxwell attempting to feed himself, aided and abetted by Jeremy and Rag. Martyn is on duty at the power station until midnight and will be brought home by an Argentine guard. After supper we all had a great discussion as to where in the United Kingdom we would settle if circumstances demanded it. I could live quite happily in Rye.

No startling new developments on BBC news, but great to hear that some more Harriers have arrived at Ascension after a nine-hour flight from UK. It is also reported that the Argentine prisoners taken at South Georgia are now at Ascension Island. BBC reception is not over great but we now have two radios on at the same time in an effort to receive things more clearly. 'Calling the Falklands' is the best bit of the day, with Peter King and Kathleen Cheesemond really doing their best to help us to bear up, under what we must admit is one hell of a strain at times. My only complaint with the programme is that when they have bits of speeches from people with posh voices, the plummier they are the more unintelligible what they are trying to say becomes. This is especially noticeable with government ministers; it's good to hear them but it would be much better if what they had to say could be read by someone like Peter King, with a voice which carries well over long distances under difficult conditions on the radio.

After supper the usual great card games commenced. Some nights we have had as many as six games going all at the same time. Cards are everywhere, but kept out of Maxwell's reach and much respected by everyone as they do play a very important part in life now. It seems to be one of the few things in which people can become completely absorbed, and so forget the present. I don't really understand card games at all, so I content myself with writing this diary in the evenings.

John Leonard popped in this morning for a chat and had some most sensible views on present situation and possible evacuation of civilians for period of fighting should it come to that. John, an American who has lived and worked in the Falklands for about 25 years, is allowed by the military authorities here to make a telephone call every other day – sometimes every day – to the American Consul in Buenos Aires, to report on the well-being of the twenty-four or so American nationals in the Falklands. John also emphasises the need here for representatives of the International Red Cross in the interests of the civilian population.

Some helicopter activity this morning, mainly over at the back of the Camber Ridge. One Puma carried a mobile field kitchen affair underneath it, complete with its still smoking chimney folded down, which looked quite odd, rather like some sinister secret weapon.

On the opposition side today, the military authorities issued the first edition of the *Argentine Gazette* – a typewritten news-sheet, run off on a duplicating machine. It was created on the orders of Gen Mario Benjamín Menéndez himself, supposedly to keep his troops informed.

Sunday 9 May – Day Thirty-eight

Cold, dull day, with very low cloud. Wind in morning from north, Force 2–3; later veered into the east for the rest of the day.

Last night tried another spell in our own beds. All very well for the first few hours, but woken at 1.30 by heavy gunfire, causing very rapid descent into bunker. Sounded like the Navy bombarding the airfield again. Shelling was in groups of six and eight rounds, with a minute or so pause between, then off again. Fairly heavy return fire from on shore.

Up just after 8. Very annoyed to have missed the BBC news at 8, even more so when at twenty past, I finally got tuned in properly, the announcer was saying that this was the end of an extra edition of 'Radio Newsreel', but she didn't say why, which was absolutely infuriating.

At 8.35 heard jet overhead, but impossible to see it, owing to low cloud. May be a Harrier to observe last night's bombardment results. Thought I also heard a helicopter. The streets are very quiet; quite a number of lorries parked, with their cold, sleepy drivers crawling out. They are as fed up as we are with this whole thing.

Did a bit more reinforcing at the front of the house, with more drums filled with earth. Put some up at the front door and side of porch, which means that we will now have to use the back door only, but all-round protection in the front of the house is essential in view of the increased number of gun-pits being dug in on the Co-op corner only a few yards away. The result of our fortifications looks a complete shambles, but at least may prevent stray bullets arriving through the house and will hopefully be blast-proof.

News at last at lunch-time. It seems that the bombardment during last night was a three-hour affair to soften up the Argentines before the attack. We only found it all extremely noisy; they must have found it very uncomfortable indeed, out in the trenches and dug-outs on the perimeter of town. The fear, the lack of sleep and food, combined with the weather, must be wearing them down quite rapidly. Also heard that one of their Puma helicopters has been shot down over part of the Task Force. An Argentine trawler, the *Narwal*, has been captured; all crew except one saved. Bombed or strafed by Harriers. It had an Argentine naval officer on board and had been within the Exclusion Zone for a week on surveillance. The Argentine reports of the trawler incident seem to differ considerably from the BBC ones.

Went to Mass again during the afternoon, having already been at 10. This is not only beneficial to the soul, but also keeps one in a routine. It would be very easy to fall into a state of apathy without some form of organisation in life. Quite a few visitors for tea this afternoon – Pat, Maureen, David, Nancy and Andrea. A real family gathering which had to break up just after 4 so that everyone could get off the streets before curfew.

The weather is lousy. Everyone has decided it would be safer to sleep in the bunker. The street lights are still on, in a night of fog and driving rain. A large Mercedes army lorry is parked directly in front of the house. Some distant firing by heavy guns about 9.30.

Monday 10 May – Day Thirty-nine

Thick fog and drizzle; wind from north-east, Force 3.

I had to look at yesterday's diary sheet to find out what day it was today – things must be getting bad.

Spent night in the bunker. Woken about 1.30 by great crashes and explosions, which went on for about three hours. The loudest we've had yet, almost as loud as the Vulcan bombs; obviously a naval bombardment. Crumps and wallops in all directions. Seemed to be mainly in lots of six, but there was one really spectacular lot of thirty, fired at two-second intervals. Very glad that we have the bunker, as this is awfully close. Had to get up top in the middle of it to go to the loo. Anya came up with me. I found it very difficult to aim straight with such a regular bombardment going on. Each crash shook the house considerably; have decided to sit down in future. In view of the closeness and the loudness, Anya and I decided to journey to and from the loo on our hands and knees, by candlelight, which added to the adventure. It is rather dangerous to stand up during these shellings, as shrapnel is likely to be flying about in large quantities, and our walls are designed to be more weather-proof than shrapnel-proof. Luckily, like everyone else, Anya is able to see the amusing side of most events. I must confess that I was very frightened of a shell burst close by while we were attending to nature.

I wonder if the thick fog had anything to do with the firing seeming to be louder. We heard during this morning that hits had been scored on the old ESRO station and at Moody Brook. No helicopter activity today; visibility down to zero at times.

Poor reception of BBC news, but understandable. British Government gives notice of a 100-mile-wide nautical restricted zone around Ascension Island, for safety reasons, because of the large number of aircraft now operating from there. The *Sheffield* and the *Narwal* have both broached to and sunk under tow during heavy weather. Last night's bombardment was, we learned, by courtesy of the Royal Navy, with 4.5 in shells. Some progress seems to be being made at the UN talks.

Ileen, Duffy and Rag had busy day in the bunker, as it seemed to be getting a bit damp. They took out all the cushions, laid down more polystyrene, along with some old carpet tiles we had in the shed, plus another old carpet, and lined the concrete and rock walls with polythene. Lit up all the fires in the house to air out the sleeping bags and pillows, etc.

Martyn arrived home with a huge box of extra strong peppermints for use in the bunker. There must be 2 lb or 3 lb of them at least. A very thoughtful lad. I'm sure that the manufacturers would be pleased to know that their sweets were of some use under such conditions.

Fr Monaghan looked very tired at Mass this afternoon. Both he and the Monsignor must be finding their duties very heavy during times such as these. There were quite a number of troops there, as well, who also looked exhausted. I think the nightly bombardment combined with our weather must be taking its effect.

Conditions very poor for receiving 'Calling the Falklands' from London this evening, but we were able to hear our ex-Governor, Sir Cosmo Haskard, speaking to us, which was most encouraging. How nice it was to hear his voice again. To our family, he was perhaps the favourite Governor, mainly, I suppose, because his son Julian was the same age as Jeremy, and many a weekend both he and Martyn would go off up to Government House to play. They must have been about eight or nine years old at the time. Lady Haskard was a splendid person too. She had that happy knack of knowing and getting on with everyone which combined respect with genuine friendship. I'm sure that many people were very pleased to hear of them again this evening.

This afternoon we managed to send off some telegrams to England, one to Mum and one to Eunice in Scotland. We naturally are rather limited in what we are able to say, but sent 'All well but gets a bit noisy at times', which about sums up the situation. We asked Eunice to phone round and advise the rest of the family and friends, as the service seems rather expensive; nearly £13 for two telegrams, so for that amount we hope they will get through.

Pat came in for a while today, very despondent as his house had been entered during last night by Argentines who wrecked everything in sight. Even his tape recorder had been put on the stove and melted. The Argentine military police have been up to the house. They may be able to get the troops concerned, but the damage has been done.

It's now 8.35 in the evening and sounds as if another naval bombardment is getting under way somewhere close by. Martyn and Rag have decided it would be a good idea to have a glass of whisky to steady their nerves – any excuse is better than none. Everyone is watching *Love Story* on the television, Ileen and Jeannie in tears, with Anya not far off having a little weep. The programme is getting the better of the Royal Navy, as no one is inclined to move yet, but I think there will shortly be a dash towards the bunker if things start landing any nearer. They seem to be getting towards the perimeter of the town, up at the back of Davis Street, at the moment.

Duffy and I stored plenty of water away during the day, as the mains were pretty badly shaken up during last night's bombardment. Everywhere we turn now in the house we seem to bump into buckets and jugs of water.

Tuesday 11 May – Day Forty

A really mucky day with thick fog and drizzle from the north-east. Wind about Force 4 all day. It has poured with rain all night, the most that has fallen since December. Conditions must be absolutely appalling for the troops; perhaps they will give up and go home. They borrowed the dockyard sludge pump early this morning to pump out some of their trenches in the town.

Duffy and I usually surface just after 7.30 each morning, in time to brew up the tea and get tuned into the BBC at 8 o'clock. This morning we heard that there had been a naval action in Falkland Sound during the night. Later reports during the day said that what appeared to be a supply vessel, probably carrying fuel, had disregarded warnings, flares and challenges to stop; so it was fired on, exploding into a huge fireball which broke through the low cloud. (There was no mention of this on the Argentine news.) BBC also said that two days ago a British frigate had sailed down the Falkland Sound close inshore, firing her guns, loosing off flares and flying her helicopter, none of which brought response from anywhere. No mention was made of the firing which we had at about 8.30 last evening. The Argentine Government has announced that all the South Atlantic is now a military zone. Anything caught within it is liable to be sunk.

With the general uncertainty of how things are going to turn out if this lot ends up in a great scrap in the town, Duffy decided to bring his paintings down here. They can be kept in my study ready to grab if we have to move in a hurry. They really are superb, and must cause him a great deal of worry as to their safety; to him they represent many hundreds of hours of work. Financially, of course, they are extremely valuable. With them stacked about, the study now resembles an auctioneer's saleroom. The paintings are mainly quite large portraits of Falkland personalities. All of them have the most realistic eyes – a speciality of Duffy's expertise – which does give the impression of being watched while in the study.

The troops have been very active all day, bringing up huge steel containers, which are being buried in deep pits, dug out by JCBs, in the paddock just along the road, on the corner leading down to the Secretariat. It seems to be some sort of priority job.

Jeremy has been on the rubbish-collecting run on the dumper all morning, while Martyn has been out attending to the very much overstrained power lines. The troops at the power station had a collection and asked him to buy five bottles of whisky and some cartons of cigarettes for them from the West Store. With the peso rate of exchange being something in the region of 2,500 to the pound sterling, he seemed to have several million pesos with him. Fortunately the troops are still not allowed into the store, but this does place Martyn in a very awkward position when asked to do things such as this by the military who are now in command of the power station; one has little option but to comply with their orders.

Noticed on the way to Mass this afternoon that most of the troops were sitting huddled together in the backs of their lorries, all very wet and dejected. Conditions all very much in our favour for morale lowering.

Got dark very early today, about 5.30. Each morning and afternoon we watch the little groups of townsfolk making their way to and from the safe houses where they spend the nights, rather like refugees, each with their little bundles and cases. Terribly sad to think we are reduced to this sort of thing. When they return home each morning they never know if they will find their house still standing, or if it has been ransacked.

During our evening check on the bunker, we found the water had risen almost up to the floorboards, so got a great bailing out operation under way with all hands for two and a half hours. Most providential that we discovered it when we did or we should have all floated out during the night. It being after curfew time, we had difficulty in getting rid of the water, which contained all sorts of little bits of rubbish. This was solved by taking up a few boards, then dipping in with buckets and tins, passing them up through the hatch, carrying them down the passage to the loo, in which we had placed an old kitchen colander which acted as a strainer for the bits. This all had to be carried out in semi-darkness as the roof of the porch is not entirely blacked out.

So ends another day. The bunker is back in shape again. We have just finished a very noisy game of Monopoly in the kitchen. The enemy have just parked another large army lorry outside the house again. Why they should choose this house is difficult to understand; there is plenty of space elsewhere. Anyway, whatever the reason, I am sure that we will all spend a much more comfortable night than the driver and his mate, who are huddled in the cab in the tiddling rain. Good luck to them. Duffy and I have an occasional peep out at them through a chink in the porch black-outs. I suppose that they may be doing the same to us in an effort to see what we get up to in the house.

The late-night news puts things almost at a stalemate position. They still talk of hope of progress at the UN. The Argentine side seems now to be handled by their Deputy Foreign Minister. It seems that the Pope's visit to England will be postponed if the conflict is still going on at the end of the month. Britain has commissioned a lady artist to sail on the *QE2* to paint and record events in the South Atlantic. It is nice to know that despite the advances of science and technology Britain can still manage with sufficient dignity to conduct its war in the grand and proper manner.

There have been a number of reports recently of cruelty and brutality to the Argentine soldiers by their officers and NCOs. A couple of days ago one soldier came in from the mountains to get more rations for his men. For this action he was stripped to the waist and made to stand all day in the freezing rain at the back of the town hall. Several people saw a young soldier at Government House being beaten with a fence batten, then kicked along the ground until he was almost senseless. There are also often disturbing incidents such as a single shot followed by a scream. It is impossible to prove what has actually happened, but does not leave a great deal to the imagination.

Wednesday 12 May – Day Forty-one

Dry, windy, clear and cool. Wind west, Force 3–4. A complete change after yesterday's appalling effort by the meteorological station.

Pat now pops in nearly every morning at breakfast-time for a cup of tea, over which we discuss the 8 o'clock news and generally put the world to rights. The troops are very thickly dug in up at the back of his house, in their hundreds if not thousands. They broke into his garage last night, causing a good bit of damage and stealing most of his tools, along with his boots. He is justifiably not very thrilled with life this morning. He says that work still continues after a fashion down at the post office, which seems to have Argentine civilian as well as military staff. All of our Falkland Islands stamps have been withdrawn from sale, being replaced with Argentine tiny blue and white things overprinted with '*Las Malvinas son Argentinas*' – The Falklands are Argentinian.

Pat does not think that the stocks of our own stamps have been destroyed, which is a bit of a nuisance as both the definitive mail ships and the commemorative shipwrecks in use at the time of the invasion were my designs. I even rushed down just after the invasion and bought a sheet of each of the shipwreck ones before they went off sale, in the hope that they might become valuable.

We were very pleased to hear Cherry Money on 'Calling the Falklands' this evening, speaking on the phone to the BBC from Southampton. She and Chris sent their best wishes and, most reassuring of all, had news of Mum, who is fine and coping with the situation very well. Then we got another message from Wendy Newbold and the boys, Lee and Scott, in Hamble, who were neighbours of ours over twenty years ago. It was very reassuring to hear from them both.

Anya's friend Diane came in for a chat after her 'O' level classes this afternoon. Philip Middleton takes a small class in the afternoons at his house, so that the continuity of their course will not be broken. Annie Chater also has children of a younger age group in – just those who live close by, as do Derek Evans, Hulda Stewart and Janice Blackburn in their respective parts of the town. These few remaining teachers are doing a remarkable job under what are now extremely difficult conditions.

Thursday 13 May – Day Forty-two

A most curious day weatherwise. Mist and fog patches drifting all around Stanley during the morning, but seldom actually coming over the town. The surface of the harbour is like a mirror, with a magical ethereal effect caused by the sun penetrating the fogbanks An absolutely superb afternoon.

I had a particularly uncomfortable night in the bunker, despite the fact that we had a lot more room, because the boys, in an act of great bravery, decided to sleep up in their own bedroom.

Plenty of water about after the recent rain, so all had good baths after breakfast – what a luxury a hot bath is now. None of us lingered very long in case of military excitement happening; not that we were afraid of being caught in the bath, but in case we missed seeing it.

Ileen and Anya shopped in the West Store. Shelves very empty but the essentials of life are still available. We have not had a supply ship in since January, so the reserves must be getting pretty low. It's great for Ileen to be well enough to venture out again. It must take a great deal of effort, especially to walk down the streets full of steel-helmeted, fully armed troops.

Duffy went up to his house to light up the fire. Everything seems to be OK, but troops are thickly dug in all around, while in front of the house, in the FIC paddock, there is what appears to be a very large ammunition dump, with crates and boxes piled high everywhere. Pits are being dug in an attempt to bury some of it. It will go up with one hell of a bang if anything should hit it. I don't blame Duffy and Jeannie in the least for feeling a bit safer down in our end of town.

A lovely incident occurred on the front road this morning when our government dockyard road-sweeping crew stopped for a smoke. A senior Argentine officer arrived to see why they were not working, and on being told that they had paused for a spell, told them to get on with their work. The sweepers' reply was to tell him to 'eff off' which confused him, as his knowledge of English did not extend that far, so he gave up and went on his way still puzzled at these new-found English words. Hope he decides to take them into his vocabulary. The results could be interesting.

Two other amusing incidents during the afternoon. Two of our locals were picked up by the Argentine MPs for being drunk. One, very voluble in fractured Spanish, was delivered safely home. The other was released on the condition that he did not go out on the streets again unless accompanied by his entire family, who would then be responsible for him.

Two Argentine paratroop officers at Mass this afternoon, complete with knives and pistols; seemed very tired and dirty. By their generally worn-out attitude, one could see that they wished this affair was over and done with. The superb weather during the afternoon has brought about an almost holiday atmosphere for most folk in the town. Troops are talking to the children on the playing-field green; groups of them are walking about in the sunshine, mostly desperate for some sign of friendliness. It's really terribly sad to see the very young boys so tired, dirty and bewildered.

Our boys took the dog for her walk, while Ileen and I took Maxwell out for some fresh air in his push-chair along the sea-wall up as far as Government House – it makes us feel very sick indeed to see the Argentine flag flying there, along with the sentries armed to the teeth among their barbed-wire barricades, in the drive and along the front of the lawns. As a sort of early-warning device against possible intruders, they have strung up thin wires around the house, some 2 ft above the ground, on which are hung beer cans, each with a small stone inside. The idea is that they rattle if touched by anyone creeping up during the night, but I would imagine that the wind blowing as it does causes some false alarms, as well as severe doses of fright. Poor Jen Williams, the gardener, must weep when he sees his once carefully tended lawns and gardens.

Just before the 1914 Battle Monument, near the steps up towards the part of town known as Little Italy, there is an Argentine Navy Puma helicopter under camouflage netting, almost on the pavement. For some reason the rotor blades are not in position. There is another, smaller helicopter – a Bell Huey, I think – on the football field. Very little helicopter flying these past few days. All of the gorse bushes are either burnt or broken down around the monument, as well as some of those along each side of the drive to Government

House. In the paddock on the seaward side are several very large containers – the type in which cargo is carried on ships. We continued our walk by turning about and going right down as far as the Philomel Store at the public jetty, past a number of troops sweeping their beloved Malvinas' streets, though they did not appear overjoyed by their patriotic action.

By the 'Upland Goose' we met Anya and Diane, who took over Maxwell, so Ileen and I decided to visit old Fred Coleman in his little shop up on Davis Street. We went in by the back door, as he was, as far as the Argentines were concerned, closed for business. He seemed very pleased to see us, and said he'd lived through two wars so might as well live through another one, though they were not exactly his cup of tea. A placid comment from a man of over eighty, living alone and almost totally deaf. It was most interesting looking out through his kitchen window, as it was possible to see a fairly large radar scanner in operation in one of the back gardens of one of the White City houses about 50 yd away. The dish bit, which was revolving, seems to be about 15 ft or so across. We have seen a smaller one, down by the public jetty, which I think controls the anti-aircraft gun, but this one up here looks more like an early-warning device.

In a funny sort of way, an enjoyable afternoon; as enjoyable as present circumstances permit, I suppose. The invasion started six weeks ago this evening. Everything seems so timeless now; we even have to ask each other what day it is.

Very encouraging news bulletin tonight from the BBC, a splendid eyewitness report on the departure of the *QE2* yesterday. Thousands of people; bands of the Scots and Welsh Guards, the pipes and drums of the Gurkhas. The most moving event ever seen in Southampton. It moved us down here as well. To think that all of this is happening because of us. Would love to have been there, though would have been quite unable to control my emotions. I had to look the other way a couple of times while listening this evening. The Prime Minister has said that she is working for a peaceful solution, not a peaceful sell-out. Francis Pym says that force will be used if necessary. At the UN, talks getting to the heart of the matter; may take a few more days. Wish they would hurry up. It seems that yesterday's air attack by the Argentines on British warships was a lot bigger than at first announced. Three Skyhawks were shot down, not two as previously announced. There were four waves of aircraft involved, one of which turned back. Sea Wolf missiles were used. The hospital ship *Uganda* is near the north of Falkland Sound.

After this somewhat buoyant day, the Argentines left the street lights on all night. Our supper concluded in a most unusual manner with a great chocolate soufflé battle breaking out at the table. It is not entirely clear how it started, but within seconds everyone had joined in throwing spoonfuls of soufflé at each other across the kitchen. The result was amazing: up the walls, in our hair, over our clothes, everywhere. Maxwell shrieked with delight, thinking it was for his benefit. It took an hour to clear up afterwards, but was a wonderful way to let off steam and tension. Thoroughly recommendable.

Drifted off to sleep with pleasant thoughts of better days last year, walking or biking down Leasom Lane in the heart of Sussex countryside, late on a summer evening, with superb smells of moist grass, bird-song and rising mist swirling in the hollows and valleys. Hopefully one day it will be possible to do it again.

Friday 14 May – Day Forty-three

A grey, murky, evil, wet day; really horrible. In the evening weather developed into a southerly gale sounding like distant gunfire.

At 7 o'clock Anya up to be sick; feeling very unwell. At breakfast with the boys sang them several verses of 'The Road to Mandalay'. They were not impressed and declined to join in the chorus; no sense of culture. Can't blame them really as it is difficult to associate this morning with flying fish and the dawn coming up like thunder.

Bit of helicopter activity at about 8.30. They don't seem to be over-keen on going too high up in the air these days in case the Harriers spring out at them. Pottered about in garden most of the morning odd jobbing. We took down some of the black-outs in an effort to lighten the house up a bit inside. Also filled lots of buckets with water as it has been announced that all supplies will be turned off at 2 this afternoon.

Huge explosion at smoko* time, 11.15; really heroic bang. The effects on different people were most interesting. Two soldiers waved and smiled thankfully that whatever it was had not hit them. Another more conscientious one ran up the hill with his rifle at the ready not knowing exactly what to do, or where to go, but felt that he had to do something. The boys were watching the television. Tyssen put his head round the door and said, 'That was a bomb', then continued to watch the programme. Rag arrived to say that he also thought it was a bomb but couldn't say in which direction. It was sufficiently powerful to have really rattled the crockery on the table.

Rag had a bullet which one of the guards at the hospital had given him as an Argentine souvenir; several other people have as well. Giving them away like this all helps in the war effort with lots of good in our direction. There are two cases of soldiers with hepatitis at the hospital.

* Traditional Falklands mid-morning and mid-afternoon break for a cigarette, tea and buns – fattening but highly recommended!

Pat in for lunch. His protests over troops breaking into his house must have had some effect, as one of his Bisley shooting trophies, pinched the night before, had been returned last night to the house. While coming back from Mass this afternoon heard and saw another great explosion in the air at about 500 ft down towards the YPF fuel installation; lots of flames and brown smoke. No fragments, so assume it was not a hit on an aircraft. Possibly a missile prematurely exploding or a projectile from a great big gun which they are towing about up on Davis Street. It's a whopping great affair which would look more at home on a battleship. Do hope they know what they are doing with it as it looks awfully dangerous.

Big boost to our morale during the afternoon when we received a telegram from Jim, Evie and Philippa at Tickhill. Most appropriate wording: 'Nil carborundum.' It's quite astonishing to think that, despite all of the great political and diplomatic upheaval in this direction, contact can still be made between the post office at Tickhill and ours at Stanley.

We examined the possibility of making another entry hatch in the passage floor to the bunker in case of a prolonged stay down there. Access to the loo would be a lot easier, as well as being out of direct range of cross-fire across the playing field from the machine-gun pits. They have now put another .50 Browning opposite us on the grass verge outside Vernon and Gail Steen's house, but have a spot of bother aiming it, as they have dug the pit too deep, so that it will only point straight up in the air. If they lessen the depth of the pit, then they have less room to shelter, which is obviously causing them some concern. There are suggestions that we should send them across a note suggesting that they leave it as it is, as it reduces the chances of them firing through our house and, with all due respect to their marksmanship, still gives the Harriers a very sporting chance as well.

News reception conditions from London very bad but managed to hear Cindy Buxton and Annie Price speaking on 'Calling the Falklands'. The talks on the Falklands at the UN have stopped for the weekend; hope they stop our bit of the war for the weekend as well. Mrs Thatcher still says No Sell-out. Thank goodness she is not going to stop *her* efforts for the weekend.

Rather a quiet depressing evening. Looked at and cleaned Dad's badges of the 7th Duke of Edinburgh's Gurkhas and the Gurkha Engineers. Is it worth mounting them at this stage?

So ends yet another day. Despite the occasional feeling of depression everyone is standing up remarkably well to life under enemy occupation. New routines are being established to cope with the changed way of life. One of the most popular and useful is the daily gathering in the Globe Bar at lunch-time, when news is pooled and exchanged, enabling folk from different parts of town to find out what's going on elsewhere. Although distances are so short, the problems involved in moving about can be considerable at times.

Saturday 15 May – Day Forty-four

Fine, crisp, clear day, but with still an occasionally watery look about it. Later turned out to be fine and windless with medium to high cloud.

Up at 7.30. I had great desire to be in Fareham to see the elegant front doors on some of the houses in the High Street.

BBC announced that yesterday there were air attacks on Stanley airport. That must have been the huge explosions we heard. They also spoke of routine air patrols over the Falklands. Argentina now says there are 301 missing from the *General Belgrano*. Air attack sounds so dramatic on the BBC, making it hard to believe that we were the target. Argentina also says that it has lost contact with one of its supply vessels for a few days. Very probably the *Isla del Estados* which was blown up in the Sound on Monday. They say it was carrying supplies for the Islanders – must have been very inflammable ones. Argentina also claims that yesterday's air attacks were beaten off by anti-aircraft fire; didn't hear any shots fired from where we are . . . BBC mentioned an attack on Pebble Island last night but no details given.

Heard several reports during the day of cases of gangrene and pneumonia among the troops.

Anya, Rag and Eli all feeling very unwell. Tyssen and I took the dog for a walk at lunch-time. Passed Martyn with the rest of the power-station crew, assisted by the Argentine Army, sorting out the wreckage caused to a telephone pole at the top of Philomel Hill which one of their lorries had hit. The troops look very tense today. The big gun on Davis Street is a 155-mm field gun, now positioned between Rag's house and 94 Davis Street under thick camouflage. Very heavily guarded so unable to get too close. It's a formidable-looking affair and will be very difficult to hit without blowing up the nearby houses. There is another one along towards Ross Road West just past the monument between Sulivan House and the doctor's old house. Another is possibly on Sapper Hill but it is quite impossible to get up in that direction now. There are notices on all roads leading off to the south of Davis Street warning of mines and the strong possibility of being shot at if found in that area. Lots of military activity up in that direction today.

Just after we had returned home there was a Harrier attack on the airfield, with bombs causing great explosions with huge plumes of smoke. Bombing continued throughout the afternoon. The Harriers also seem to be after the missile site just at the back of the power station. The missiles were uncovered today. A bomb landed up there just about 2.30, which didn't destroy the site but must have given them all one hell of a fright. The final bomb of the afternoon landed opposite over the harbour at the back of the Camber; spectacular bang with lots of smoke; think they may have got an ammunition dump by the sound of it. The blast wave travelled across the harbour almost bringing our front porch down. Fortunately most of the glass is loose or the lot would have collapsed.

Everyone in town is rather blasé about bombs now; we all turn out to watch. A lot of the troops seem too apathetic to react very quickly. They are scared stiff of the Harrier raids. We passed a lorry outside the post office this afternoon with one poor chap in the back who was either badly wounded or shell-shocked; he just gave a feeble wave and vacant look as we went by; very very sad indeed. No one seemed to be bothering overmuch about him.

The new bunker hatch has now been cut in the passage floor. The carpentry is not over-great, but it will serve the dual purpose of being another entry and extra escape hatch.

Very little helicopter activity during today. Two have been parked on the football field; one armed with missiles, which took off when they bombed the missile site during the afternoon, but landed again two minutes later. The other flew over to the back of the Camber after that had been bombed, but didn't stay long. I think that an F-27 got in during the day and landed at the airport.

Over the road, work still continues even after dark by floodlight on the General's Bunker – so nicknamed by us because it seems to be the main accommodation for senior Argentine officers at night and during periods of military excitement in the daytime. This is being still further reinforced with some more bales of wool, brought up by the lorry-load from the jetty warehouses. I doubt if they have any idea just how much money they are writing off by burying these bales in the earth and leaving them to stand in the pouring rain.

Each bale is worth somewhere in the region of £500. They had been stowed in the warehouse from the various farms, waiting for shipment to be sold in England. I notice also that some are being used down on the corner opposite the town hall to form some sort of a barricade. Useful military thinking I suppose, as the stopping power of the tightly packed wool must be considerable. The farmers would go mad if they could see it.

Uncle James from the met office popped in just before curfew for a chat as he usually does nowadays on his way home. He is Ileen's sister Joan's husband, Jimmy (Stephenson), who has always been known to us as Uncle James. Tall, thin and bearded he is known for his outspoken opinions – brief and to the point. He works under extreme pressure as the Argentines have smashed and stood on most of his equipment, yet they still expect him to provide them with their met information. It is unclear why they do not have their own meteorologists here. According to James the activity this afternoon caused a red-alert state, but the Argentines occupying his office were in the middle of a game of chess. One man leapt up ready to fly into action, but the others persuaded him that his solo effort would not contribute greatly to the success or otherwise of the attack, but would have a serious effect on their game of chess, so he came back inside and sat down. James has told us that during previous raids this particular chap is prone to getting carried away with the excitement. Once he poked his machine-gun out through the window, which created a terrible draught, so they told him either to close the window and go outside with his gun, or to stop mucking up their war by making a nuisance of himself.

We have come to regard James's daily visits as most important, as the met office is situated on one of the highest points in the town, from which an excellent view of the airfield can be had. He is the only civilian allowed in that area, he says, not because of his meteorological skill, but because his binoculars are much better than the Argentines', so they often ask to borrow them. It does not seem to occur to them that they have the power to confiscate the binoculars, especially as James carries them every day in a restricted zone. A curious set-up.

Wonderful news on the BBC at 7 this evening. The result of the raid on Pebble Island last night was eleven Argentine aircraft destroyed, as well as a large ammunition dump, carried out under appalling weather conditions, backed up by a naval bombardment.

The Argentine version is that only three aircraft were damaged and the attack was repelled. It seems that Chile has offered the research vessel *Piloto Pardo* to evacuate the Argentine dead and wounded from Stanley, which they put as forty-one dead and thirty-eight wounded. The UN people say today that the first few days of next week could be decisive. 'Calling the Falklands' is now being permanently jammed by the Argentines. Reception is very difficult but we were able to hear Eunice speaking. She has received our telegrams. Really lovely to hear her voice again.

There were a few explosions about 9.30, but have all decided to be brave and daring and try for another night in our bedrooms. Heard an aircraft taking off just after 11 which sounded like an F-27.

During the day there has been some very disturbing news circulating in the town that the Argentine troops at Goose Green have locked everyone up in the Social Club Hall. If this is true then the people out there must be having a pretty rough time of it, as there must be over a hundred of them, and the hall is not very big, with only two toilets if I remember rightly. It's very difficult to get more details.

Sunday 16 May – Day Forty-five

An absolutely superb day. Warm, sunny and cloudless. Warm enough to go out with only my tweed jacket on. Just a fine layer of white frost over everything – all very healthy and tingling like an advert for toothpaste.

Was about to write up these notes at the start of the day, about 8.25, when things got rowdy and noisily interrupted by a Harrier bombing attack on the airfield. Really spectacular sight. Great stacks of smoke and flames, heavy anti-aircraft fire from all over the town. Everyone downstairs in a big heap, some down the bunker, others outside to watch with the neighbours, Rudy and Camilla. Their teenage daughter, Katrina, was up on the fence with our boys cheering them on. What a good start to the day and all for no extra charge.

Mass at 10 o'clock. Good attendance by locals as well as plenty of troops – mainly senior officers who joined in the singing of several of the hymns. Tyssen behaved magnificently in his duties as altar boy when great bursts of anti-aircraft firing opened up from the guns opposite the chapel behind the town hall. He didn't even flinch, which is more than can be said for most of the Argentine members of the congregation. We locals pretended not to notice it and hoped that our shaking was not too visible. I saw a couple of pieces fall out of the stained glass windows at the back of the altar.

There was another outbreak of firing after the service, while we were chatting on the porch steps. One had to appear not too enthusiastic as the white puffs of anti-aircraft fire were bursting well below the vapour trails of the Harriers. I was so pleased that we had all made an extra effort to dress as we normally would have done for Sunday Mass, which tended to confuse the Argentines even further: what does this stupid British family think they are doing, strolling through the streets in their Sunday clothes during an air raid?

The Harriers have really had a field day, bombing mainly in the airport area, but occasionally dropping one somewhere else, so that the Argentines would not become too complacent about things. An unusually large number of folk turned out for Glory Hour in the pubs at lunch-time, taking advantage of the sunshine plus the entertainment – not only the British bombing but also the Argentine confusion. Glory Hour is another Falklands tradition brought about by the licensing hours which only permit the pubs to be open for one hour on Sundays from 12 until 1 pm. The effects of the sometimes swift hard drinking are often quite spectacular on new arrivals in Stanley. Lots of people out for walks, which was making some of the Argentine officers seethe with rage by the look of them. Funnily enough they have not issued an edict ordering everyone off the streets during an air raid. Went to Mass again at 3, during which there was another great outburst of firing and bombing which Tyssen again took in his stride while serving.

Joined Harry Milne for a cigarette afterwards as we and the Argentine troops carried out our daily watching of each other from chapel steps to the town hall. They are really getting quite tame; when we wave they wave back. Even the senior NCOs give us a wave and a nod. We will have to keep this up now; if we do not appear each day they will become suspicious and wonder what we are up to. Harry said that it was his birthday and thought that this morning's spectacular bombing might have been in honour of it. Harry was due to retire on 1 April, after a number of years as manager of the Stanley FIC, and hand over the controls to Terry Spruce, but these recent military events have disrupted things somewhat. I think now what has happened is that, although officially retired, Harry is still at work ready to provide extra assistance should it become necessary. It really has been quite fantastic at times today, with everyone in our part of town out on the road with cups of tea watching the progress. At breakfast time we did offer one cold-looking soldier a cup of coffee, but he regretfully had to decline and get on with the war. He was most awfully cold and unhappy, having spent the night in the back of a lorry outside of the house. I don't think that he had seen frost before, as he was wiping bits from the fence top with his finger. He was not over-impressed by it either.

Ileen, Tyssen and I took the dog for a walk around the town during the afternoon. The troops were very courteous, some even slowing down as they passed us in their vehicles. At tea-time, just before curfew, Tyssen and Eli, along with some other lads, were playing football on the green in front of the house when some young soldiers asked if they could join in. Eli ended up with one of their tin helmets on. What a lop-sided, crazy turn-out this affair is.

Duffy and I dug out a bit more of the passage entry cum escape hatch this morning before lunch, so that we now have good access without banging our heads or getting stuck. It is very reassuring to have this done as, in the event of cross-fire or panic firing from the gun-pits around us, things could get rather dodgy if we had to go through the front porch. As an additional precaution we today also shovelled earth between the drums built up in front of the porch; a tedious business as we had to carry the earth in buckets from the vegetable garden; there isn't a wheelbarrow in sight these days. It's going to be a terrible mess to clear up afterwards. What I was proudly developing into a lawn has now disappeared completely, and the vegetable garden has a large hole from where we have been taking the earth, but at least we are a bit more blast-proof now. It is not that we don't trust the Harrier pilots, but should they have a hiccup and drop one of their bombs nearby it may help to cushion the effect somewhat. The same can be said if one of the Navy shells should happen to land in town. It was heavy work, so we had frequent stops for a smoke, then additional stops to watch the bombing and the vapour trails.

The Argentine helicopters seem to mainly concentrate on the football field now. They don't venture far; always very low.

Unable to hear 'Calling the Falklands' at all tonight as conditions terrible. Reception of the news was patchy, but were able to hear that an Argentine ship has been bombed; the crew took to the boats. Another Argentine ship at Fox Bay was not bombed but strafed with cannon fire because of its close proximity to the settlement. Bombing raids have also been carried out at Darwin. Ambassadors are still dashing back and forth across the Atlantic at bewildering speed in an attempt to resolve our situation. The *Canberra* is reported to be in our waters which is very reassuring news. The Argentines have decided not to give us any news this evening, only a football match on the television, so the entire household is playing either cards or chess, with a record of Tennessee Ernie Ford singing in the background, while I write this at the kitchen table. Anya and Rag are both feeling much better today, but Jeannie is feeling unwell.

No street lights on this evening; would not be at all surprised if we have another naval bombardment during the night.

Have just got hold of more news of the events at Goose Green. Terry Spruce has received a note which was brought in during the day, in a discreet manner – about which the less said the better. There is no other means of communication with Stanley as the telephone lines have been cut.

The situation at Goose Green is appalling. Since 1 May 115 people have been confined in the hall. Brook Hardcastle and Eric Goss were released yesterday but the others are still confined. Brook is hoping that more will be released today. Everyone confined has kept well, but all have weight loss. Houses have been looted and foodstuffs stolen. Brook asks for a shipment of general stores 'as *soon* as *possible*, please'. During the last raid on Darwin two Harriers were shot down and approx. forty Argentines killed. Work on the settlement has not been carried out; no rams put out. Helicopters bring dead sheep into the settlement every day. Farm is a complete shambles, dead carcasses everywhere – cows have been blown up by mines. All fences in a bad state, or completely damaged.

Hundreds of Argentine soldiers are dug in on the Bluff and Carters Hill between the school and the settlement. Rockets are mounted on tractors and there are very good anti-aircraft guns.

Terry Spruce is going to discuss this with the Monsignor in the morning, as he is the one person with the most influence on the Argentines here at the moment. Hopefully something can be arranged to sort this lot out as soon as possible.

Monday 17 May – Day Forty-six

Another superb day – brilliant sunshine, no wind, very little cloud, closing with a spectacular sunset.

Up at 8; bombing commenced at twenty-four minutes past. One on the airfield, another on the Canache. Very impressive explosions. The crockery jumped about on the breakfast table again. What a splendid way to start the day.

Had a disturbed night. My prediction was correct; the Navy opened fire at 2300 hours. Our Lady of the Nightie (Jeannie – so nicknamed because of her flowing night attire) appeared in our bedroom at 2301, plus everyone else in the house, seeking guidance. We told them to return to their beds, which they all did until 2305 when another salvo whistled low over the house and so began another great and rapid descent into the bunker. From what we can find out this morning the Navy seemed to be concentrating mainly on the Moody Brook area for several hours. Possibly the ones which seemed to come over the house were warmers. I must confess that the rhythmic firing of a 4.5-in gun still has a soporific effect on me after a while. It is only when the Argies open up in return that sleep is disturbed, with the change in tempo.

Shopped with Ileen at the West Store during part of the morning. Lots of troops about in the streets drying out after their night in damp and wet dug-outs. They seem to be generally enjoying the sunshine, though they all look as fed up as we are with this dreadful affair. Yesterday, apparently, President Galtieri made an inspiring speech from Peru saying how his troops would all stand till the last man. He ought to be here to see them now, hungry and steaming with the damp, marching in groups of fifty down through town from the trenches to the dockyard to have the compulsory shower. Their clothing is sodden, boots falling to pieces; many have no laces, just bits of string. The shower is variable according to the state of the tide, as the inlet hose leads out into the harbour. Water is drawn up through this, passing through iron pipes over a diesel burner, then trickling down through a perforated pipe over the unfortunate soldier, who drys himself on his wet, filthy towel, and puts all his wet clothing back on again, then off up the hill to wait for his enemy.

The troops out there must be mainly conscripts; in no way could one describe them as trained soldiers. They are purely cannon fodder and so obviously expendable. The average age seems to be about seventeen. I know that their purpose here is to kill us if necessary, but it is impossible not to feel sorry for them as they pass by. They are exhausted in mind and body, almost pleading for any sign of recognition or acknowledgement from the local people. Having said that, one then thinks about what they are doing to our people at Goose Green. By the sound of things they have got some of their 'Heavies' deployed out there. The 'Heavies' in Stanley still strut arrogantly about, along with the officers – dry, well clothed, and well fed. It does cause them to lower their dignity a bit when we pass the time of day to them, to which they have to respond. There is an immense gap between the officers, the professional soldiers and the conscripts which it is hard to describe adequately. This whole situation gets more extraordinary and bewildering as the days go on. On the Goose Green business, I believe that the Monsignor has discussed it with Padre Bagnall and that they are going to see Gen Menéndez about it today. Not much is being said by anyone on the subject. It does not pay to be too inquisitive at the moment. In fact the less one knows about some things, the better it is.

As it was so pleasant a morning we had our smoko sitting on the front doorstep – quite unheard of for this time of the year. Everyone, both us and the troops, watching for more air activity, but nothing happened.

About 2.40, a jet aircraft rather like a Dominie (though some say it was an F-28) flew flat out up the harbour from the direction of the airport towards the west at about 100 ft or less.

There were three very young what appeared to be second lieutenants at Mass today. One was dressed up with weaponry and grenades all over him. They seemed pleasant enough. One spoke English, so we decided that after the service, a cigarette and a bit of light conversation were in order, to see if we could learn anything useful, which we didn't, except that they were living up on the hill in a hole, and very cold – serves them right, they shouldn't have joined. We also thought that they may have been sounding us out, so kept the conversation to a very formal level.

About 4.50 this evening a C-130 Hercules took off from the airfield in a most spectacular manner, turning sharply to fairly leap up over the Camber Ridge, which it crossed at almost zero feet; we could see the dust coming up from the ground. What pilots; whoever was driving this one was handling it like a fighter. Then some twenty minutes later, as Duffy and I were putting up the black-outs, we saw another C-130 flying very low down the harbour to land. Despite the number of bombs we have dropped on the airport, it is apparently still usable, but it may well be that the Argentines, in desperation to get more supplies in, are forced to try their luck on what is left of it. Just as the sun had finally set, it took off again, after only thirty-five minutes on the ground. Superb flying, hopping over the hills into a most wonderful sunset. The aircraft very dark with yellowy orange cloud-banks. Must make a painting of it one day.

BBC news fairly clear. The UN talks now reaching final stages; results should be known before the end of the week. Also says that a British destroyer came close inshore to carry out a bombardment on the Falklands last night among what may have been minefields. The gunfire started a blaze onshore but they were unable to determine what it was.

Tuesday 18 May – Day Forty-seven

A damp, foggy, horrible day; visibility almost nil at times. The fog turned to a thick drizzle, with the wind increasing from about Force 3 in the morning to 5 during the evening, mainly from the north-west.

The house feels very cold and damp, so Rag and Duffy brought down two of the gas cylinders from the back of the garden and connected them up, so that we were able to get some heating going through the front of the house. We were ready to disconnect them quickly and roll them out of the way if any firing or bombing started up.

Bought another bag of flour from the West Store. It is said that the Argentines are about to take over the old bakery for their own use, which if true is likely to cause a shortage of flour as they may be unable to get their own brought in. Lots of very wet, despondent troops about the streets. Many look absolutely all in. We hear frequently from the BBC now that this period is a process of attrition against the Argentine forces. This is really evident nowadays; it is working well. According to our dictionary it means 'friction; abrasion; gradual exhaustion'. A most suitable method – having a visible and powerful effect on the troops. What a well-chosen word.

Two great explosions at 10.20 this morning. One down towards the airport and the other seemed to be up past the Beaver Hangar towards the 60-acre paddock near the butchery. Don't know what they were, but it had a spectacular effect on the Argentines, causing a great exodus down the hill from their dug-outs – running like hell, according to those who saw them.

Our kerosene stock is getting rather low, so decided to get another drum in, which meant going down to the Argentine fuel plant (YPF). Our Land Rover refused to start, probably owing to the claggy weather, so Marvin Clarke kindly took me down. Everything is very tense in that area, especially from the FIC offices onwards. Very thankful to have got the fuel, as I have a strong feeling that YPF may start to ration or even close down shortly.

We had just got back about 5.15 when there were two tremendous explosions, the blast of which seemed to force the whole front of the house in and then back out again. It had a most interesting effect on everyone. Some headed for the bunker, others to the front porch windows to see if any glass was left. I dashed upstairs to the front bedrooms, passing Duffy on the way down with young Maxwell, and arriving just in time to see great columns of smoke and flames erupting from behind the ridge at the Camber right opposite the house. Tyssen says he saw big bits of stuff flying about. It was obviously a Harrier bombing run, in absolutely foul weather conditions with failing light. I think they must have hit an ammunition dump. The effect on the troops nearby must have been horrific. It was quite dark by 5.30. Maureen and David had come down for tea, and so were able to watch this spectacular happening from our vantage point. I am still unable to understand why the front porch did not collapse with the blast. It's a lot stronger than I thought.

'Calling the Falklands' was fairly clear tonight. They really do give us an excellent round-up of the day's news. The UN President has stopped his meetings to allow Argentina to consider British proposals. Argentina's reply is expected in a few hours. A definite answer on the issue is to be had by Thursday. The Task Force is said to be assembling to the east of the Falklands. Mrs Thatcher still will not be moved on her stand towards the issue. Another Sea King was lost this morning. They do seem to be rather accident-prone. The crew, fortunately, were saved. More Harriers from container ships have now joined the fleet.

A lousy play in Spanish on the television this evening, so listened to records of Tony Hancock, which provided a few laughs. Later BBC news said that a spokesman on *Hermes* has denied that there is a danger to the people of Stanley during bombing raids around Stanley. The British community in Buenos Aires want a ship to come to Stanley to take away the children to safety in Argentina. Our response can be imagined.

Really must clean the silver tomorrow. It's so tarnished that it looks like gold.

Duffy and I are seriously considering applying for work in the dockyard on Monday, as funds are getting very low, though we are safe in having on hand a good stock of flour and fuel.

There was apparently an accident last night among the troops, when one soldier shot another.

Wednesday 19 May – Day Forty-eight

Muggy, damp and misty. A little wind from the north-west, Force 2–3. Got wetter during the evening.

Slept in bunker, not very well despite having taken a Librium and two Mogadon tablets last night. Very depressed all morning. Decided to fight it by not listening to any world news and having a good clean-up in the study, though it may be all blown to bits in a few days. Mood not helped as my pencil sharpener has been moved, and one of my *Jane's Fighting Ships* has not been replaced in its proper position. I really must not allow myself to become so aggravated by such trivial things. Used the last of the lavender polish on my bookcase. The brass and silver also now look a lot better for a bit of cleaning. The study tidy and smelling of polish helps to combat the shambles outside on the streets.

Bucked up considerably during the afternoon. Everyone helped out on building a fence alongside the path, to keep the dog off the grass now that it is getting wet and muddy. Mass at 3. Several hundred troops down by the town hall preparing to go off into the hills. Pathetic sight – tired, cold and hungry, with blank, confused faces. Many of them must have been in the same clothes for six weeks now. Great deal of military activity about the town all afternoon; seems to be some sort of an alert. The Navy have been bombarding Argentine positions to the south of the town most of the day. This, combined with the Harrier attacks, is really alarming the Argentines.

I don't think that I mentioned that yesterday the *Forrest* turned up at the public jetty, taken over and manned by Argentine military, painted a very dark matt green, almost black, which completely alters her shape. There had been reports that she had been sunk. She looks very ugly now, so different from her former red hull, white upperworks and buff funnel. She is also very dirty indeed.

We were shocked to learn that during last night Stan and Daphne Cletheroe's house was shot up during an outbreak of firing at that end of town, for reasons which are not clear. It must have been a terrible experience for them as they are both well into their seventies. They had not long gone to bed when the first shots passed through the headboard, only inches above their heads. More shots ripped through the bedroom furniture, badly damaging the wardrobe. Others passed straight through the house, in one wall and out of the window, taking the glass along with them.

Some of these Argentine machine-gun crews are downright dangerous. One lot down on the sea-wall occasionally get their gun jammed into automatic fire, which causes them to let go of the thing in fright, leaving the gun to whirl about, up, down, and sideways until the ammunition has run out. They lie flat on the ground until it's all over. This sort of hose-pipe effect of the bullets has an interesting and spectacular effect on the crews of other guns nearby.

Thursday 20 May – Day Forty-nine

Damp, misty and cold; generally murky. Wind north-north-east, Force 4.

Things seem to be getting a bit desperate. Late last night in the bunker we listened to the BBC. Talks at the UN seem to be in a state of collapse. The reviews of the daily newspapers predict an invasion by the British forces today. Shortly before midnight the boys decided that the time had come for drastic emergency measures to be taken. They crawled up through the hatch we had cut in the passage and passed down two bottles of whisky, two cases of beer and a bag of frozen sausage rolls from the deep freeze. They were then kind enough to ask if the rest of us would like anything for our well-being and survival. Someone suggested a cup of tea might not be a bad idea, so without too much fuss some flasks were made up and passed down. It was a cosy, jolly little affair; eleven of us huddled in sleeping bags by candlelight. We had put off the lead lamp so as not to wake Maxwell. Grim news bulletins were still coming through on Duffy's very fine radio. We drank our drinks, some of us smoked, then at 12.30 the Royal Navy opened fire not very far away, for their nightly pounding of the Argentine positions. So once again to the rhythmic roars and crashes of the salvos we drifted off to sleep. An absolutely foul night outside, with a full gale blowing from the north-east – the most unpleasant quarter of all.

It is Ascension Day – six weeks after Easter. How time flies by. Although sometimes this occupation seems to have been going on for years. It all depends what mood one is in; time is just one big jumble nowadays. Everyone says that they slept well last night. The bunker is splendidly warm and well ventilated; if there were less of us sleeping down there it would probably be very cold, but as it is, an even balance seems to be achieved between the fug which we create and the passage of fresh air sweeping in from under the house.

Great activity among the troops this morning over at the bunker which they have dug alongside the Co-op Nissen hut warehouse.

It's a huge affair, with the roof bit extending half-way up the side of the hut. It must easily accommodate fifty or sixty men. But this morning they are filling it in at a great rate, with lots of arm waving, and vehicle movement which started well before daylight. They seem to say that they had a fire in there, but this seems most unlikely considering last night's appalling weather. Never have I seen the Argentine forces filling in a hole before. All very curious . . .

We all managed to have baths this morning as the water in the tank was boiling. We were hoping all the time that there would be sufficient fresh water to refill the tank. The water situation in the town is now critical.

The news bulletins are still grim. The President of the UN has put forward some of his own proposals to Mrs Thatcher and the Argentine Government during the night by telephone. These are now being considered. Mrs Thatcher has told Parliament that Argentina has rejected nearly all the British proposals, and that the Argentine proposals are unacceptable . . . What now? Argentina expects an imminent invasion by the British forces.

Sent off a couple of cables home today in the remote hope that they may get through. They are suddenly much cheaper, only £6.70 for two. There is a very carefree atmosphere in the post office on the civilian side. The post master, Bill Etheridge, and Lewis Clifton are both manning the counter, which has now been split into two parts, one for the troops, the other for civilians. The military side was decidedly sombre and crowded. Every soldier carries a rifle. It's a wonder that with so many of them jostling about in there that there are not some accidents. The air is thick with their dreadful cigarette smoke.

Rag is now temporarily working at the Butchery and arrived home with some fresh meat and kidneys, which were very welcome.

The lunch-time news is most interesting. Chile reports finding the wreckage of a British Sea King helicopter in the Straits of Magellan near Punta Arenas. A search for survivors is taking place. The big question is, what was it doing 450 miles from the Task Force? Chile has made a diplomatic protest in Santiago.

At Mass this afternoon I told the Monsignor that I was strongly thinking of writing to Rome, pointing out their lack of courtesy in not inviting him to be present tomorrow at the Mass for peace between Britain and Argentina. As representatives from both those countries will be there, it would have been not only polite, but also expedient to have had the head of the Catholic church in the Falklands present. It's like having a play with one of the principal characters absent. Transport difficulties are no excuse, as the Argentines are still continuing to fly their aircraft in and out.

The present situation is so confusing. I happened during the day to be walking up the road at the same time as Capt Hussey of the Argentine Navy. We had a most amiable chat. He says that Capt Gofoglio is still here. Also told me to ask at any time if I need any assistance with the protection of the shipwrecks in the harbour. His English is excellent and his manner such that it was difficult to believe that we were the invader and the invaded, as we walked along discussing the maritime heritage of the Falklands, with our respective countries poised on the brink of war.

Most of the troops are still desperately hungry – some are down to one meal per day. One soldier had an Oxo cube which he was trying to make last as long as possible by sucking it for a while, then putting it back in his pocket. Two soldiers knocked on Stan Cletheroe's door for food today. I wonder how he received them after having his house shot up last night?

Very little air activity; no bombs today – yet. The days are getting very short now – dark about 5.30 in the evenings and dawn about 8.15.

Cigarettes are now rationed in the West Store to two packs per person per day. This will not affect us greatly, but we have tended to smoke considerably more than usual lately. Cigarettes have assumed a much higher priority among the essentials of life.

Have felt much better disposed towards life all day, possibly because I have been again recollecting some of the pleasant memories of our holiday at Rye. It is a fortunate thing to be able to rummage about in one's memory, taking out fragments and going slowly through them.

Friday 21 May – Day Fifty

A really fine, brilliant, cloudless day. A very hard frost first thing this morning. What little wind there has been was from the west, Force 2–3.

Wonderful news. The British are ashore at San Carlos, the last place that anyone would have expected them to turn up, but they are here. How odd it seemed to hear San Carlos mentioned on the world news. Since early this morning reports have been on the BBC of something big happening. The first was at 9 this morning, when they announced that raiding parties had been put ashore during the night on the Falklands; then later, that a major landing had taken place at San Carlos with not too much opposition. Troops ashore in substantial numbers; Royal Marines and Paras. By noon heavy equipment was being ferried ashore, including anti-aircraft weapons, etc. But there have been major air attacks on the Task Force by the Argentine Air Force. Also, tragically, another Sea King has been lost while transferring troops; twenty-one dead, nine saved. There is no mention of where the raiding parties left troops, but there have been mentions of attacks on Fox Bay and Darwin Harbour.

Just on breakfast time there was a very loud explosion with lots of dense smoke, in the direction of the Mount Kent. No lorries on the streets during the morning, but quite a bit of running about and whistle-blowing among the troops. There was some odd firing but nothing exciting seemed to happen. It was so pleasant that we took our smoko out on to the front steps to enjoy the weather and watch the Argentines. We are, like everyone else, feeling really jubilant at the great news of the San Carlos landing. This is what we have all been waiting for.

Ileen, Anya and Jeannie have been busy preparing food all day, ready for a possible extended stay in the bunker. The boys and I continued to build the fence in the back garden. The Argentines have put four of their helicopters in the shelter of the rocky ridge over at the Camber, well camouflaged, but the rotor blades glint in the sun which rather gives them away.

Towards the end of Mass this afternoon, we heard the sound of a jet aircraft overhead with no firing breaking out, so assumed that it was an Argentine. Afterwards, while outside on the steps, there was a great burst of firing from the airport, with clouds of black smoke. An Argentine TV crew were filming it from the back of the town hall. We heard later that they had shot down one of their own planes and then opened fire on the helicopter which had gone off to rescue the pilot. They are getting rather jumpy.

Late this afternoon we suddenly discovered that we had an Argentine soldier stationed outside the house, apparently some sort of guard, done up like a miniature arsenal with pistol, rifle and grenades. This was not really on, so invited him in for a cup of coffee. He was a bit hesitant at first, but a plate of cakes went a long way in helping him to make up his mind. He didn't speak a great deal of English, but we were able to have sort of a fractured conversation, during which he told us that all was well with his army; everything was going fine; no problems. We were not entirely convinced. He stayed for nearly an hour, then somewhat furtively took up his position outside the gate again. We had thought of offering him a cigarette, but he would have gone up like a Brocks benefit night with all that weaponry strung about him.

I think that the Argentines may be keeping an eye on us, as so many young people, especially lads between eighteen and twenty, come to the house during the afternoons. They may suspect that there is some sort of subversive movement being set up. They do seem very afraid of this sort of thing. We do, I suppose, look a bit suspicious, for besides Jeremy, Martyn and Rag who are permanent, there are also Peter Roberts, Graham Bound, Ramon Miranda, Cousin Zachary, etc., who all pop in for a beer, cup of tea or a chat and also to pinch whatever cakes or buns may be lying about.

Reception of 'Calling the Falklands' completely unreadable this evening. 'Radio Newsreel' was a bit better, which gave a most dramatic account of the landing at San Carlos. I wish now that I had made a recording of it. Losses must have been heavy on both sides. Argentina has lost seventeen aircraft in today's action; Britain has three ships severely damaged and two small helicopters lost. I do wish that it would all come to a rapid end.

Saturday 22 May – Day Fifty-one

The day got off to a bright start but got considerably duller later on. Very heavy frost during the night; there was still thick ice on the water butts in the garden late in the morning. Wind from the east, Force 3.

Ileen and I took the dog for a walk before lunch, keeping fairly close to home in case of air raids. Stanley House is now very closely guarded; it's quite startling to see camouflaged heads popping up from behind the fence pointing rifles at you. We wished them all Good Morning.

Chatted for a while outside with Terry Spruce and Mike Butcher. Terry says that his wife Joan and young son Mark are both well out on the farm at North Arm. Mike Butcher and his wife Trudy are finding life rather tough going, up at their house on Dairy Paddock Road which is now behind Argentine lines as it were, being on the south side of Davis Street. They are surrounded by hundreds of troops and a good number of anti-aircraft guns. To move out from their house to another part of town would be asking for trouble, as the Argentines would move in on Mike's welding and light engineering business very quickly. He has enough trouble at the moment keeping an eye on his plant, stock, and machinery.

Our guard was posted outside again this morning. Soon got him in by offering food, and he told us he was getting only one small meal per day. He sleeps in a trench half full of water, up on the hill. His clothing made great wet patches on the carpet. For over three hours he sat mesmerised by the warmth and food while Jeremy, Martyn and Robert took his weapons to pieces and examined the grenades. We did think of leaving some of the bits out, but thought better of it. He's been much more truthful today. This charity exercise was worthwhile. It gives us some idea of the state of the war from the Argentine side.

Have just heard the dreadful news that one of our Type 21 frigates – I think they said it was *Ardent* – was sunk yesterday after being hit by fifteen missiles. MOD says that we brought down twenty Argentine aircraft. Later news broadcasts say that a 10-mile square beach-head has now been established, with no interference from the air. Five thousand troops are ashore with Rapier missile systems, plus artillery, three commando regiments and two para battalions.

The Argentines have started reporting the landing, but only mention 200 troops, increasing to 700 by the late evening broadcasts. President Galtieri appeared on their television during the afternoon with reports saying that he looked weary and disturbed. Should think he has cause to after hearing the news of the San Carlos landing. If things go along at this rate he will be at the labour exchange looking for a new job in a week or two.

There was a splendid scene at St Mary's this afternoon, when the Monsignor caught some troops attempting to carry off some sheets of corrugated iron from his new house. I've never seen him so furious; they dropped the lot and took off rapidly.

Have found a new way of occupying my time when the others are playing cards during the evening. I listen to music from the tape recorder through headphones, which is very refreshing. Tonight's entertainment was the band of the Black Watch; really splendid. This must be the first time in my life that I have ever had to look around for something to do.

Sunday 23 May – Day Fifty-two

Damp coldish day, but bright. Wind east, Force 3–4.

Up at about 7.45. Fine dawn observed from Tyssen's bedroom window with a cup of tea. Watched the people from the safe houses returning to their homes in little groups. Everyone up early. Polished shoes for Mass and wore collar, tie and tweed jacket. Left my umbrella in the church porch; hope no one pinches it. When we were standing on the church steps after the service having a chat, two Harriers passed overhead very high, glinting in the brilliant blue sky. Seemed to be possibly a photographic reconnaissance run. No response from the ground except that we, and the troops across the road, watched with interest.

Quite a bit of firing from the west during the later part of the morning; must be patrols from the Task Force. BBC reports that the British morale is very high.

Two Argentines called at the house, one a civilian who never normally speaks until he is obliged to, when we pass the time of day to him, and an air-force pilot who required accommodation. Had to truthfully tell them that we are overflowing with people as there are eleven of us living here now.

Impossible to hear 'Calling the Falklands'. Later in the evening we got bits of the BBC news. Supplies are pouring into the beach-head. The supporting ships have been under attack from about thirty aircraft. One frigate has been damaged. Four Mirages and two Skyhawks have been shot down, along with one Puma helicopter which exploded in mid-air, and another which caught fire when landing. More Argentine prisoners have been taken; described as being cold, wet, dejected and suffering from exposure. Some had not had any food for three days. British patrols continue to probe inland. Two other Mirages have probably crashed.

The Argentine radio says that the British are ready to surrender, having now been surrounded by Argentine artillery, but then says their planes find them difficult to locate. All very confusing and conflicting.

While writing this up am listening to *Il Trovatore* on the headphones. It seems odd to try and grasp what terrible things are going on outside while listening to such great music.

There has been no sign of our Argentine soldier today. Perhaps it was noticed that he spent such a long time inside the house yesterday. It really was rather difficult to get rid of him; we had to suggest that he left in the end.

Monday 24 May – Day Fifty-three

Cold and brilliant; very little cloud. Wind west, Force 2–3. Splendid sunset.

Up at 7.30 as Duffy has managed to get work in the dockyard. I am going to see about work there tomorrow. Had very disturbed night. Loud explosion about 11.15, then about half an hour afterwards small-arms and machine-gun fire opened up – very close indeed, in the direction of the Drill Hall; the nearest that we have had yet.

Found this morning that St Mary's presbytery had been shot up by the Argentines, from the Drill Hall only 25 yd away, because they thought that they had seen something move there. We counted twenty-nine bullet holes in one wall. The damage was incredible, especially in the Monsignor's study, where the bullets had thrown all the books right across the room from the bookcase. One shot went straight through the toilet, shattering the bowl. Monsignor's only comment was that it was fortunate that neither he nor Fr Monaghan had been in session. He had a very lucky escape, having just gone upstairs to bed. Some bullets had come in through the outside wall of the house, gone through the bathroom wall and finished up embedded in the kitchen door. Fortunately Father was sleeping that night at the 'Upland Goose'. It was a fearsome sight this morning to see the old chap on the warpath after the military authorities.

A most spectacular bombing attack on the airfield this morning, about 9.30. I had just gone outside to the dustbin when Harriers streaked through the harbour entrance, about 50 ft high, turning towards the airport where there was a colossal explosion. It was just like the pictures. Great sheets of bright orange flame, then plumes of dense smoke billowing hundreds of feet into the air. God only knows what they hit, but whatever it was it went off in a most awe-inspiring way. Martyn rushed in moments later saying that he'd had a grandstand view of the whole thing from on top of the power station Land Rover. Four Harriers were involved, which he confirmed came through the Narrows like a dose of salts, then must have opened fire with their cannons before releasing their bombs, as the water looked as though it was boiling, down by the hulk of the old iron sailing ship *Lady Elizabeth*.

The whole incident happened at fantastic speed; fifteen or twenty seconds, then it was all over. Jeremy said it was watched from the dockyard with a divided reaction. The Argentines took cover while the locals greeted it with great excitement, with lots of shouting, cheering and leaping.

At lunch-time it was announced that all water should in future be boiled before drinking. Our shaky old water mains are being jostled about a bit by all these goings-on. The joints must be collapsing. More Harriers over during the morning. Everyone turned out to watch but no one fired back. The airport guns must have been knocked out during the first raid this morning.

More Harriers over late in the afternoon between 4 and 5 o'clock. Very high up. Quite a bit of firing from the Argentines this time, with some very near misses.

There was apparently a meeting in town today between the military chiefs about the indiscriminate shooting at night. One report says that the port captain was obliged to lie on the floor for some considerable time until his own troops had finished firing through his house. Stories do tend to become exaggerated, but in view of recent events this one has a ring of credibility about it.

Reports coming in on the BBC of a great air battle over San Carlos. Wave after wave of Mirages and Skyhawks attacking the Task Force ships, being repelled by Harriers, missiles and gunfire. Seven have been shot down, with another turning away trailing smoke. HMS *Antelope* has sunk after receiving a bomb in her engine room yesterday which exploded today during attempts to defuse it. It has been confirmed also that another frigate, HMS *Ardent*, was sunk during the initial landings at San Carlos. More ships have now joined the Task Force, bringing it up to an even greater strength than before. A spokesman in England has said that the days of the Argentine occupation are numbered. Their air force is taking a heavy toll while their navy is locked in port by British submarines.

News from Argentina is still confused, with some reports of dissatisfaction among the military leaders about allowing the bridgehead to be established at San Carlos without opposition.

Tomorrow is Argentina's Independence Day. I wonder what sort of spectacle we can expect from either side.

There has been an unsuccessful attempt by the Argentines to get fresh meat for their troops into Stanley from the farm at Fitzroy, some 25 miles away, by driving in sheep overland. They started off with 350 and arrived with 30.

Tuesday 25 May – Day Fifty-four

Very foggy start to the day, just able to see the other side of the harbour. Cleared by 9.30 to a damp but brilliant day again. Rather cool. Wind west, Force 3–4.

Another quiet night in the bunker. Heard lorries moving around on the streets about 6 o'clock. They seem to park them up at the west of town during the nights, then bring them back just before dawn. Able to see the odd flashes of matches as they light up their first cigarettes of the day in the cabs. Perhaps they park on hills for easier starts.

The troops looked a bit smarter this morning as it is Argentine Independence Day. There was a parade at the Drill Hall and another in front of the FIC office block, where one soldier let the side down by shooting another in the foot while fiddling with his pistol, which rather upset the dignity of the proceedings. Anya got up early and went down to Mass on her own, which she sometimes does now. She really has developed the most remarkable self-confidence recently in going out on her own in the present conditions, which have brought about an atmosphere of tension, anxiety and, recently, some hostility among the more professional soldiers.

Robert and I had frequent interruptions to our work putting the finishing touches to our fence, as things got very interesting and noisy, with Harriers again bombing the airport and the surrounding area. There was some spectacular manoeuvring by the Harriers, which were very high up before they came in to do the bombing. Very little return fire from the Argentines. This afternoon there was an interesting display by two Argentine Pucaras which started to fly very low and very fast around the harbour in an apparent attempt to show off to the civilian population, but their heroics soon collapsed about their ears when a couple of Harriers suddenly appeared overhead and for some fifteen minutes kept them pinned down on to the surface of the harbour. I think the Pucaras had to jettison their bombs as there were a couple of very loud explosions, before they eventually managed to creep up over the end of the harbour to land on the airport. The Harriers seemed to be having a field day, with lots of action and bombs all over the peninsular area. The effect on both troops and equipment must be absolutely fearful. The Argentines really ought to call it a day and give in with some dignity before they are pounded into a shambles down there.

I did try to make a recording of some of the noise but for once the anti-aircraft gun up at the back of the garden did not come into action. It is, I think, a 30-mm twin-barrelled Oerlikon, which makes a fair old din when it gets going. The rate of fire must be about 400 or 500 rounds per minute.

Independence Day is being played in very low key, both here and in Argentina. No great speech as was expected from Galtieri.

Argentine air attacks continue on the Task Force at San Carlos. Three Mirages down with another confirmed for yesterday. HMS *Bristol* has now joined the fleet, with extra warships, which make up for more than the losses suffered during the action. No mention of the *QE2* yet; possibly these supporting ships could have accompanied her into the South Atlantic. Wonder if Geoff is with the fleet anywhere; I did send a telegram to his home three weeks ago but doubt if it got through. We grew up together and have always managed to keep in touch, albeit only a card at Christmas with occasional very rare meetings at ten-year intervals or so. He now lives in Cornwall with wife Susan and children Guy and Kate. This sort of situation, dangerous though it may be, must be what every naval officer would wish to become involved in.

The BBC news today is very much a case of up and down spirits from one broadcast to the next. There was another mass air attack by the Argentine Air Force this morning. A British Type 42 destroyer is badly damaged and in difficulties. Argentina has now lost fifty fixed-wing aircraft. Mr Haig of the US predicts an early victory – presumably for us. The Pope is to go ahead with his visit to Britain. Plymouth, the home port of both of the frigates lost in the last few days, is deeply saddened. The British have now established a bridgehead of 60 square miles at San Carlos. No opposition yesterday from the Argentines. The news is dominated by the Falklands; no one else seems to get a look in nowadays.

Wednesday 26 May – Day Fifty-five

Dull, patchy sort of day; dry and cold. Wind west, Force 3–4.

It's now just before 11 at night and I'm writing up today's events in the bunker. Not a great deal of elbow room with eleven of us in here but managing fairly well. Today has been overshadowed by the horrific news of the sinking of the *Coventry* and the *Atlantic Conveyor*. *Coventry* suffered fifteen bomb hits and has lost twenty men; she had previously downed five Mirages. *Atlantic Conveyor* was sunk by Exocet missiles. No more details yet.

Last night was very noisy, with a heavy and close naval bombardment. They seemed to be firing at two-second intervals. Occasional return fire from land, but not a great deal; they must be too busy keeping their heads down.

Went to the dockyard to see about getting work this morning, but not very successful. My name will be put on the list; come back next week. What a mess the dockyard is in – thick mud everywhere, troops and vehicles all over the place. Bedraggled troops queuing up at the compulsory makeshift showers; others queuing at mobile kitchens from which a sort of stew is being dished out in very tiny portions. Some troops have lit small fires in odd corners where they are trying to keep warm and dry themselves out a bit. The dockyard used to be the butt of many jokes when it was under civilian rule, but that was 500 per cent better than this military shambles. Malcolm Binnie, the yard foreman, is doing a heroic job against heavy odds in trying to keep essential services going with his small gang. The unglamorous rubbish collecting and dumping is probably one of the most important and often dangerous tasks being regularly carried out now. The sudden rise in population has presented, among other things, a great deal more rubbish and filth. We are fortunate that vermin have not made an appearance.

Another bombing attack on the airport about noon and more bombing raids while we were at Mass this afternoon. Just before the Elevation a Harrier flashed down the harbour; all the guns opened up, but presumably missed as there was a tremendous explosion as it dropped its bombs. Tyssen, serving on the altar, never flinched, and Father never paused, continuing as if all was as normal. A young Argentine military padre, who often attends Mass, also remained apparently unaffected by the commotion, though like us he was probably dying to get outside to see what was happening. A few minutes later when the service had ended we saw a great mass of smoke and flames up towards Mount Kent.

We had a visit from the military today when an army lieutenant and a captain called to obtain details of the household for a census and to issue us with identity cards. They were very civil and rather embarrassed about it all, but we must have documents like all good citizens. We all went into the study where we gave our details, which were entered on official forms, then on to our cards which lacked our photographs in the appropriate spaces. This does seem to leave a bit of a loophole.

Both officers spoke English, so we were able to have a reasonable conversation, during which we smoked cigarettes. The formality of the proceedings was upset a little when I offered one of them a light. As he leaned forward across the table the leg of his chair unfortunately broke, which he took in good part. This helped to relax the atmosphere considerably. We learned later in the day that their reception by the householders was noted, so hope that the chair-leg incident will not be held against us. As they were leaving, the senior of the two said that one day he would enjoy returning to be able to spend a holiday in Stanley, possibly to stay with us as a guest. Such is life in these amazing days. During the form-filling, a Harrier passed overhead but everyone was too polite to notice it.

Have noticed several attempts recently by the Argentines to catch the logger ducks in the harbour for food. This is profoundly disturbing. Fortunately they are not being very successful, but there are some of the soldiers who seem to be using them for target practice.

We bedded down in the bunker at 10.30. A fairly good routine has been established in getting down there without too much fuss in the darkness. Jeannie takes Maxwell down first to get settled, then Anya, Ileen, Tyssen and Eli, followed finally by Duffy and the remainder of us, by which time everyone has got into their sleeping bags with their torches, books, etc, placed handily. For some unexplained reason this evening we have thirty-three pillows in here with us.

The BBC news has announced that the Task Force is poised for the attack on Stanley. May be an interesting night.

Thursday 27 May – Day Fifty-six

Dull, cloudy and damp. Very cold. Wind west, Force 4, decreasing during the afternoon.

Think the attack on Goose Green may be underway. Intense activity in Stanley. Helicopters flying out the Argentine Special Forces from the racecourse with vast quantities of ammunition. Big panic on. One soldier was killed when he rolled a drum of petrol over a mine. Another soldier injured himself while cleaning his rifle. Lots of movement towards Mount Kent and in the Estancia direction where presumably the Argentine front line must be. Very long and loud explosion about 4.45 this evening, rather like heavy cannon fire, over in the Murrel River area. Tyssen says he saw flashes in the sky. I've never heard an explosion like it before. An Argentine aircraft, which sounded like a C-130 Hercules, got in and away again during the night.

BBC news again is a mixture of encouragement and tragedy. Canberra bombers have attacked San Carlos. Helicopter pads have been set up within the bridgehead. Scorpion tanks and more artillery are ashore. The *Atlantic Conveyor* has been found still afloat and upright. It is now presumed that twelve people were lost on her. She was said to have on board thirteen helicopters plus Harrier spare parts. Twenty men have been lost on the *Coventry*. Galtieri will have an awful lot to answer for when this is over. The Pope is due to arrive in England tomorrow, then on to Argentina. We pray that he will be able to persuade Galtieri to stop his madness. Later news during the day said that the Royal Marines are moving towards Stanley and the Paras towards Darwin; no mention of where the other 3,000 British troops are. The survivors of HMS *Sheffield* arrived in UK today.

Pat came in as usual at breakfast time. He had three Argentine magazines showing dramatic pictures of Stanley and the terrible mess that the airport is now in. Also a news item that the Argentine naval vessel *Alférez Sobral* has been either very badly damaged or sunk. She was in Stanley about ten years ago. Nestor Barrico was her captain; he gave me a fine model of a ship's cannon. One of her young officers, Raul E. Scheller TFCB (I don't know what these initials mean), came up to the house and later gave me a book on the history of the Argentine Navy. They were both very pleasant officers; wonder what they are doing now?

Managed to have a bath this morning, which was somewhat curtailed by a Harrier bombing raid. Lots of anti-aircraft guns firing from nearby, which sounded exceptionally loud in the bathroom, so got outside rapidly and damply to watch events. As usual the firing was enthusiastic but thankfully inaccurate. During all the commotion a young soldier came up to the gate and asked if we could give him something to eat. He seemed to have lost all interest in the current proceedings. We gave him some bread; what else can one do in such circumstances? One is compelled to make decisions between humanity and politics. I hope he had time to eat it before being caught and dealt with.

Tidied up in the garden again. It is remarkable that one of the bushes by the front gate still has buds and flowers on it this late in the year. Sent off cables to Mum, Eunice and Geoff. Probably a waste of time but if they do get through it will help to reassure them somewhat. The post office is full of troops; everywhere is filthy with mud, water and foreign cigarette smoke. There is an air of extreme apprehension among the troops.

'Calling the Falklands' fairly clear. Had message from Noreen which bucked us all up. According to the Argentine news Gen Menéndez says that the British blockade is causing difficulties and shortages for the local population; his supplies for the troops are satisfactory. (He seems to have got the situation reversed.) They also say that the Argentine troops are now poised for a counter-attack on the British bridgehead. We shall wait and see . . .

Despite the seriousness of our present position, there is a wonderful air of what I suppose might be called a community spirit among everyone. We are all cheerful and seldom a day passes without some small episode which causes great amusement. This goes not only for us as a household, but for everyone in town; though having said that, we have noticed recently, especially when shopping, that some people have suddenly got a lot older in appearance, but they still put on a brave front. No one knows what the next few days or weeks will bring, but we try to keep our thoughts and fears to ourselves.

Friday 28 May – Day Fifty-seven

Wet, windy, misty and cold. Generally lousy weather all day. Wind east, Force 4, increasing during the afternoon.

Goose Green has been retaken by the Paras. Wonderful news which reached Stanley by lunch-time. Young Ramon rushed in to tell us. The word got through when Gail Steen was allowed by the Argentines to get in touch with her husband Vernon from the hospital to let him know that Alan's operation had been successful. Vernon managed to pass on the news during the conversation by simply saying, 'The flag's at GG again.' It is very difficult to believe that it's true. It was confirmed this evening on 'Calling the Falklands'. The Paras have taken both Goose Green and Darwin. No details are available yet, but it is definitely confirmed. The Argentine news reports fierce fighting during the day. Reinforcements were flown from Stanley during the day and drove the British back 7 miles. Later BBC news again confirmed the British success, saying there were both British and Argentine casualties, and Argentine prisoners taken.

Very heavy naval bombardment last night from 11.15 until 1.30 this morning, the heaviest yet. Illuminants were being used. We were able to hear the whistle of the shells going over the house and then see the bright flashes of the explosions through gaps in the black-outs.

Up at 7.30 to tune into the BBC. Nothing is being released by the MOD on Falkland movements. The Pope has arrived in Britain. Four Royal Marines and one Royal Engineer were killed yesterday at San Carlos. Twenty men were injured. MOD says that yesterday's attack on San Carlos was by Mirages and Skyhawks, not Canberras. Two Skyhawks shot down, and one Harrier pilot forced to eject, possibly towards Port Howard.

Two Pucaras took off from Stanley just after 8 this morning. Some say that a C-130 Hercules got in during the night. Great helicopter activity on the racecourse, moving some more troops out towards the mountains, presumably to the Argentine front line. With the wind increasing during the day it has been difficult to distinguish between the gale blowing and distant bombing or shelling.

The town water supply was shut off at midday. We had to empty our hot water cylinder to prevent loss through the overflow, so we filled up everything possible from the hot taps, then had to replenish the supply tank in the attic with cold water, which we had standing by in the two bathrooms downstairs. A very complicated operation, involving much tramping up and downstairs with buckets. As an additional reserve we brought in a large old milk churn from the garden, which is placed between the downstairs toilets, filled with water from butts, buckets and drums which we had put under the down pipes and guttering from the roof of the house. It's a bit grotty but quite suitable for flushing purposes.

Most of the day has been spent in water logistics. Came upon a great find this afternoon behind Harry Ford's greenhouse next door, where he has a 40 gall. drum to catch the water from the roof; so quickly transferred that to buckets and tins, which are now stowed in the house. I'm sure Harry won't mind us using it. He and Betty are at Fitzroy; we haven't heard anything from them for weeks but presume that they are well. Some time last week the boys, who often pop around next door to keep an eye on the house, found that Harry had some fine tomatoes still in the greenhouse, so quickly liberated them lest they should fall into the hands of the enemy, as they so nicely put it. It was, we thought, a justifiable cause, so we all thoroughly enjoyed them. Rather we should have them than some prowling Argentines.

The sale of petrol has been stopped at YPF; no more left. This is going to be a bit awkward for the Argentines as most of their vehicles depend on it. They will now start to commandeer our diesel Land Rovers, I suppose.

Martyn has had a very busy day repairing broken power lines throughout the town. He also has been paid by the military government, in Argentine Pesos, which he has put straight into his bank account here in the hope that the money will retain some of its value. I broke into our last £10 note; the tourist business is not too good these days. Fortunately and thankfully the boys are keeping us afloat, but I would be much happier earning my own money. There may be some sort of a job when I apply at the dockyard again on

Monday. It's a most odd experience as I have never been out of work before. Our entire capital was put into establishing this new business and the little reserve which we had has now gone – not quite, though, as I still have £8.35 left from the £10. Things are not so desperate as I had imagined!

More news has just come on that another 1,000 troops are to leave England next week for the Falklands, including Royal Engineers to repair the roads and runway. HMS *Hecla* is due in Montevideo on Monday with casualties from the Falklands. The Pope has called on the Queen; he spoke on the radio in very good English; still hopeful of this terrible dispute reaching a peaceful settlement.

Everyone in town has taken great interest in last night's bombardment. It really was quite spectacular. Late this afternoon there was a lot of firing, banging and what sounded like bombing, away to the north and to the west of Stanley. We got our heads down, trying to ignore it, until it was time for supper. We can possibly expect another noisy night, so are all getting odd bits of sleep in during the day. While on the subject of getting heads down, it seems that Gen Menéndez moves about quite a lot, sleeping each night at a different place, in case of attack I suppose. Apparently you can always tell where he is because the only black Alsatian guard dog is stationed with its handler at whichever house he happens to be in. I have seen it a few times at the house opposite the Drill Hall where the Growcotts and, before them, the Clapps used to live. The Argentines have dug a tremendous hole in the back garden, in which they have put a sort of steel shelter covered with earth and rocks.

Quite a lot more people have built bunkers under their houses. We were talking to Mark Hullock the other day, who has now moved into Vicky and Ian Townsend's house up by the Monument, as they are in England. Mark has dug a hole under the floor in among the foundations, as he says it tends to get rather exciting up that end of town some nights. How much more self-confidence he has since this lot began. He lives in the house on his own, and works in the dockyard, usually on lorries or on the dumper crew. Always shouts and gives a smile and a wave as he passes. It is odd to say, but as in the case of several other people, this situation has revealed a tremendous strength of character; so much more than when he came out here with us from Rye a couple of years ago rather than leave school and face the dole queue in England. That was a very big move for him to make at seventeen; none of us thought that we would have a war thrown in as well.

Anya's great friend Diane comes in most days for a chat after being over at Philip Middleton's house, where he still continues teaching his 'O' level group, despite the difficulties. The schools may be closed but the few teachers that are left still do their best to continue the work in their immediate areas.

Going back to Goose Green – we were appalled to learn that the people there were still imprisoned in the hall. Little notice seems to have been paid to the protest by the Church or the enquiry into the situation promised by Menéndez a couple of weeks ago.

Saturday 29 May – Day Fifty-eight

Cold and raining. Wind from the west, Force 5.

There are unconfirmed reports that Douglas Station and Teal Inlet are in British hands. Great news, but we are all of us deeply saddened by the terrible loss of lives in this conflict so far. We have just heard about Col H. Jones and the Paras, who were killed in what appears to have been a brilliant attack on Goose Green yesterday.

The Argentine troops are very apprehensive, in some cases very frightened, here in Stanley. One broke down and had to be carried away by his mates. Another wandered up the road in tears, dragging his rifle. There are hundreds of them about the streets, clustered in pathetic, depressed groups, their clothes and boots sodden with rain and trench water. Very little spirit seems left in them. They are now realising that the push is about to hit them – and hit them hard.

The hospital ship *Uganda* was apparently in Middle Bay at the northern end of Falkland Sound a couple of days ago for half an hour, to pick up casualties. The Argentines have protested that it was interfering with their military operations.

Went for a sleep upstairs at 11 this morning, but just about blown out of bed by a most violent explosion when the Harriers bombed the paddock down by Ashworths' dairy once again. The house seemed to lift off its moorings. It is fortunate that the houses here are of fairly flexible construction; brick buildings would have suffered serious blast damage. Found that all of the cushions in the bunker were very damp, so brought them up into the house to dry out. My suspicions about the taking over of diesel vehicles were confirmed this morning when a captain and lieutenant called to enquire if our Land Rover was diesel or petrol. Luckily it's petrol, so they went on their way. They seemed extraordinarily pleasant and wished us luck as they left.

There have been several bombing attacks around the perimeter of the town today by the Harriers. Ileen, Jeannie and Anya are putting up blankets around the front-porch windows, to improve the black-out and prevent glass from flying about.

A bit of a display was put on this afternoon by some Argentine aircraft, Pucaras and Guaraní, which flew low and fast around the town several times, then some really daring flying right on the surface of the harbour. They disappeared from sight behind the government jetty and hulk of the *Charles Cooper*, which meant that they must have been about 10 ft or 15 ft up.

A lot of firing suddenly opened up from down towards the bottom of the harbour. I think that the over-keen gunners may have shot one of them down, as there was quite a bit of smoke. The Argentines seem to have had a number of own goals lately.

The food situation among troops in Stanley is becoming increasingly desperate. Jeremy says that yesterday when he was tipping out the rubbish at the dump the soldiers were waiting for his arrival to go through the rubbish with sticks for bits of food.

Sunday 30 May – Day Fifty-nine

A brilliant day. Sunshine with tingling blue sky. Light dusting of snow this morning; quite thick on the mountains by the look of it. Very cold. Wind from the west, Force 2–3.

A very noisy night indeed. Naval bombardment commenced 11.20, then continued without let-up for five hours. They seemed to be aiming at saturating the area between Moody Brook and the airport. The occasional few shells passed over the house, but no really good whistlers.

Had morning tea while waiting for the dawn to come up, watching from Tyssen's bedroom window. There were – and still are – some very cold troops moving about the streets. They seem quite fascinated by the snow, scraping handfuls from the top of the fences in order to examine it. Many of them are distinctly puzzled, not having come across it before.

The first bombing attack of the day was just after 9 o'clock, out towards the airport. We all went along to Mass at ten; lots of Argentine officers there, with military police standing in the porch. Across the road outside of the gymnasium are stacked a lot of Blowpipe missiles in cases. Lingering about long enough to count them is impossible; perhaps that's why the MPs were in the chapel porch. There is an extremely tense atmosphere in the town; the troops are very jumpy. In fact before Mass this morning one of the officers asked the Monsignor why the church bell was being rung. I think that it took him a great deal of restraint and patience to explain that it was the normal practice to ring the bell of a church on Sundays, not only in Port Stanley, but all over the world. Maybe the Argentines thought that it was some kind of signal to a possible resistance movement in the town.

We all spent the day preparing for further action, filling more drums with earth. Placed three across the top step against the front door, stuffing the gaps with timber and rocks. Also placed more drums and rocks at the west end of the porch, where we have one of our escape hatches. We've moved vast quantities of earth. Goodness knows what we will do with it all when this lot is over. The troops are now digging in solidly all over the paddock on the Co-op corner; it's fairly bristling with weapons. They have also dug another machine-gun pit opposite, on the grass outside Vernon Steen's house.

Lots of air activity. Just before 11 there were huge explosions towards Mount Kent, possibly a bit to the north of it. There was a great deal of smoke which hung about for a long time. Shortly afterwards saw two Harriers over the town. I think they must have hit an ammunition dump in the mountains. The airport has been plastered by bombs for much of the day, with very little return fire at the Harriers. This has all been accompanied by a very heavy bombardment by the Navy. Lots of sporadic small-arms firing going on up towards Mount Kent/Estancia direction.

Down by the town hall and in front of the police station there are troops sweeping the street. This seems to be a genuine attempt to keep the streets tidy, with rubbish bins placed about the main parts of the town. There are also notices in Spanish about keeping the town clean; some have an illustration showing two people alongside a rubbish bin. At the top are words to the effect of, 'Clean Up the Malvinas Campaign'. In the West Store one of these notices has been cleverly adapted for local consumption. It is headed 'FALKLAND ISLANDS GOVERNMENT – CLEAN UP STANLEY.' The people standing alongside the bin have been converted into a kelper and a Royal Marine who are in the act of shoving an Argentine soldier into the dustbin. We all have a pretty good idea who is responsible for the conversion but no one is saying a word. There will no doubt be repercussions from the military authorities.

With the recent wet weather the condition of the streets is becoming appalling. They have been badly battered by the heavy military vehicles, especially by the APCs which, although only here for a couple of days, by their sheer weight caused almost irreparable damage by breaking up the surface of our roads, which were only designed for Land-Rover traffic. The result now is that the water has got in underneath, along with the hard frosts, causing huge pieces to crack up; other sections are sinking. The mud brought into the town by the troops on their boots is fantastic. If we have 4,000 troops here, then that is 8,000 boots – assuming that each soldier has been issued with two legs. The result is ankle-deep mud in many places now, when the really bad weather of winter is not yet here. The majority of roads have a couple of inches of thick, soupy mud slopping about on the surface.

New curfew instructions have been announced, to become effective tomorrow. All persons to be off the streets by 4 o'clock in the afternoon, until 8.30 next morning. The population are to remain inside their houses during the hours of darkness. These instructions are to be strictly complied with. We will end up like battery hens at this rate. This latest notice really serves only to reinforce arrangements already being carried out.

Also issued today was a new instruction which reads as follows:

SECURITY ORDER No. 1 FROM THE MILITARY GOVERNMENT FOR THE PROTECTION OF THE CIVILIAN POPULATION.

– All the inhabitants of Puerto Argentina (ex Stanley) are informed that those living or having their homes on the southern sidewalk of Davis Street and towards the South, will have obligatorily to move to another place in the town.

– All those homes affected by this order must be closed the best possible way in order to avoid illegal entries or robberies.

– This order has to be accomplished before Monday the 31th of May at 3 pm.

– Those who need help to move their belongings can ask for it at the Secretary General's Office (Mr Mora).

– The Military Government at the proper time will let it be known to those affected by this order when they can return to their homes.

– The purpose of this order is to protect the civilian population because of the tendency of the latest British bombardment.

– Once the situation is normalized the Military Government will contemplate those cases in which damages were caused by our Forces on private property.

Last night's bombardment must have really made the Argentines' eyes water, especially up in the trenches and dug-outs at the back of the town. It was rather scary at times down here; it must have been bloody terrifying up there. The firing by the Navy is uncannily accurate. Their shells are landing right on the very edge of the town.

There is the possibility of a total house curfew as the British troops continue their advance towards Stanley, so spent much of today storing more water in the house. We also put half a dozen

5 gall. containers of paraffin under the house – well away from our bunker exits – and brought a couple of sacks of potatoes down from the shed into the kitchen. It's all a bit like a jumble sale in the house now, but at least we have the essentials of life on hand. Water is the big problem with eleven of us here, but I think we can manage – we will have to. The supply was cut off again at 4 this afternoon. We have to keep a careful eye on our plumbing system, as this shutting on and off, combined with filling the supply tank by buckets, has disturbed the sludge of years which has accumulated in the pipes, now causing slow running of the taps, in some cases no running at all. So we have to keep watch on the hot-water system, so that it does not run dry; if it does the boiler in the stove is liable to explode. Damage by enemy action is one thing, but to have your kitchen blown up by your own stove is another.

The black-out regulations seem to be being tightened up, so nailed more blankets and cardboard over the windows. Our preparations for the forthcoming attack on Stanley are just about as good as they can be in the circumstances. All we can do now is to sit back and wait. The situation seems so unreal – like preparing for a siege. After curfew we were leaning over the front gate enjoying the sunset when an Argentine colonel and a lieutenant colonel came along the road. They asked us in good English about life in general. They seemed as disenchanted as we are with the situation. Bit late now – they shouldn't have started it.

The news this evening from the BBC was interesting. There was a dramatic account of the taking of Goose Green. It was a fourteen-hour battle. It is confirmed that the Paras had only 600 men and took 1,400 prisoners. They suffered 12 dead and 30-plus wounded. Their commanding officer, Lt-Col H. Jones, was killed while attacking a machine-gun post. The description of how his body was carried down into the settlement, led by a soldier with rifle pointing towards the ground, was an accomplished and poignant piece of broadcasting. It reminded me so much of Charles Wolfe's great poem, 'The Burial of Sir John Moore'. I will not be able to bring myself to read it or to listen to it for a very long time yet. (We have a superb recording of Simon Cooke reading it, which we made some years ago when he was the officer commanding the Royal Marines of Naval Party 8901.)

It was appalling to hear again on the BBC confirmation that the people of Goose Green had been locked up in the Social Club for the last four weeks; their homes have been broken up and looted. It seems that the Argentine surrender was arranged on the R/T between the British and Argentine forces by Eric Goss and Alan Miller.* The prisoners were paraded on the Goose Green airstrip, where they sang their national anthem before laying down arms under the direction of an air comodoro. Many seemed cheerful at the prospect of going home. After the parade there was the pathetic sight of hungry, tired and bewildered prisoners searching for their dead and bringing them in.

The Harrier pilot who ejected some three days ago has turned up after living in the Camp, evading the Argentines. He had to leave his aircraft as the cockpit was a mass of flames. Didn't say where he turned up.

Also confirmed that Douglas Station and Teal Inlet are in British hands. It was also stated that the bombardment of Stanley last night was the heaviest carried out yet – no wonder it sounded so noisy.

On the Argentine news they admit to having lost contact with their troops at Goose Green. They also claim to have bombed HMS *Invincible* – Britain says this is untrue.

Ian Strange, the painter and writer who lives up near the cemetery, has had the pet sheep pinched, probably for food. He and Maria were looking after it for Janice Jaffray. They think that it must have been carried away, as they deliberately tethered it near the house so that they would hear any bleating or movement after dark.

* The farm managers of Goose Green and Port San Carlos respectively.

Monday 31 May – Day Sixty

Fine, clear and very cold for most of the day. Wind east, Force 4. Snow on ground again this morning. Occasional snow squalls.

Woken and shaken about 5.45 this morning by Harriers on a low bombing run at the back of Davis Street. Three incredible explosions all very close together, even louder and more alarming than the Vulcan bombings, which were about 3 miles away (these were only about 300yd away). Caused all the ladies to get up and pass water by torchlight. They returned with cups of tea and buns. So refreshed, we all slept until 7.30. Then got up and watched a vicious snow squall sweeping in from the west. Got the fires going and fuelled up the stove. Topped up everything in sight with water when it came on again at 8.30, in case of further stoppages. Tyssen and Eli up early to play in the snow.

Went with Anya to the West Store in morning for a few essentials, as we may need to have things on hand for the next few days. British troops are reported to be on Mount Kent. They can see us; we shall be awfully glad when we can see them. Occasional firing from that direction. No more meat to be delivered from the Butchery, as it is too dangerous for anyone to work up there now. Fortunately we have a good stock in the deep freeze.

Duffy, with Les Biggs, Timmy McCallum, Nidge Buckett (Ron's wife) and other volunteers have been most of the day bringing people with their belongings down from Davis Street to houses down in the town. They all have been doing a wonderful job these last few weeks under very difficult and dangerous conditions. Nothing is too much trouble for them, no matter the time, the day or the military obstacles. Robert has brought his cat here to stay, a huge grey affair called Tinkles who seems to fit in well with all the other wildlife in the house. He carried it down in a large suitcase.

Plenty of air activity. While in the West Store heard missile go off which missed; made a very loud bang. Jeremy arrived home mid-morning in his dumper for a warm and a cup of tea. He says that the dustman's job is becoming increasingly dangerous. The troops down towards the rubbish dump are now even less fussy about where they open fire.

The Pope is having a great reception in England. He always mentions the people of the South Atlantic but never uses the names of the places involved.

Great excitement at lunch-time. Four Harriers bombed the airport. Saw the whole thing. They made a fantastic sight coming in at about 30 ft or 40 ft up, very fast. Rather like being at the Farnborough air show, with action thrown in. Great explosions, smoke and flames. Think they must have got the Pucaras which were flying about yesterday. Lots of return fire.

Owing to the early curfew, Mass is now at 2.30 each afternoon. Just as we were leaving home to attend we saw two Harriers very high, then lots of anti-aircraft firing broke out and two missiles were launched, causing great detonations and flashes in the sky. Thought they had got one Harrier but he thankfully reappeared through the smoke. Then just as we were about to go into church another missile was launched, causing a huge ball of flame with dense white smoke; seconds later a tremendous explosion. All the Argentines cheering like mad; we felt sickened and sure that they must have scored a hit. Felt awful all through Mass. We arrived late; Tyssen who was serving said that the whole church shook so much that the stands on which the flowers were placed all but toppled over. More firing broke out during the prayers for peace. Afterwards we found that both Harriers had got away safely; the missiles had exploded some distance below them. I think that the Argentines must have bought some old stock off someone, as their missiles are fortunately not very successful; many seem to go up a few hundred feet, then either go off bang or whirl about all over the place, which is highly dangerous for themselves, as they have no idea where they are likely to come down. They don't seem to have much control over them once they have been launched. One came down at Eliza Cove among their own troops the other day.

Took the dog for a short walk before the new 4 o'clock curfew. Very different attitude among the troops today; solemn and serious. They are digging in everywhere. They started on the children's playing field, but Jeannie went out in a great temper pointing out to them in no uncertain terms that because of them, this was the only safe place left in town for the children to play, so they should dig their holes elsewhere. They were so taken aback by this outburst that they dug in outside the fence. They are now burying huge steel containers all over the town. One just opposite, next to the R/T station, digging with a JCB till late into the night by floodlights. It is fortunate that we reinforced our defences outside yesterday. The Co-op corner is now like a fortress; they can't possibly have any room left to dig any more gun-pits.

Another moving piece of reporting on 'Radio Newsreel' on the funeral at San Carlos yesterday of the seventeen men killed in the Goose Green battle. They were buried in the evening on the mountainside. No firing party. Handful of earth thrown into the graves by the RSM, flanked by members of the Paras, Royal Marines and Royal Engineers, against a background of the sunset and a frigate in the bay with her guns silently turning, trained skywards in case of another Argentine attack. The large numbers of prisoners at Goose Green are causing problems; not enough identification labels for them, so that they are having now to use the brightly coloured P & O cruise labels, which must look rather odd. They are being taken in batches to San Carlos where they are put aboard a British ship. Most are painfully thin. One said he'd only had one cup of rice during the past two days. Another ship left England today for the Falklands; no details disclosed other than that she was fitted with a helicopter landing pad.

The Argentine news continues to claim that the *Invincible* was hit during their raids on the Task Force yesterday. Britain continues to refute their claim and says that no ships were damaged. They say that two Exocets were fired by the Argentines, which were brought down, and that no ships were damaged. One Super Etendard and one Skyhawk were shot down as well. The *Atlantic Conveyor* has now sunk. The commander of the Argentine Air Force is today visiting bases in the south of the country; says there are plenty of good pilots left. According to the Argentine radio, they are expecting an attack on Stanley in the next couple of days . . . Will tomorrow be another glorious First of June?

During today the Darwin Road has been shelled and bombed, also the Airport Road, as the Pucaras have been landing there. Martyn is on fire duty tonight. Once more we have had to carry out the water operation on the storage tank as the supply has been cut off again. The troops took over Willy Bowle's house today. His furniture is being piled up in the garden outside. He left with his family for Darwin soon after the invasion, so must have been locked up in the Social Club with thc rest of the people out there.

There was a most unusual bombing of a frigate of the Task Force yesterday, when a C-130 Hercules flew over, opened its back door, then the crew threw the bombs out.

Late evening. Have suddenly remembered it's Whit Monday. Fun-fairs on the village greens in England; also the Royal Thames Yacht Club Cherbourg Rally; wonder if they still hold it? . . . I remember in 1965 sailing down from Deauville to Cherbourg in very thick fog, arriving just in time to catch the tail end of the festivities on the *Fiumara*.

Tuesday 1 June – Day Sixty-one

Grey, overcast, cold day. Wind west, Force 3. Dusting of snow on the mountains. Thick ice on the puddles in the town remained all day.

Another night in the bunker and our sixty-first day of Argentine occupation. Woke at about 2.30 to loud firing; seemed to be a combination, possibly, of artillery up in the direction of Mount Kent and a bombardment from the sea, with return fire from the Argentines. All very noisy and quite impossible to sort out whose shots were whose. Not at all like the usual steady crash every two seconds from the Navy. Drifted off to sleep again after half an hour or so, only to be woken by Anya throwing a book at me for snoring. Eventually up at about 7.45. Not a bad sort of morning; very little activity among the troops. We had good baths to the accompaniment of heavy gunfire from the mountains, possibly from the sea as well, as we could see the shells landing and bursting on Wireless Ridge.

The Argentine hospital ship *Bahía Paraíso* arrived in Port William early this morning, then came in to the harbour towards lunch-time. Fine modern-looking ship; white with cream superstructure and large red crosses, helicopter deck aft. Bridge forward, two cranes amidships; large after-structure. Seems to be about 5,000 tons; had been cleared by a British boarding party before being allowed into Stanley.

The Argentines continued throughout the day to dig a great hole in which they have buried the steel container over by the R/T office. Earth and sods are now piled up on top of it so that it resembles a natural hump in the ground – it's distinctly unnatural as far as we are concerned. We noticed this morning that there are now many rifle positions in this part of town which are sort of individual jobs, just a hole in the ground some 3 ft or 4 ft deep, in which is placed an old petrol drum with the top cut out. This does prevent the sides of the hole from caving in, but has the disadvantage that when there is rain or melting snow it fills very rapidly with water which is unable to escape. Some troops have tried knocking holes in the bottom, but these do not seem to be successful. It must be an awfully chilly experience to leap into one of these things half full of water at the commencement of a bombing raid, especially now, as we noticed several soldiers having to break away the ice before they could start bailing their positions out.

Went along to the dockyard this morning to see what the job prospects were, but nothing doing. Come back next week, says the colonel. This does cause one to feel a bit despondent, but there is not much that can be done about it. Met our dentist, Robert Watson, with his wife, Kathy, when I came out of the dockyard. They really are extremely kind, offering in the most Christian way without hesitation to assist in our financial situation should it be required, but I explained that the boys and Duffy were helping out. Our heads are above water and I naturally want to be responsible for the main income by getting work of some sort. It is most comforting to know, though, that in an occasion of need Robert's offer still holds good. Later in the day met Harry Milne who must also have heard of my dockyard visit and told me to let him know if we needed any financial assistance. It's good to have friends; we really appreciate it.

It appears that three aircraft managed to get in and out during last night. Two C-130 Hercules and another type which no one seemed to be able to identify. They took off without lights during the early hours of this morning. Credit must be given to Argentina's superb pilots. They must have landed in complete darkness on what is left of the runway. They were very fortunate to have escaped detection during all the firing that was going on. There is, as ever, the very strong possibility of being shot down by their own anti-aircraft gunners, who are still keen to have a go at anything that flies.

A very loud and noisy artillery exchange interrupted lunch, causing everyone to rush outside to see what was going on. Having lunch does sound a bit grand for these days. It actually consists of the eleven of us trying to fit around a kitchen table designed for six. Everyone is talking at the same time, so that no one is able to keep up conversation on any one subject; so it's a case of selecting a moment when someone is pausing for breath, then joining in on their conversation; sort of a vocal blind-man's buff. Most interesting but inclined to get one totally confused. Only the remnants of sanity remain at our mealtimes now. The din was so great that today we became aware of the artillery goings-on, not because of the crashing of the guns, but because the vibration made several things fall off the table.

During Mass this afternoon firing broke out, accompanied by lots of cheering from the troops. Anya, who had been to Mass this morning, met us immediately afterwards to say that a Harrier had been shot down; she had watched the pilot eject and come down by parachute towards Eliza Cove. Shortly afterwards a Chinook took off to bring in the pilot, so we rushed down to the football field to watch it return. Quite a crowd had gathered, including an Argentine TV team, who were very excited at the prospect of filming the British aviator, as they put it. Their disappointment and embarrassment was extreme when an Argentine fighter pilot appeared at the back hatch of the Chinook in a not too happy frame of mind. It seems that once again they had shot down one of their own aircraft. Some little time beforehand the Harriers had brought down a C-130 Hercules just off Mangeary Point as it was coming to land at the airport; possibly the fighter shot down had been an escort.

Many people saw this afternoon's action. There still seems a possibility that a Harrier was brought down as well, but there has been no sign of another pilot being brought in. Had this happened the entire town would have known about it, as the Argentines would have naturally been overjoyed at their success. Some people have drawn sketches of the type of aircraft that they saw the pilot eject from; some resemble a delta-wing fighter, while others have definite wings, without much doubt a Harrier. If it was, hopefully the pilot is OK.

There is a curious atmosphere in the town today among the troops; they are quiet and uneasy. They may have heard the news that there were 250 Argentines killed at the retaking of Goose Green. Quite a number of Argentines are being taken from their field hospital at the hostel on to the hospital ship, by helicopter. Constant to-ing and fro-ing.

We had a most odd and somewhat moving experience this afternoon when taking the dog out for her walk. Two young officers came up to us and in fairly good English more or less apologised to us for what was taking place, saying that it was not the fault of many of them. They are here against their wishes and want no part in the present events. They are sure that the British will be here tomorrow. They have been told that all prisoners will be killed. I'm sure that if we had said come home with us and hide in the shed they would have done so.

On the BBC news we heard that large quantities of napalm have been found at Goose Green, presumably for use by low-level bombing with the Pucaras. These Argentines really do have a cheek . . . They were making a terrible fuss the other day about the British using cluster bombs, saying they were inhuman and wicked – napalm is not exactly Sunday-school-treat sort of stuff is it? Mount Kent was taken on Monday with the minimum of force. A C-130 Hercules has been shot down some 50 miles north of the Falklands by Harriers from *Invincible*, which rather disproves the Argentine claims that they have badly damaged her with bombs. There was a news report directly from Goose Green which was a bit distorted by atmospherics, but it seems that someone there was tied up for some considerable time for an offence concerning a wireless.

Times are bad when we have to get the news from Goose Green via London.

All the town electricity went off for quarter of an hour during supper-time which caused a great rush for the candles. Several daring raids were carried out under the cover of the darkness on various plates around the table. Eggs, slices of bread and all sorts of things disappeared, causing fierce outbreaks of fighting in the kitchen as the offenders tried to conceal their spoils.

Wednesday 2 June – Day Sixty-two

Misty, damp and foggy; very thick at times. Wind from the east, Force 2. Cold.

Slept fairly well despite a naval bombardment and an artillery barrage somewhere to the south-west. Up just before 8; did the now-routine water gathering, unblack-outing and fire-lighting performance. There was a great deal of activity during the night around the hospital ship; seemed to be unloading, which started late evening and continued till about 4.30 this morning. Lots of boat movements between ship and the jetty. Lorries on streets. Unable to see much because of black-outs and curfew.

The hospital ship sailed about 9.30. There is still some doubt as to what sort and how many aircraft were brought down near Stanley yesterday. Lots of new troops digging in down at the east end of town. It looks very much as if they arrived yesterday on the hospital ship.

Jeremy arrived home at lunch-time with the news that the troops were washing their clothes in the town reservoir, so we are again advised to be sure to boil all our water. Several families in town are sick, which quite possibly has something to do with polluted water supplies.

Edwina and Colin came up for tea with young Gladys. They seem cheerful enough, but are, I think, still dazed with the shock of having their farm burned down by the Argentines at Mullet Creek. They are temporarily staying with Marge Morrison down at Police Cottages which are safe houses. I went down with them after tea as some very close firing broke out, which was rather alarming for the children. I got a bit jumpy myself a couple of times but hoped it didn't show.

The firing started while Tyssen and I were taking the dog for her walk. There was a lot of it, coming mainly from the direction of Sapper Hill and the Camber – all small-arms stuff but very rapid. We increased our pace smartly on the way home: It was unusual to see that, during this time, the former survey launch of HMS *Endurance* – the *James Caird* – was very close into the beach on the other side of the harbour, just about opposite the Upland Goose Hotel; there was a lot of activity around her.

By 4 o'clock this afternoon fog was lifting, the firing increasing and the sun appearing – all at the same time. The wind died away completely, leaving the air absolutely still. The sun was setting out towards the north-west, giving the most weird effect in the drifting fog; all orangy and wispy. To the west over Mount Kent was a perfectly blue sky with brilliant banks of pure white fog rolling along in the valleys, the artillery barrage going on in the background giving an eerie, sinister effect. Quite fantastic; in some ways very like a Salvador Dali painting. Rudy and Camilla came out to watch and to chat over the fence. We couldn't go any further because of the curfew. Perhaps it is as well that we can't, as we could see quite clearly the bullets entering the water in the harbour. I managed to record some of the noise fairly successfully. There is some very heavy artillery being used, maybe mortars as well. I can't really distinguish between the crumps and bangs, although I think that the deafeningly harsh barks and the crashes are from the really big 155-mm guns up on Davis Street.

We closed down outside and got the black-outs up earlier than usual in case we had to make a quick trip into the bunker. There must be a great battle going on up in the mountains to the west of us; it's getting very close indeed now. We also had an early supper, but apart from a couple of extra loud bangs activities seemed to slow down. For some reason the soldiers brought the fire engine out about 5.15. Shortly afterwards a troop of horses suddenly came out of the deep twilight on to the playing field, where they stayed for an hour or so. Poor brutes must have come down from the hills scared out of their wits by all the firing. It's impossible to go out to them as anyone on the streets after the curfew is liable to be shot.

On the news there are unconfirmed reports that British troops advanced 40 miles with heavy equipment during Monday night. The BBC correspondent describes conditions on Mount Kent as being like the trenches of World War I; the mud is unbelievable. They are now so close to us that with their binoculars they were able to see the Argentine troops having their lunch. Mrs Thatcher is talking of another Shackleton Report, looking to the future and to a longer airfield. After the Goose Green episode she says that sovereignty will no longer be on the future agendas of any discussions with the Argentines, or words to that effect. Some Argentine troops have been killed at Goose Green while moving some of their own ammunition, which afterwards one of their officers said had been 'a bit unstable'.

Rene Rowlands, our neighbour from the days when we lived up on Hebe Street, stopped by to join us for a chat and enjoy the sunset on her way home from the hospital where she visits her father each day. With the advancing years his sight has gone, a great tragedy for such an active man. He must be eighty-five or so now. How bewildering the present events must be for him, and also the other elderly folk, some of whom have never left the Falklands, even for a holiday. Rene has red crosses painted on pieces of card attached to the back and front of her bicycle, on which she pedals to and fro each day no matter what the weather or military activity – from either side. She travels slowly, almost majestically, not altering course an inch, so that the troops have to move out of the way quite sharply at times. It's rather like steam having to give way to sail.

Thursday 3 June – Day Sixty-three

Cold, misty, damp and foggy. Wind from the east, Force 2. Identical conditions to yesterday.

Violent awakening in bunker just after 6.30 this morning by heavy cannon and anti-aircraft fire from very close by, as aircraft could be heard overhead – we presumed that they were Harriers. The noise was both vicious and deafening for a few minutes, then deep silence.

Jeremy still goes to work for half the day, but Robert is unemployed as the butchery has become too dangerous to work in with all the shells flying about up that way. Martyn popped in briefly at breakfast-time on his way from the hospital, where he has been on fire duty, to the power station. They had a check at the hospital last night by Argentine commandos.

The Special Forces – 'Heavies' – arrived at the hospital for a spot-check on identity documents during the late evening. It all got a bit confusing, so Les Biggs had to drive with one of them in the ambulance down to the jetty to pick up the Argentine, Dr Mario, from one of the ships, who with his knowledge of English was able to sort things out. The street lights were all off, and Les was not allowed to use the ambulance headlights, which caused them to run into a large bit of airstrip metal which was poking out from the machine-gun nest in Neville Bennett's hen run. This went straight through the windscreen, fortunately missing Les and his escort.

On returning to the hospital the 'Heavies' closely examined Leslie's map of the Falklands showing the progress of the war as he saw it, with sinking ships, exploding aeroplanes and the great British advance proudly illustrated by Union Jacks. They were not amused and confiscated it. Leslie was not amused either.

There were quite a number of Argentine burials at the cemetery today; Jeremy saw them as he passed by on his dumper. They must have been victims of yesterday's action. The great effort of pegging out 1,000 graves, not long ago, seems to have gone by the board now. The burial arrangements are a lot less organised. Now only the officers' graves get marked with a cross. Other ranks are put two or three to a grave. There may be some sort of a mass grave as well for rapid burials. All graves are very shallow; just a couple of scoops with a digger and that's all.

We were very surprised and pleased to get a delivery of meat from the FIC today. Goodness knows how they have managed to do it under the present circumstances; maybe they are clearing the freezers of everything. Sent off cables to Mum, Eunice and to Tony (Ileen's brother) in Australia.

There has been steady gunfire for most of the day, mainly very heavy barrages coming down from Mount Kent way. After Mass this afternoon, the fog had lifted and we were able to see the terrible sight of shells landing with deadly accuracy in the Argentine trenches in the Moody Valley area. Huge spouts of earth being flung up, and with binoculars can see bits of men among the debris; occasionally whole bodies, but mainly bits. There is very little return fire. Lorries were coming down the road with the dead and wounded, while other lorries were going up the road packed with young conscripts to fill the gaps. It seems to be mainly conscripts left in town now. As we watched, half a dozen of them came from the dockyard carrying armfuls of crosses, heading towards the cemetery. This is hardly the way to inspire an army, either those carrying the crosses or those passing by in the lorries towards the front line. It was sickening to watch. This sort of thing would never happen with our forces. It's difficult to make out what is actually going on up in the valley; a large section of the Argentine troops seem to have crumbled and are now trapped in it. Lots of them are wandering about on the rocks and ridges with no thought of taking cover, clear targets for snipers' fire.

The latter part of this afternoon was identical to yesterday. The sun started to go down at about 4.15; the cloud lifted, sending the fog rolling about the valleys, during which time the Harriers took advantage of the break of weather to bomb the airport. Thus we had great eruptions at either end of the harbour – we are now getting used to the house and the ground shaking. Stood watching events over the fence with the neighbours and the soldiers across the road. The children played outside on the street. Although it was after curfew the soldiers didn't seem to mind, or care for that matter. A Chinook took off from the football field for the airport and returned shortly afterwards flying very low. So low in fact that it had to go up in order to land on the football field again. A very brave pilot to have made the trip, as firing was by this time going on at the back of the Camber ridge as well as at Moody Brook. The Chinooks now fly with their rear ramps down, having been fitted with a heavy-calibre machine-gun in the back; looks like a .50 Browning. We could hear the Harriers about somewhere, but were unable to see them. The harbour was absolutely still, so still that we could see the bullets from automatic weapons making identical lines of splashes over on the north side. Goodness knows what is happening or where they are firing from; perhaps they are practising. This whole thing is crazy. All this going on while we are passing the time of day to the troops across the road.

Old Mrs Stacey's house was broken into during last night, all her food stolen and the windows at the back broken. The Monsignor went to use his typewriter today and found that a bullet had ploughed its way through it during the firing on his house the other night.

The BBC news has been varied and interesting throughout the day; British troops can choose their own time to push their attack. All is now ready, with heavy equipment brought up to the Mount Kent area.

Gen Menéndez has told his troops to fight to the last man. He warns of an imminent British attack. Harriers this morning dropped leaflets on the Argentine lines with surrender passes which contain a note pointing out that although Britain is anxious to avoid further bloodshed, if they want to fight on, the British are quite willing to carry on. British Government has had no reply to yesterday's message urging the withdrawal of Argentine troops within ten to fourteen days to avoid further useless and senseless loss of life and to help Argentina make a face-saving withdrawal. A Vulcan has been forced to land at Rio de Janeiro. Said to be on a reconnaissance mission, and had been given permission to make an emergency landing. It will be allowed to leave after it has been disarmed, but no details given of what was being carried.

The people of the Cayman Islands have given a cheque for half a million pounds for the Falklands victims fund. Sidewinder missiles are now being fitted to the RAF Nimrods on the South Atlantic patrols.

The Auxiliary ketch *Penelope* (FIC-owned) arrived during the night from Darwin with an Argentine crew.

Friday 4 June – Day Sixty-four

Misty and damp; foggy at times. Very cold. Wind north-east, Force 5, decreasing late in the evening.

Last night was very noisy again. Seemed to be the now almost nightly duel between the Royal Navy off the south coast, and the Argentine artillery out on the Common.

Jeremy says we are now entering our tenth week of occupation, a not very encouraging – but unfortunately true – pronouncement at breakfast.

Ileen and I spent the morning scrubbing out the church. It was absolutely filthy with the thin, wet mud swilling about between the pews where the floor is slightly recessed, which prevents the water from draining away. The carpets in the porch and up the aisle are saturated, so we took down some old carpet tiles from the shed, which the boys laid as a sort of temporary track on which people can now walk. It does not look very elegant but at least may help to keep the place a bit cleaner and drier. No one objects to the mess as it cannot be otherwise in the present circumstances, but if things can be done to help save the carpet and keep the floor dry, then so much the better. Many troops use the church during the day; some come to pray for a few minutes, some just sit and shake. One sat in front of us shaking and trembling in a combination of exhaustion, fear and cold. Another cried uncontrollably. Most are very young. Their damp clothing smells of wet earth and camp fires.

The Monsignor showed us the remains of a couple of his theology books. He said that the bullets had got through them far more quickly than he had. His breviary also has an Argentine bullet embedded just over half-way through it.

The fog lifted a bit during lunch-time, allowing the British troops to open fire on the Moody Brook area again from the mountains. What a fearful mess it must be up there, the earth, rocks and mud being flung high into the air in all directions.

Several hundred troops are moving into the paddock over the

road behind Malvina House. Lots of tents being pitched there; can't be very pleasant as the surface of the ground with all this wet weather is like a rice pudding (ie, texture is the same but the colouring different).

Jumbo Whitney delivered us a drum of paraffin today. He says that there are now only eleven drums left down at the fuel depot, so must try to get another one. We rely on the paraffin stove in the kitchen for cooking, hot water, heating, etc. If we do run short of fuel and are unable to use it things will be extremely difficult. As this situation is likely to become more a reality than a possibility, we must tomorrow make some sort of contingency plan to overcome it. The electricity supply is sometimes erratic these days, with no real certainty of how long it is likely to continue. The staff up there are doing a fantastic job but just at the back of the station the Argentines have a missile site which is bound to be a target at some time. The effects of any attack on that will certainly not do the power station much good.

It's been an odd sort of day; feeling very tired; possibly lack of sleep or tension.

A big treat for everyone this evening – they have not shut the water off. There is a euphoric atmosphere in the house as people rush about having baths and flushing the toilets. You don't realise what a joy these simple things are until you have been without them for a while.

Saturday 5 June – Day Sixty-five

Weather appalling; cold and wet with high wind.

Last night's water must have got the better of me. I've had to spend the day in bed with what is locally known as Galtieri's Revenge, a particularly savage dose of sickness and the runs. Most people in town have had a bout of it. It is said to be caused by the bad water. The boys are confident that they will remain fit, as they drink mainly beer.

Lots of distant gunfire out towards the south-west – Bluff Cove and Fitzroy way.

Martyn is now on permanent fire duty at the hospital during the nights, as he has the knowledge to operate the emergency generators should the power station be put out of action. Lots of people sleeping in the corridors over there now.

Sunday 6 June – Day Sixty-six

Evil weather – wet, windy and cold.

The anniversary of 'D' Day; I wonder if it will have any significance for us . . .

Still in bed feeling lousy. Had to miss Mass. Dr Mary Elphinstone called during the day. Confirmed that the sickness is caused by the bad water. The best cure is starvation. If the germ can't eat it can't live, so therefore to drink only boiled water for the next few days. She is a very sensible young woman.

Distant heavy firing during the day; may be mortars.

Monday 7 June – Day Sixty-seven

Still in bed. This is a particularly wretched sort of ailment, leaving one quite useless; very hot. Dr Mary called again this morning; what splendidly cold hands she has.

Fr Monaghan brought me Communion just before lunch. He is doing a fine job in visiting – especially the old people, many of whom are so bewildered by this situation that they just enjoy being able to sit and have a cup of tea and a chat with someone.

Felt so rough that I haven't even bothered to look out at the weather. This must be the first day since the invasion that I have not recorded what it's like.

Firing again to the west.

Tuesday 8 June – Day Sixty-eight

Dr Mary called about lunch-time. Her starvation theory for gut bugs works, as was feeling a good deal better, especially later in the day. Tried getting up for short periods throughout the day.

The boys arranged for the safe delivery of another drum of paraffin, so we have sufficient for the next two or three weeks, but will have to use it carefully. Seven drums are left for public consumption.

Had a quick bath late this afternoon, which was a bit disturbed as the security police arrived at the door wanting to know how many people were sleeping in the house each night.

The young soldier who had guarded the house called again this morning. He seemed to have escaped while coming down into the town for the compulsory shower. He arrived at the back door asking if he could possibly have a wash and a shave. He is with an anti-aircraft gun crew on Sapper Hill. Food is dropped to them by helicopter every three days. He is very serious and afraid, speaking of many casualties. He sat and had some tea and buns after his clean-up. It is wrong to assist the enemy, but when faced with a situation like this one is placed in a very difficult position. Humanity comes into it somewhere. By what we were able to learn from this Argentine, morale is at a very low ebb; conditions are appalling. The steady, powerful advance of the highly trained, well-equipped and fed British troops, combined with the Harrier air strikes, the naval saturation bombardments, and the ferocious weather, is causing grave problems within the Argentine forces.

Sufficiently interested in life to listen to the news again today. Fitzroy and Bluff Cove have been retaken by the British. There are now 4,000 troops moved there, protected by Rapier missiles. The Argentine troops are said to be completely cut off. Strange story of a United States based supertanker being attacked and bombed some 150 miles to the north-west of the Falklands by a large four-piston-engined high-wing aircraft. The tanker is in ballast with an Italian crew. HMS *Hydra* is on the way to assist her.

With the fighting getting closer, combined with the increasing intensity of the nightly naval bombardments, more people are moving into safe houses. Down at the Upland Goose Hotel, Des and Ning King have over twenty 'regular overnighters' who feel a lot more secure within the thick stone walls of the 150-year-old building. Space is a bit cramped but camp beds and sleeping bags are the 'in thing' now, not only in the 'Goose' but in nearly all of the safe houses.

To date, in excess of twenty-five homes have been broken into by Argentine troops, mainly during the hours of darkness. The sight for the owners next day can only be sickening – excreta plastered about, remains of a fire often in the middle of the sitting-room carpet, and general dishevelled mess.

Wednesday 9 June – Day Sixty-nine

Bright, fresh sort of day. Quite cold. Wind west, Force 4. Good sunset.

Up and about at 8.45, feeling considerably better though rather tottery on my feet. Things are really getting close now. There was a ground-level bombing attack by the Harriers on the Argentine gun positions at the back of Davis Street about 10 this morning. Tremendous noise, but it was all over in seconds; by the time we had got to the back door it had finished.

Very noisy and constant firing all day up towards the Two Sisters and Moody Valley. The effects of the vibration beginning to show in the house, with the doors sticking – even the front gate won't close properly.

Cleaned and hung the bell outside for the first time since Friday. This is the first time that it has not been regularly cleaned for ages. It's usually my first job of the day. It came from the schooner *Sparrow Hawk* built in England in 1874 for mail and passenger services in the Falklands. The bell was found many years ago in an outhouse in Stanley and given to us, since when it has always hung in the study of whichever house we happened to be living in. When we bought this house it seemed fitting that it should be called *Sparrow Hawk* with the bell hung outside the front door.

Shopped briefly at the West Store. The *Bahía Paraíso* is due in again shortly, to evacuate more wounded and with members of the International Red Cross on board. Argentine medical staff are buying huge quantities of new sheets, brooms and disinfectant. A great cover-up exercise is about to take place.

Things had quietened down a bit during the afternoon, so took the dog for a walk down towards the football field to look at the helicopters and the activities there, then along Ross Road past the Secretariat, which has got all sorts of fortifications dug in and built up in the front of it. A parapet cum dug-out made from shipping containers reinforced with sandbags, guns poking out all over the place. They have built the same sort of things around Government House. Shipping containers are placed in a line along the edge of the Government House paddock, from the front gate down as far as the Hospital Corner. On the west side of Government House where Sir Cosmo and Lady Haskard had planted their trees some years ago, there are dug-outs roofed over with turf. Communication between the dug-outs is by means of a series of trenches. Telephone wires are strung everywhere.

Militarily it's probably quite effective; it looks an absolute shambles, but nonetheless, heavily defended. Part of the lovely gorse bushes up by the Memorial to the great naval battle of 1914 have been burned out. In among the remains are concealed gun positions. It must be extremely uncomfortable crawling through the gorse to man them. The Argentines still have one of their Puma helicopters, with its rotors removed, under camouflage netting, tucked away on the stretch of grass on the left of the road as one goes up towards the Monument Hill. It's painted blue and white with some kind of corrugated alloy on the sides; different from the others. The houses to the west of the Monument are suffering badly from the effects of shrapnel from the British shells landing along the racecourse, which is in a frightful mess. The Argentines have been using it as a helicopter base and have also dug ten or twelve huge pits, about 30 ft long, 10 ft wide and 6 ft deep, in which they have buried thousands of boxes of ammunition. The mess is hard to describe.

We turned to head towards home via the Ross Road up as far as the bottom of Philomel Hill. The Labour Union headquarters have a machine-gun position built up outside, with a friendly sort of occupant who has stopped being fierce and now gives us a wave each day as we pass him with the dog. The town hall on the upstairs floor is a sort of barracks now, full of troops; outside at the back are several anti-aircraft guns. The gymnasium seems to be the headquarters of the Argentine Special Forces. There seem to be two sorts – those with the maroon berets and those with green berets – though their numbers have diminished somewhat since the retaking of Goose Green. There appear to be only about forty of them left here now. They have a badge on the door which is a green fir tree against a white background.

The police station, opposite the gymnasium, seems to be another sort of headquarters. The telephone exchange has gun-pits dug around it. Stanley House is liable to be dragged to the ground by the sheer weight of the telephone wires leading into it. A great pity to see such an impressive old house reduced to such a state. After Government House it is the next biggest in Stanley, built somewhere in the 1880s for the Colonial Managers of the FIC who lived there continuously until the mid-1970s. Since then it has been used as temporary accommodation for a number of projects, but now seems to have reached the bottom of the barrel. It's a bit disconcerting to walk alongside the fence these days as there are sentries posted every few yards in and around the trees and bushes, who pop their heads out and sometimes ask for a cigarette. I think they may have anti-aircraft guns in the garden. More troops are dug in down by the FIC slipway, opposite the West Store. The gardens of Jubilee Villas and the next couple of houses down have each got their own machine-gun posts. The area to the east of the public jetty, enclosing the PATA buildings and the FIC jetty office and warehouse complex, is completely sealed off as a military zone, like Fort Knox to get into. Our final leg home was along John Street, packed with military vehicles. The senior school heavily guarded at both entrances with machine-gun posts; built up at the front and sides with sandbags and concrete paving blocks.

The back of Stanley House was a hive of activity. Troops everywhere; the same system of guards as in the front, every few yards in the bushes behind the fence. The Drill Hall and the junior school are now joined into one big military section full of troops and vehicles. The guard dogs are kept here; they look to be the best fed of anyone in the entire Argentine military organisation, in absolutely splendid condition. Skooch, being a lady, enjoys the attention from these magnificent animals each day as we pass by. I think that the guards are impressed by her apparent self-control, as being deaf she can't hear them barking and only becomes aware of their presence if she happens to look their way or the wind happens to bring their scent in our direction. So quite often she appears to pass haughtily by. The broadcasting studio now has a painted sign proclaiming it to be something or other in Spanish. And so, back to the Co-op corner and home.

Everyone commented after Mass this afternoon that this occupation seems to have given the old Monsignor a new lease of life. Usually at this time of the year he is stricken with colds, accompanied by all sorts of aches and pains, but now he is so full of life, ready to meet every challenge, helping people out left, right and centre, no matter which church they come from, not that he has really ever concerned himself about that sort of thing anyway. Fr Monaghan usually takes the afternoon Mass, so Monsignor waits on the church steps until the last possible moment so as not to miss any excitement, which for some reason always seems to erupt at the same time as the commencement of Mass. Many are the occasions lately when Father has had to send Tyssen out to remind the Monsignor that it is really time to get the Mass under way. Then, if during the service things sound as though they are hotting up, the Monsignor does a sort of racing finish in order to be back outside again. We have seen him standing on the steps pointing at Harriers and blessing passing soldiers all in the same movement. He really is a tremendous source of inspiration to everyone these days. The Holy Father would be proud to see him.

We were just about to set the table for supper when the security police arrived at the back door to check that all of us in the house had documents. A most odd sensation to hear a knock on the door after dark. We shouted to ask who it was before opening the door; all very sinister, rather like the sort of things you read about in books but never expect to happen to you. There were three officers, all very polite, who showed us their authorisation papers allowing them to carry out this check. One took down our details, which were recorded on a form; another wished to look through the house, so Martyn took him round; and the other went outside, presumably to have a look around – he was, I think, a captain in their Parachute Regiment. They all seemed satisfied and left after fifteen minutes or so. I imagine that they may be looking for British Special Forces in local houses. No luck here I'm afraid; it's a cross between a lunatic asylum and a zoo.

Robert's cat is settling in very well but will insist on going into the study, where he walks about on the mantelpiece, disturbing all manner of things, then plays with a dried rockhopper penguin's head which I have there. He carts it about the house, so that we find it turning up in the most unusual places. One of the penguin flippers has disappeared altogether; goodness knows where we will eventually find that.

The news from the BBC is not good tonight. Yesterday there was a lightning raid by the Argentine Air Force at Fitzroy. The logistic landing ships *Sir Tristram* and *Sir Galahad* were both abandoned because of fire after being bombed. Heavy casualties are feared. HMS *Plymouth* was attacked and damaged at San Carlos with five of her crew wounded. The Fitzroy attack was apparently so sudden that no one had time to put on any protective clothing. There was extreme bravery by the helicopter pilots in daring rescues, picking up men from the sea through dense smoke. Two landing craft were also lost. It sounded horrific. Four Argentine aircraft were shot down yesterday.

We also heard on the news that the *Monsunen* is at sea again, manned by a local crew. A rope which was around her propeller had been freed by Bob and Janet McLeod at Goose Green. She now sails under the Union Jack and the flag of the 5th Infantry Brigade.

At 9 o'clock this evening there was the most enormous explosion not far away. It really would be much more convenient if each side were to have different types of bangs; as it is we are unable to distinguish what bangs are whose. Whoever this one belonged to, it was a whopper.

Thursday 10 June – Day Seventy

Good hard frost last night. Bright day with high cloud. Wind east, Force 3.

Corpus Christi. Also Malvinas Day.

Very disturbed night with heavy artillery exchanges until about 3.40 this morning. The firing was very irregular as opposed to the rhythmic thump of a naval bombardment. Last night they seemed to be loosed off in lots of twenty. A helicopter was overhead about 3.30, and remained over the town for about half an hour, after which I dropped off to sleep.

Up at 7.45. Three Pucaras took off at 8.30 – flying fast and hugging the ground towards Mount Kent where they dropped their bombs, returning to Stanley about 9. Watched them with Pat who was in for his morning chat and daily review of events.

Capt Hussey, the Argentine naval port captain, telephoned me at 10 asking if I would meet him at the FIC jetty. Went along to a background of Harriers bombing the perimeter of the town. Capt Hussey explained that some of the troops had unfortunately cut part of the poor old *Fleetwing*'s stern away for firewood before he was able to issue instructions to stop them. Now a hulk, *Fleetwing* is historically important as one of the last remaining examples of the famous sailing vessels built at Portmadoc in Wales. Built in 1874, she arrived in the Falklands in 1911. The timber is remarkably sound and clean. In these difficult circumstances it was most kind of him to have called me along to discuss the matter. He stopped any further damage being done and left me to look at the rest of the vessel. This was fine, but the whole of that area is a military zone, so getting out was a bit of a complicated business. I had a pass to get in, but not one to get out, so for half an hour or so I had armed protection – I suppose that I was under arrest – until the guards sorted out what I was up to, and how I came to be in there, after which they let me go. I was very pleased to get back home; they seemed a bit too efficient for my liking. I should have remained with

Capt Hussey. During the time we were speaking together, there were some particularly vicious bombing attacks up towards Mount Kent, which we both tried to ignore.

Rather a confusing day. So much so, that after Mass this afternoon I realised that I was still wearing my pyjamas under my jeans.

The Monsignor was very angry after Mass to find that some soldiers had installed themselves under his new house being built in the paddock to the front of the old presbytery, so he went out and got them shifted in a very short time. Took the dog for her walk. Very tense atmosphere in the town. Chatted for a while outside the hospital with Mike Bleaney's daughter Debbie who is a nurse, to the sound of helicopters taking off from the football field, plus a great barrage going on up the road towards Moody Valley, plus small-arms fire from over the back of the Camber Ridge. The Tiger Cat missile battery up behind the power station was on full alert with the missile covers off.

Two Harriers over at 4.30, very high. A bit of firing at them from the ground batteries. Went indoors to draw the study curtains a few moments later, just in time to see them flash through Fairy Cove gap, firing their cannons and being fired at. They couldn't have been more than 40 ft up. Fantastic sight silhouetted black against the setting sun. A superb view of them as they banked steeply to turn. A great roar of their engines and the bombs which they dropped. It was all over in fifteen seconds; just one great crashing, banging and roaring, then tranquillity. Totally unreal. Very difficult to believe that it had happened.

'Calling the Falklands' remarkably clear tonight. As usual a good meaty news summary. The MOD declines to report on the losses in Tuesday's air attack at Fitzroy. The Pope is on his way to Buenos Aires for a two-day visit. This will be the final chance for Argentina to withdraw from the Falklands with dignity. The RAF Vulcan impounded last week in Brazil has been released with its six-man crew. The missile has been kept in Brazil.

Friday 11 June – Day Seventy-one

Fine and bright with high cloud; very cold. A hard frost persisted throughout the day. Wind from the west, Force 3. After a superb sunset the wind died away.

A very noisy night with bombardments from all quarters. All very close. Anya hadn't slept very well during the night so tucked her up in the boys' bedroom downstairs with a hot water bottle at 8.20, then suddenly all hell seemed to break loose down the road by the town hall. There was a great roaring, crashing and machine-gunning. I grabbed Anya and shoved her from the bed down the hatch in the passage into the bunker, then from the front porch saw huge bits of the police-station roof flying about through the air with flashes, flames and lots of smoke. There was intense small-arms fire outside, then three spectacular eruptions as the Harriers bombed the Pucaras at the airport, which burned furiously and exploded. There seemed to be a British helicopter over behind the Camber Ridge, with the Harriers concentrating on the airport. Really thought that the British attack on the town had started, but it appears that a missile had been fired from the helicopter.

It really was the most fantastic sight; quite beyond description. The whole incident only lasted a few minutes but it seemed to go on for ever, like a slow-motion film. The noise was incredible. Argentine troops opened fire from the streets with their rifles at the helicopter and – somewhat optimistically – at the Harriers, which caused the Coseley boys to take rapid shelter in Harold Bennett's garden on the corner of King Street, to avoid having their hair parted, as one of them later put it. The Coseley is a bungalow converted into bed-sitter accommodation for single men. Peter Roberts arrived here shortly afterwards, rather shaken, as a soldier had opened fire just behind him. Peter told him not to be so bloody stupid and to watch where he was pointing the thing, then leapt into the ditch. Martyn told us of one poor soldier trying to shelter behind the fuel oil pipe which runs down alongside the football field. Uncle

James was seen walking to work through the middle of it all.

Went shopping during the morning, mainly to view the damage to the police station, which was quite spectacular. Half the roof has been blown off, as well as a large portion of the front of the main building. Bits and pieces hanging out everywhere; furniture and wallpaper plus plumbing, all mixed up together. The Argentines are very upset about all this and do not encourage us to linger. It's going to take them a while to sort things out. There is something of a holiday atmosphere in the streets and the West Store. After seventy-one days help is very close by. Relief of tension shows on everyone's face. We do not know what the casualty rate was at the police station.

Very noisy morning altogether, with Harriers bombing the front line up in the mountains to the west. The Argentines fired a missile from somewhere at the back of the town, but after gaining a bit of height it did a few wobbles then headed off over the common where it unfortunately came down among their own troops. They have excellent weapons but lack the expertise to control them. During the bombing raids there is great jostling between the troops and locals for the best positions for viewing and shelter.

Argentine helicopters with red crosses on them busy all morning flying between the hostel and the *Bahía Paraíso*, which is anchored up opposite the cemetery. A large number of troops could be seen on her decks. Only one was wearing a Red Cross armband. More reinforcements perhaps?

Another interrupted lunch, with spectacular bombing runs on the airport by the Harriers – what superb aircraft they are. One moment they are at the end of a vapour trail, then they have disappeared completely, suddenly reappearing out of nowhere at startling speed, dropping their bombs. Neither we nor the Argentines have any idea where they are going to pop up next.

Very noisy at Mass again this afternoon. The church was shaking so much that more bits were dropping out from the stained-glass windows behind the altar. Tyssen must surely be eligible for some sort of medal for serving so many times under fire. He is quite unshaken by it all, though last night he was very upset, not through being frightened but after having seen the troops shooting the kelp geese and logger ducks in the harbour for food. He has a great love of our wildlife.

A curious atmosphere in the town; the troops are very withdrawn and quiet. Lots of the military things have disappeared off the scene. John Street, which yesterday was like something out of the Western Front, was almost back to its former self. All the defences around the schools had gone. Very few of the troops have any weapons visible. The International Red Cross people are walking round the town with some senior Argentine officers. I do hope that they are not being taken in by this flagrant charade, put on for their benefit by the Argentines. They do not appear to have been allowed to make contact with many locals.

As we were passing the old ambulance garage, some rather cocky troops again let off a few rounds from their rifles in an attempt to frighten the dog; she of course didn't hear a thing. Like the last time, it had more effect on us, which we tried not to show. From their point of view it was a stupid thing to do, as the military today are doing their very best to present an atmosphere of tranquillity. I suppose this morning's spectacular at the police station must have caught them on the hop a bit. There was a lot of concern for us from the troops as we passed the Secretariat during a bombing attack; we thanked them for their kind thoughts and carried on. The Brits are not aiming at us; it's the Argentines that they are after.

There are a couple of disturbing reports circulating today that the women and children of the town may be moved into Waverley House for safety, or that the entire civil population of Stanley may be moved into the town hall. Both stories have an ominous ring to them. If either of these things happens it's going to be very difficult to decide just what to take with us; we have so many things which we treasure that the prospect is absolutely bewildering. I have made up an emergency envelope in which are our passports and the insurance documents of the house and its contents, which are fully detailed so that in the event of losing everything we do have a record on which to base a claim for possible compensation. The majority of our bits and pieces are beyond any monetary value; some are quite irreplaceable.

Then there is the awful problem of what to do with Scooch (the dog) and the two cats; they could not be allowed to remain untended in the house to endure any of the horrors which seem likely to come this way very shortly. They would have to be put down. The outlook is grim, but a situation which has to be faced up to and the necessary precautions taken. Each hour now the British firing is getting closer; the net is tightening around the Argentine forces, who are now virtually trapped in Stanley by the skilful pincer advance being carried out under the direction of Gen Jeremy Moore. There is no escape.

One of the Argentine doctors at the hospital who went up to the front line yesterday is so disturbed by what he witnessed that he is returning to Argentina on the hospital ship.

We counted twenty-seven Harriers over Stanley today, which has kept the anti-aircraft gunners busy, but they seemed to get fed up towards the end of the afternoon with their lack of success. They more or less gave up trying to hit them. A missile was launched at 4.25, which was one of their old stock again as it soon fizzled out. After that they gave up trying.

Uncle James came by at 4 o'clock in a most indignant mood. The military had arrested him for an hour. He does not know quite what for but they kept him in the police station, where to pass the time he read part of a James Bond book, then told them he would have to go, as he was required to start work at 3 o'clock. So off he went. I don't think that they have come across people like James before. He asked them for a lift up the road – and got one!

We all watched a very low bombing run by two Harriers on Fairy Cove at 4.20 this afternoon. Almost identical to yesterday, streaking up from Moody Valley. Just one long stream of noise, then absolute silence. During one of the raids today, a young Argentine soldier on road-sweeping duties was given a rifle to shoot at the Harriers. A desperate move really, as he was more danger to the Argentine Army than the aircraft.

It was very amusing in the West Store this morning when the lights suddenly went off. The Monsignor was there and shouted in his very loud voice, 'Ah, the FIC aren't paying their bills again', which brought a great laugh from everyone. It's things like this that do a lot towards keeping our spirits up these days.

The BBC news was very crackly today, but heard a most interesting report that someone in Chile had intercepted a telephone call on what was apparently an open line, from Gen Menéndez here in Stanley to Buenos Aires. He said that the morale of his troops was very low; there are no replacements, no mail, etc; if things continue like this they will crumble very shortly. This is the best news we have heard since the Task Force arrival at San Carlos. The *QE2* has arrived back in England with some of the survivors of the warships recently lost in the Falklands. The captain of HMS

Coventry described how, when his ship was heeled over, a helicopter landed on her side to pick up survivors.

Mrs Thatcher does not require an Argentine surrender. If Gen Menéndez so wishes he may withdraw his troops in an orderly and dignified manner from the Falkland Islands.

Saturday 12 June – Day Seventy-two

Very cold, very wet, very dismal. A hard black frost this morning. What little wind there has been came from the north-west.

A most awful day. James came in early this morning to tell us the terrible news that Sue Whitley and Doreen Bonner were killed during the night when shrapnel from a shell went through John and Veronica Fowler's house, in which they were staying. Old Mrs Mary Goodwin, well into her eighties, has also been very badly injured. So has Steve Whitley (Sue's husband). I think that the Fowlers may have been injured as well, but everyone is so badly shaken that it is impossible to think straight and form a proper picture. It was apparently very difficult for them to make contact on the telephone with the hospital to get an ambulance.

Last night was the most incredible, frightening one yet. Hundreds of shells were fired, which screamed and whistled over the town for hours on end – it's non-stop. They are still going strong now. A steady naval bombardment had been going on for some hours – we could tell it was the Navy by the regular rhythm of the firing. At about half an hour past midnight it suddenly ceased; then, just as they stopped, street firing broke out right outside the house, on the playing green. It was savage and right alongside us. We didn't dare move out from the bunker. Return fire came from up along John Street; more firing opened up from the direction of Pioneer Row, at the back of us. It was a fierce exchange which went on for about half an hour. The only thing we can think of was that a British forces patrol had penetrated the town. It left us all in a cold sweat of fear; not knowing or being able to see what was going on added to our anxiety. We were very thankful for the bunker. The Navy didn't seem to open up again, but the British and Argentine artillery fought fiercely throughout the night. Through the partly opened hatch we could see the flashes of the explosions. We have successfully blacked out the side windows of the porch but are unable to make the roof light-proof.

Got up at 4.30 for a procession on our hands and knees to the loo. Outside the ground was white with frost which later turned to freezing rain, causing the frost to turn black and leaving the ground in a treacherous condition. It was almost impossible to stand up anywhere outside for most of the morning. We eventually got up just after 8. I doubt if any of us slept at all.

Things do not seem quite so bad in the daylight, though a full-scale battle is now raging all around us; the town itself is still. Rather like being in the very centre of a cyclone. We are being completely ringed by shell bursts and explosions on the Argentine positions. They, meanwhile, are putting up fierce resistance. We can see their shells exploding quite clearly to the west of us, on the Two Sisters, Mount Tumbledown and Mount Longdon. Just after daylight a hundred or so troops marched along Pioneer Row singing and cheering – shouting something about the Pope. They were on their way down from the trenches at the back of town – all very wet and filthy. Possibly someone had told them that the war was over. All very odd.

Martyn was called out to work just after breakfast. (That's not really the right word as everyone was too shocked to eat anything; all we could do was to smoke and drink tea.) Power lines had been hit, causing loss of electricity in parts of the town. It's very dangerous indeed working up poles on overhead lines in this lot, but the staff of the power station are willing to have a go at it in order to keep the electricity flowing. They had a very tough night up there. Because of the intensity of the shelling, the military at the station would neither take Ted Carey home at midnight, nor collect his relief, so had to stay up there. During the early hours of the morning, shells were landing all round the place; shrapnel started coming through the roof, breaking up the main switchboard and damaging the cooling radiators. One piece went through the knee of his overalls. Then a little later more shrapnel punctured one of the 1,500-ton oil storage tanks outside, so Ted had to go out and do what he could to patch that up. The Argy guards refused to go out with him as they reckoned it was too dangerous. At daylight they found the bodies of four dead Argentines outside who had apparently been trying to keep warm in the air which was discharged through the radiators.

Les Harris, Assistant Superintendent at the Power Station, with the rest of the staff, all managed to get up there about 9 this morning, and were having a brew of tea when the Argentines fired a

Tiger Cat missile, from the launcher just to the back of them, at a Harrier. This exploded prematurely, sending chunks of it through the power-house roof. The Harrier dropped a cluster bomb, the nose of which also went through the roof, landing in the station and bringing the tea-break to an abrupt end. Ted eventually managed to get home, where he found his house had been peppered and damaged by more shrapnel. Considerable havoc was caused to that part of town last night. Most houses had their windows blown out or were badly damaged by shrapnel and blast. Joan, James and Zachary live up there, but we are unable to get through on the telephone; the lines have probably been shot away.

Later today the following notice was issued:

> By order of the Military Government all inhabitants living on the west side of the Monument Battle will have to leave their homes before 4 pm of today. The enemy's shelling make these houses unsafe and a serious risk to all those who live there. This order is Mandatory and cannot be refused. Those who have no place to go in the City will have available as a first place to go The Cathedral, The West Store, The Colony Club, and the Saint Mary's Church Annexe.
>
> This order is issued as part of the responsibility of the Government to ensure the security of the Civilian population.
>
> Signed: The Military Government.

The intensity of the shelling is such that the whole town seems to be shaking. So many things are being toppled from the shelves that we took everything down, including the pictures from the wall, which we have packed in boxes and stowed under the house. The house is bare and bleak, and incredibly untidy. After last night's street fighting we thought it best to use only the hatch in the hall to get in and out of the bunker, as to be caught in a burst of firing through the front porch would be fatal. We moved my filing cabinet to the porch wall in line with the front door, which may stop a few stray bullets, then nailed up a strong old trestle table to the front door, which gives it a double thickness. We have also taken the carpet tiles up from the hall and porch, stacking them around the inside walls, along with the furniture. We further reinforced the protection outside with all the old timber we could find lying about.

It was interesting to see this morning that Argentine troops were on the streets collecting the empty cartridge cases from the street fighting last night. They were putting them in bags.

Went along to Mass at 2.30. The church is a pathetic mess, with pools of mud and water on the floor; smelling dank with the sweat and fear of the troops. We had intended to continue cleaning up there this morning, but present events make it impossible. Everyone who has no good reason to be out is keeping off the streets this morning. There is no water for the foreseeable future. The power lines to the filtration plant are shot to pieces; it's far too dangerous for anyone to go up to attend to them.

The bombardment continues without a break; it's getting a bit trying on the nerves. Everyone is standing up to it in the most remarkable way. Tyssen and Eli reading old comics in the sitting-room as if nothing was happening; it's absolutely amazing. Jeremy is finding it difficult to walk, as this morning he fell down the bunker hatch during some particularly exciting moment. We had to spend an hour or two bailing out the bunker again this morning as the water was almost up to the floor. We must have got 200 gall. out with our chain of buckets. We are doing our best to find water in one way and get rid of it in another. Some of this morning's we put into drums, but it's very muddy.

Harriers have been bombing continuously throughout the day, mainly on the Argentine artillery positions at the back of Davis Street and Callaghan Road. Kathy and Robert Watson's windows were all blown in just after 10 this morning. The little house where Danny Borland used to live was badly damaged by shrapnel, as were the domestic gas bottles, which went off in a most spectacular manner. Marlene and Jen Williams have moved down to St Mary's from their house to the west of the Monument. Someone asked why they didn't bring much luggage, to which Jen replied, 'If your house had just been bloody well blown up, I bet you wouldn't stay around to pack your things.' James came in briefly this afternoon to say that he, Joan and Zachary are still well, but conditions are getting a bit difficult. That sort of thing coming from James means that things must be pretty desperate. He pulled out a handful of shrapnel from his pocket to show us, which he had picked up in their house. He got involved in an argument this morning with an Argentine officer, who ended up by punching him, which has annoyed James very much. It seems likely that tomorrow they will be forcibly evicted from their home, to move down to Nancy and Raymond's – it will be an epic manoeuvre, with their two dogs, goodness knows how many cats, the two tame geese, the hens and a budgerigar.

The icy roads today have caused some spectacular disasters among the Argentine drivers. One lorry towing a mobile soup kitchen went through Terry Binnie's back fence, ending up in his garden, resulting in a fearful mess of fence battens, fresh vegetables and hot soup, plus a very frightened lorry-driver.

It is very noticeable that, now that we are being surrounded, the Argentine forces are pulling back tightly into the town itself. The final scrap, which cannot be far off, looks as if it will take place in our streets, sheds and gardens.

The Panhard armoured cars – ten or twelve of them – were all moved close into the back garden fences of the houses on Ross Road West, until Danny's house was hit. The flaming gas bottle nearly set one of them on fire, so they moved into town, taking up positions on Villiers Street.

The news from London today has been a bit sketchy, as it is another weekend. However, we have heard that the British advanced 5 miles last night, and are now at Mount Longdon. The Pope has left Argentina to return to Rome; his pleas for a peaceful settlement in the South Atlantic have seemingly gone unheeded. Argentina reports that its shipping was attacked in Stanley harbour yesterday by Harriers. There were messages on 'Calling the Falklands' for Sue and Steve tonight; the news of last night's terrible events cannot yet have reached England.

The British have been pounding Sapper Hill with their heavy guns, from the west, for most of this afternoon. Half of Stanley turned out up on the back road to watch. It is really rather dangerous but far too good an opportunity to miss.

Spoke briefly to Ian Strange today. There has been some very heavy shelling by the Navy up in their end of town by the cemetery. He's been looking after Angus Jaffray's hens, which today have at last started to lay, after one particularly close salvo landed alongside the henhouse, blowing the door off and the windows out. Shock treatment, I suppose.

Sunday 13 June – Day Seventy-three

A cold, bright day with very high cloud; a light covering of snow on the ground. Wind west, Force 2–3.

Had a remarkably good sleep, the best for many weeks, although there was apparently continuous heavy firing through the night. The first I heard of it was at 7.40 this morning when I woke up.

It's been a day of non-stop intense firing from all sides. According to one news broadcast, this is the heaviest artillery exchange and bombardment since World War II. They are quoting incredible numbers of shells having been fired during the past few hours, running into many thousands. (That's only from the British side; the Argentines are sending over thousands in return.)

A great umbrella of shells is now over Stanley, being fired non-stop in three directions: by the Argentines, outwards towards the advancing British Army in the mountains; from the British Army, which is firing on the Argentine positions; and from the Royal Navy, who are pounding the southern perimeter of the town from the sea. Overhead the Harriers ceaselessly pound the Argentine positions, with cannon fire and bombs. It is impossible adequately to describe the noise, which is now almost constant. The air is filled with the stinging smell of cordite. Every few minutes the Argentines fire their 155-mm monsters from up at the back of the town. These guns don't go bang, they bark with a deep twanging crack, which grates on one's nerves after a while. Our house, and I suppose everyone else's, shakes and shudders continually. If we hadn't taken the pictures down the other day they would certainly have fallen down today. Besides the bangs, we have the whistles as the shells fly overhead, then the crash of the explosions, deafening ones from the British shells as they land on the Argentine positions, and distant crumps as the Argentine shells land in the mountains. By the look of it they are using a lot of air burst, which can plainly be seen in the crisp, still air. Possibly the noise is even more intense today, as there is not sufficient wind to carry it away. Stanley is circled by erupting earth, smoke and flames. The Argentine army is trapped, beneath this torrent of unrelenting fire – so are we.

About 11.30 this morning poor old Wilfred Newman's house up on Davis Street received a direct hit and burned to the ground very quickly in a great mass of smoke and flames. The British are obviously trying to hit the Argentine 155 mm that is between the houses up there. Another shell went through the roof of Harry Milne's garage, in which he had all the new furniture for his house stored. Another damaged Bob Stewart's and Derek Evans' house. From here it looked very much as though Pat and Maureen's house had gone up, so Jeremy went up on to the roof with the binoculars to see what was happening. It was impossible to see accurately which house had been hit, as Wilfred's was next door to Pat's. Two Argentine military police then arrived, saying that looking through binoculars was not allowed. They insisted on going upstairs to see how he had managed to get on to the roof, then they wanted to confiscate the binoculars, but fortunately their attention was distracted by something else being hit close by, so they went off in a hurry. Blast them and their stupid regulations. Something big has just gone up at the back of the new hostel; masses of black smoke and flames high into the air. I think an Argentine helicopter may have received a direct hit.

Just after lunch – which none of us had, or even thought about – Nidge Buckett brought old Fred Coleman down to stay with us. Up until this morning he had refused to budge from his house, but had to be forcibly removed as it was getting so dangerous up there on Davis Street. He's well into his eighties and very deaf and was most apologetic that they had not allowed him the time to change before bringing him down. He did, however, manage to grab his best cap, put an overcoat over the top of his pyjamas and bring a bottle of rum. We soon had him settled in front of the fire with a hot rum and his carpet slippers, watching the television. He had not seen television before and was most impressed, saying that he was unable to hear a thing but enjoyed the pictures. He looked so splendid and comfortable sat there among the chaos of the sitting-room. It's surprising that they have managed to keep the television going under such frightening conditions.

We are now all of us feeling the strain of things, even the boys. Ileen is bearing up wonderfully well. Surely it can't get much worse than this. It was perhaps a stupid thing to do, but we all went to

Mass this afternoon, trying to carry on as normally as possible. It was rather noisy but the volume of the responses was in accordance with the volume of the gunfire. The church creaked and swayed a lot.

Walking back towards home afterwards was a sad, uncanny experience. In the cold, through the mud and the slush in the pale, wintry sunshine of late afternoon. The noise of the Argentine guns seemed louder, as more and more they were being drawn in towards the town. Their smoke created a haze in the air; their smell stung our eyes and our throats. The British guns on the mountains pounded on relentlessly as they advanced inexorably towards Stanley. It was so difficult to grasp that all this was happening in our once serene and tranquil Stanley. It was like having a nightmare – sitting on the outside of a situation looking in, paralysed, unable to do anything whatsoever to stop this awful holocaust which hourly is increasing in its violence, so that soon it must explode in a great fury all around us.

Despite the tension, life still goes on. The Ashworth family still deliver the milk whatever the discomforts. Dennis Place and his lads from the filtration plant are still out dodging shells in their efforts to keep the fresh water supply flowing. The hospital and its staff are prepared for whatever may come. Les Biggs and Chris McCallum are still working every daylight hour assisting the old and the infirm to places of safety. Duffy and Nidge Buckett are doing the same thing, as, no doubt, are many others in the town. It is difficult to know, as we are restricted very much to our own parts of Stanley. People are still able to raise a hopeful smile. Late this afternoon one of the Harriers dropped a green flare over the town; could this be significant?

At curfew this evening we were able to see the Royal Marines barracks at Moody Brook still blazing. It's been on fire for most of the day; there seems to be very little left now. The garage at the hospital has been cleared out during the day to accommodate more Argentine wounded. The Beaver hangar is said to be a mortuary, with hundreds of Argentine bodies in it. Today's icy conditions have caused several more spectacular disasters among the military vehicles. Many are in unusual positions on the hills and in gardens. The shaking and vibration today has been too much for our lovely Wedgwood carving dish; the inner section has split into two pieces. A great shame as it was over 150 years old.

BBC news today announced that 400 prisoners were taken a few nights ago when Mount —— was taken – owing to the awful reception conditions it was impossible to get the name. We now have Mounts Kent, Longdon and Harriet. The losses at Fitzroy on the *Sir Galahad* and *Sir Tristram* were about fifty. This figure was deliberately kept secret. HMS *Glamorgan* was hit during the bombardment on Friday night. Nine were killed but the ship is still serviceable. There was also a most interesting item on the International Red Cross who want to establish a neutral zone in Stanley to accommodate the civilian population. Great Britain agrees but there is no definite comment from Argentina yet. Also talk of possible evacuation temporarily; could this be on the *Uganda* or the *Canberra*? There are only 500 people involved. The MOD says this would in no way affect the plans of the commander of operations in the field. If things continue as they are it would be a sensible idea, as the final outcome of this battle is going to be a very fierce and bloody affair, with the people of Stanley caught in the middle of it; the town could well be wiped out completely.

An air of anxiety and restlessness hangs over the town tonight. The guns are still pounding away. I think that we will get settled down under cover early and leave the washing up of the supper dishes until morning.

Monday 14 June – Day Seventy-four

Damp, cold, grey day, with snow squalls. Wind West, Force 2–3.

Artillery fire all night long without let-up: the Navy from the south coast; the Argentines drawing their heavy guns into the town during the night; the British advancing from the west towards Stanley. Sleep was impossible: shells screaming and tearing overhead, the bursts rocking the house every few seconds; deafening noise from the Argentine guns – loud twanging cracks only yards away; crashes and crumps from the British shells landing. It was like being in the very centre of hell itself. By looking through the black-outs we could see the sky alight with explosions, flares and tracer. The final stage in the battle for Stanley seemed imminent.

Up from the bunker at 7.30. As dawn broke we were able to see the appalling shambles all around us. The air was thick with smoke, dense with the pungent reek of cordite. Ileen, Jeannie, Anya and children remained in the bunker. Old Fred was sleeping soundly in the boys' bedroom, blissfully unaware of the chaos raging outside. We had plans to get him into the bunker at the last moment, but at eighty-six he said he would have found it a bit difficult to have managed, unless it was absolutely necessary. He insisted that, as long as he had his tobacco and the rum near at hand, life was still pretty good. The boys, Duffy and I looked out over the front fence towards Wireless Ridge and Moody Brook, where the sky was red with tracer, great thick streams of it curving almost gracefully from one side of the harbour to the other. The noise was incredible. Huge spouts of water being flung up just down in front of the government jetty as shells landed in the harbour. The Argentine howitzers seemed to be firing non-stop all around us. Their armoured cars were moving up into a position on Pioneer Row just at the back of us.

Jeremy and Duffy were about to set out for the dockyard, more to see what was going on than with the prospect of going to work, and got as far as the front gate when they met up with Mark and the

Coseley boys who said in a classic piece of understatement that work was suspended for the day. Minutes later, back in the house, we saw from the study window the amazing sight of hundreds of Argentine troops streaming like ants along Wireless Ridge, down through Fairy Cove towards the Camber. They were running before the British shells which were landing just behind them – almost keeping pace with them, throwing up great mounds of earth and rock. Many of the Argentines were falling. A huge fire was blazing out of control at the back of Government House; then the ambulance shed was hit and burned fiercely. The smoke was intense; several houses seem to be on fire at the west end of town.

Martyn was called out at 8.30, as the power station was damaged. He went off cheerful as ever, though somewhat cautiously past the hundreds of Argentine troops who were assembling on the children's playing field with heavy weapons, mountains of ammunition boxes, rocket launchers, and goodness knows what else. It was by this time frighteningly apparent that the fighting was about to reach its climax; Stanley was about to be written off the map. With the vast amount of arms and ammunition on the playing field the Argentines would have been able to put up a devastating fire-power, to match that of the advancing British troops, had they not crumbled within the next hour.

Ileen, Jeannie and Anya were taking more food, clothing and water into the bunker. We thought it best to leave Fred sleeping as he was. Tyssen and Eli were sorting out a few books to occupy themselves with. Maxwell was shouting for his breakfast. Jeremy and Duffy, plus Rag, were giving a running commentary on events, ready to shout a warning if it was time to dive into the bunker. For some unexplained reason I was in the kitchen at the sink, washing last night's supper dishes. This must have been at 9 o'clock, as from the BBC we heard that the International Red Cross has got a response from the Argentine Government that there was to be a designated 'Safe Area' for the civilian population of Stanley. What a hell of a way to find this out; the rest of the world has been told, with the exception of us here in the middle of it. The Argentines could at least have let us know; it would not have been difficult, there are enough of them here.

An Argentine officer then shouted from the front gate, so I went down to see what he wanted. He told us to take cover; get our heads down as there was going to be one almighty scrap, or words to that effect, which was quite obvious, but it was nonetheless considerate of him. Less than five minutes later another Argentine officer arrived at the back door, backed up by about fifty or more troops in the garden, and told us to get out of the house. He and his men fairly bristled with weapons. They all had bandoliers of ammunition festooned about them like spaghetti – not once around their bodies but several loops of the stuff. Once more the heavy responsibility of being head of the family became awfully apparent.

We had no time to equip ourselves with anything other than a sleeping bag each. Duffy had his Mini van outside, into which we bundled poor old Fred, still half asleep in his pyjamas and dressing gown; he'd managed to put his hat on and grab the rum. Jeannie grabbed the children; Ileen and Anya somehow managed to get a tranquilliser down the dog and put her with the cats into the bunker. Jeremy and Rag turned off the water and electricity, then stuffed the other eight of us into the Mini. The whole operation must have taken about three minutes, probably less. It went like clockwork; everyone was marvellous, no panic whatsoever. Fred did remark what a silly bloody carry on it was, but thank goodness the rum was safe! He even confessed to being able to hear the noise of the firing, so it must have been loud.

The journey through the town to the Safe Area was an epic one. Jeremy and Rag ran alongside; we seemed to be hanging out from the doors and windows. Half of the Argentines were in full retreat through Stanley, dropping their weapons as they ran. Some were smashing their equipment at the roadsides. More and more troops joined them; others, still determined to put up a fight, were attempting to go in the opposite direction. We seemed to be caught up in a seething military mass. How Duffy managed not to run anyone over I don't know. It was an incredible sight and noise. According to the news the designated safe building was the cathedral, but we saw the back door of the West Store open, so stopped the Mini and heaved ourselves in.

Ileen was very upset, so was whisked off immediately by Isobelle Castle, the store manager's wife, for tea and sedatives. She was distressed mainly by the thought of leaving the poor dog and the cats trapped under the house in the bunker. It was an awful feeling for us both to have been forced from our home with the family at gunpoint, leaving everything that we had worked and saved for during the last twenty years. We had no choice; you can't argue while looking down the barrel of a rifle. The staff of the store were nothing short of marvellous, coping fantastically. They had no idea what was happening to their homes either. There were 126 of us in there altogether. We were allocated space in the ladies' millinery department. Terry Spruce, the FIC manager, and David Castle, the store manager, cannot receive enough praise for their efficiency and understanding in handling the situation. They had things running like a Sunday-school outing. Video had been set up for the children out among the scales and the bacon slicers, with hot soup and sandwiches prepared for everyone at lunch-time by the ladies of the staff.

Towards noon, Terry called everyone together to give a situation report, such as he was able. No one was entirely sure what exactly was happening. The population had been advised by the Argentine military authorities to remain indoors. Argentine troops were milling about everywhere. There was no more firing. Negotiations seem to be under way for a surrender of the Argentine forces. White flags flying in parts of the town. The situation was confused and seemed to be balanced on a tightrope; one false move from either side and everything would have broken out again. All we could do in the store was to wait. In the afternoon, about 2.30, Vice-Comodoro Bloomer-Reeve called in to inform Terry Spruce that definite negotiations were progressing for a surrender; these would take time; we were to be patient and all remain in the store.

This news was passed on to the old folk still in their homes by the faithful team of Les Biggs, Chris McCallum, Nidge and Ron Buckett, assisted by Duffy, Jeremy and Rag. It was highly dangerous to be on the streets, probably more dangerous than at any other time, but there was no way of letting people know what was happening other than to go out and tell them. The anxiety and uncertainty of not only the old folk, but of everyone else who was not aware of the situation, had to be relieved. In the store we all listened hourly to the BBC, clustered in little groups around the few small radios. The British forces had halted their advance just outside of the town. Everything seemed to hinge on the outcome of the meeting up the road between Gen Jeremy Moore and Gen Menéndez – this was taking place no more than five minutes walk from where we were all sitting. It was so hard to grasp. The BBC confirmed that the white flags were flying.

An uncanny stillness had fallen over the town. It took some time for it to sink in that the firing had at last stopped; the silence seemed just as deafening. The air was still; the smoke and smell drifted like a mist. It was very cold; the mud was freezing on the streets. An occasional helicopter flew overhead; someone thought they had seen a British one. Argentine troops huddled in groups, bewildered and uncertain as ever. Later in the afternoon the power station caught fire. We supposed that Martyn was still there; we hadn't seen him since early this morning. Jeremy, Rag and Duffy went off to join other volunteers to help fight the blaze.

The town electricity was cut off, so out came the candles, Primus stoves and the Tilley lamps. They created a curious flickering atmosphere in the store. Families and friends sat among the shelves of food, household goods and millinery; some dozing, some smoking, others preparing makeshift suppers. It reminded me very much of Van Gogh's great painting of 'The Potato Eaters'. Despite the circumstances we were a happy crowd; it was almost a social occasion, with people moving from group to group nattering and gossiping. It was so noticeable among the older folk that some of them had not met up with each other for months, or in some cases even years. They chatted and laughed as they recalled events of old times.

At 6.30 this evening Capt Ramanov of the military police arrived with Ron Buckett, who now seemed to have been accepted as the liaison officer between the civilian population and the military government. A window had been found open at the back of our house and Capt Ramanov insisted that I went with him to check if anyone had been in. Fortunately no one had, but why he insisted on my going with him is quite beyond me.

It was most eerie driving with him in his Mercedes through the streets; pitch black as the electricity was still off. I wondered if he remembered the afternoon in the police-station yard a few weeks ago when Martyn was arrested. There were groups of Argentines everywhere, vague shadows in the darkness. For some reason we stopped at the remains of the police station for a few minutes while Ramanov had a discussion with some other officers by torchlight, then off up Ross Road to the hospital corner, which was lit up like day, with the power house still blazing. There were several power lines damaged, causing great green flashes to shoot across the sky towards Government House. George Butler's house was also on fire, out of control. Here we met up with the boys, along with the rest of the fire brigade, who were obliged to give up fighting the fire as the house was packed with mortars and ammunition. The gardens were full of booby traps with trip wires. The house was an inferno with the exploding ordnance causing eruptions of flaming debris to be thrown over a wide area. It was a miracle that no other houses were burned down when the bits landed.

On reaching our house, we went through it carefully with Ramanov leading the way. He was not satisfied until we had looked in every room. No one had been in; nothing had been touched. When we looked into Anya's bedroom he asked me to confirm that I thought no one had been in. It was like a church bazaar jumble stall, as it usually is, but a bit worse, as all the shelving along one wall had collapsed where we had stood on it yesterday getting a better view of old Wilfred's house when it was burning. We checked on the dog in the bunker; she was fortunately still under the effects of the tranquilliser. The cats had disappeared altogether, probably hiding under the house. What a muddle the place was in; our rapid and unexpected departure this morning left no time to do anything. There were dirty dishes, drums and buckets of water, clothes, boots and shoes. So we secured the window and went off back to the West Store.

Capt Ramanov seemed to be genuinely distressed, not only about our particular plight, but about things in general. The tables had turned. The appalling reality of the effects of Argentina's Malvinas recovery operation had got through to him, in much the same way as it had hit the people of Stanley seventy-four days ago. He must have been acting on someone's orders to check on the house with me; whose orders we shall probably never know, but he conducted himself well and, in fairness to him, it must be said that his concern and helpfulness this evening did not seem to be a last-minute effort to save his own skin.

I must confess that I was extremely glad to reach the comparative safety of the West Store again; being outside along with the Argentines caused a most disturbing feeling. The boys, with Duffy and the rest of the fire-fighting crew, arrived back shortly afterwards, wet through and freezing. The power station fire was out; George Butler's house had to be left to burn and blast itself to the ground. With the booby traps and the explosives, there was no other course open. They had not been back long when they were called out again, this time to Giles Mercer's peat shed, which suddenly caught alight. Again the West Store management came to the rescue by providing dry clothes off the shelf and, better still, hot rum to thaw out a bit. Back again an hour later, then off again to another peat shed on fire; more rum, more dry clothes.

It looks very much as if the fires are being deliberately started by some of the Argentine troops. There has been no fighting since this morning. If they had been caused by troops sheltering in the peat sheds, they would not have had such an intense hold by the time the fire brigade arrived. Just before 10, they arrived back once again, saturated and exhausted, and even colder as it had started to snow. Food, hot rum and more dry clothes dished out by the store. Ileen, Anya and Jeannie had got Tyssen, Eli and Maxwell settled down in their sleeping bags under the racks of ladies' coats and dresses.

About 10.20 we were having a cigarette and a mug of tea discussing the excitement of the day when there was a knock at the back door of the store. The immediate thought was that it was another fire being reported. Terry Spruce opened up and in walked Patrick Watts, followed by a small British soldier who said, 'Hullo, I'm Jeremy Moore. Sorry it's taken rather a long time to get here.' Told us that a surrender had just been signed. More British officers then crowded in. The reaction was fantastic. People cried, others cheered; others just stood mesmerised, all by candlelight among the bags of flour and crates of food. He introduced his officers and then it got through to us. We are free, liberated. Everyone shook his hand, most of us beyond words. He was hoisted on to shoulders and given a drink. Terry proposed a toast to Mrs Thatcher, then to the Queen, then to the Task Force – it was such an emotional moment that I forget the order in which they came. It was hard to describe our feelings. Many wept; Ileen kissed the General, Jeremy was among those hoisting him shoulder-high. Jeannie and Maxwell got photographed with him. I was stunned with relief. It was hard to believe, almost impossible to believe – but it was true. It was also a tremendous relief to learn from one of the officers that Ileen's brother Terry was safe and well. He had met up with the 3rd Paras and fought with them in the great battle for Mount Longdon.

After the General had left and we had not long settled down the fire brigade was called out again. The dockyard was ablaze. We were told not to go out on to the streets until morning. Sleep was virtually impossible with our confused thoughts. The tension of seventy-four days was suddenly gone.

These notes are a bit confused as they were jotted down at odd times throughout the day on bits of paper. The main bulk of the diary is scattered about the house in the hope that if the Argentines did come across it they would not find it all.

It must be placed on record at some time the great work which Neville Bennett and Lewis Clifton have done in organising the volunteer fire brigade. Nothing has daunted them and they are still out doing what they can to save the dockyard.

Tuesday 15 June – FREEDOM

Very cold. Snow squalls. Very little wind, from the west.

At 9.30 this morning we were allowed to come home from the West Store, through the streets filled with abandoned weapons, the gutters choked with ammunition – it's everywhere, millions of rounds which we crunch underfoot each time we go out. We've brought some weapons in from the road to get them out of the way – seven FN rifles, two sub-machine-guns, several pistols. Martyn arrived home with a large general-purpose machine-gun which he insists on keeping in the bedroom. Tyssen has a collection of tin helmets and bayonets. The novelty will hopefully wear off. I suppose that we will have to give them all in at some stage.

We found our house completely untouched, though in the back garden there were long rows of excreta where the troops had relieved themselves. It must have been jolly draughty as they had not even bothered to squat in the lee of either the fences or the bushes. They have done the same thing in the town hall and the post office. It's such a frightful mess that they have had to get the fire engine to hose the whole place out. They have even fouled inside the drawers of the postmaster's desk and piles of our undelivered mail, which have had to be destroyed.

What a joy it was to take the black-outs down from the windows; the house seems strangely bright with all this daylight streaming through it. The water and electricity supplies are intermittent. There are now several thousand British troops who will require it; they are welcome to all they want, they deserve it.

British helicopters started arriving this morning early. We went down to the football field to watch them. It was a wonderful sight, as are the British troops now streaming into the town, tired but jubilant, having yomped and fought their way in from San Carlos. We, and everyone else in town, invited them in for tea and buns; we must have brewed gallons during the day. By mid-morning the tanks were arriving, along with the Snow Cat type vehicles – I think they are known as BVs – each one piled high with equipment and weapons, Union Jacks flying from their wireless aerials. The battle-scarred HMS *Plymouth* and many other ships are arriving in the harbour. What lies we have been told in the past when so-called experts have said that the harbour is not big enough to take large ships. There must be ten or more of them anchored out there, stretching from Government House to the Narrows and beyond. Port William is crammed with them.

The house is in such a shambles it should really be sorted out, but we left it for the sheer joy of going out on to the streets again in safety. There are thousands of Argentines being rounded up. Some still have their weapons. A few are a bit aggressive, but the majority are relieved and smiling, some even shaking hands as they pass by. There is mud and wreckage everywhere, great piles of it. Buildings are still burning; the smoke is still thick in places. Fires are being left alone as dozens of booby traps are being discovered in sheds, houses, gardens. Some of the Argentine troops must have had a busy time yesterday while the surrender was being negotiated. Anya and Diane were photographed outside the wrecked police station by one of the military photographers. They came across some Argentine bodies during the day.

This afternoon we went up beyond the Battle Monument to meet Terry who we heard had arrived in town. Everything was in a fearful mess. Half the roof was gone from the house recently converted into two flats for Pat and Brenda Whitney and Jimmy Sornsen. A large shell had gone through poor Jimmy's flat, doing a vast amount of damage. On Racecourse Road the house recently occupied by the Brysons was burned to the ground, still smouldering. Very few houses had windows left intact. Most had been riddled with shrapnel and small-arms fire. Water and mud everywhere; probably burst mains. Some Argentine dead bodies lying by the side of the road. Abandoned equipment everywhere: webbing, sleeping bags, blankets, boots, underwear, toothpaste, personal papers – all had been abandoned during the final crumble under the British onslaught. A lamentable sight, but I suppose this is the end result of any attempt to remove a stubborn aggressor from one's territory.

Up along the ridge of rocks in the 3 miles or so from the racecourse along to Moody Brook are hundreds of dug-outs. It looks like some straggling shanty town built from old oil drums and firewood. The ground is full of shell craters from the British

105-mm guns and the Navy's 4.5s. The casualty rate among the Argentines encamped up there must have been very high indeed. The four new houses down by the Beaver hangar completed just before the invasion are in a mess; two have disappeared altogether; just blackened ruins remain.

Built in among the wreckage of the foundations are a couple of large turf huts. Looking at these and the construction of some of the Argentine dug-outs it is plain that they have been built by those who really know what they are doing in making the best out of other people's rubbish. Many Argentine troops must have been gathered in during great purges of the shanty towns around their large cities. Perhaps this explains the somewhat exotic toilet habits of some of them; to many the marvels of modern sanitation must have been a bit of a revelation. It also goes some way to explaining why some were uncertain as to where exactly they were. I suppose their geography was a bit limited as well. No wonder many of them didn't look very enchanted about taking part in the recovery of the nation's beloved Malvinas Islands. I bet half of them didn't even know where they were.

The Beaver hangar is like a colander; there are more bullet holes than tin on the roof and sides. Enormous red crosses are painted all over it. The wreckage of the two Beaver aircraft lies outside on the slipway; both hacked to pieces by machine-gun fire.

On the other side of the road are many of the Argentine howitzers, some tipped up drunkenly by the effects of the British bombardment. There must also be ten or a dozen wrecked Argentine helicopters of various sorts all along the racecourse. One of their Chinooks is up in the gorse behind Government House.

We finally found Terry in one of the houses on Ross Road West into which the Paras and Marines are moving for temporary shelter. He is bearded and well; very pleased with life, especially as the 3rd Para Brigade have given him the honour of being the right marker when they march through Stanley for their thanksgiving service in the cathedral in a few days' time.

On the way down the road we had a quick look at the old Government Store area, which we used to call the Army Camp. It's full of heavily fortified positions, with tons of military stores lying about. There are hundreds of cases containing mines. The thick mud up there makes it almost impossible to walk.

Down in the centre of the town the British have unlocked the shipping containers brought in by the Argentines. There is sufficient food in them to have lasted the troops for months, if not a year or more. Hundreds of tons of it. Three containers alone were crammed full of flour; another four were completely full of sacks of potatoes. These containers are about the size of a caravan. Others contained cheeses, jam, tomatoes, macaroni, cigarettes, tinned fruit, sides of bacon, powdered milk, corned beef, stewing steak, cooking oil, sacks of sugar, and hundreds of crates of ration packs. I've only named a few of the things. It is absolutely fantastic – the quantities are staggering. It's not in dribs and drabs, but by the crateful. Besides the foodstuffs there are other containers full of equipment – boots by the thousands, enough socks to keep us going for ever, gloves, working gear, it's all there. Yet the troops were starving and dressed in clothing which was falling to pieces. Other containers are full of ammunition of all kinds. We only passed a few; there are scores of them scattered about the town. The Drill Hall was another eye-opener – stacked to the roof with provisions. Even crates of surgical cotton wool and torch batteries.

Even though it is filthy and ravaged, the town seems quite beautiful tonight. Odd street lamps are on but not many; most of the streets are in darkness. People have taken down their black-outs. Flickering candlelight shows in the windows of the houses. The Argentine troops are being rounded up by the thousands. The British still continue to pour in, on foot and by helicopter. The public are advised that, because of the large numbers of Argentines still being dealt with, we should remain off the streets, but at least we now again can open our doors in safety, even go out and stand in the garden in the dark – really daring stuff. Even the dog can go out for her nightly tiddle again. Such are the sheer joys of liberation, little things possibly to other people, but things which are not fully appreciated until you are suddenly denied them. After supper I stood in the garden for a few minutes trying to take everything in, when there was the wonderful sound of a bugler playing Lights Out. It was very still, more snow was just starting to fall, the notes carried up over the town, then were taken up by more buglers from other regiments. The British Army is in Stanley. It's so difficult to grasp the fact that they are really here and that it is all over at last.

And so ends this momentous day, one a lot of us thought that we might not ever see. To me the best moment was this afternoon as we passed by Government House and saw the Union Jack flying once more. A terrible price has been paid to get it back there. It makes one feel very humble to realise that this whole conflict has been for the freedom of the tiny population of these islands. We are deeply thankful.

Sadly we heard this morning that old Mrs Mary Goodwin passed away yesterday from wounds received from shrapnel on Saturday night at John and Veronica Fowler's. A tragic way to end her eighty-odd years.

APPENDIX

Extracts from the Argentine Gazette

No 1 – 8 May 1982

Editorial

The Argentine Gazette has one purpose: to fill an information need for the Members of the Armed Forces. Thus, our first objective will be to tell the truth according to true facts, and to give a new historical and social understanding to the Malvinas Territory. False information creates absurd or imaginative illusions, while a pure information service shows the background and helps to maintain in us a virile alertness to the just and noble battle which we have begun and which must not cease.

Our Baptism of Fire

The Argentines of yesterday were able to cross the Andes and travel the seas to bring liberty to the continent. The Argentines of today have the task of recapturing that part of our territory snatched away by England 149 years ago.

In the hearts of our men beat the same ideals as yesterday's. No one abandoned his post. Beneath the bombs or artillery fire, each man did his duty with honour. Now the enemy knows the precision of our fire, the capacity of our arms and that the oath we have sworn is not empty words.

Each man should be satisfied; in the hour of testing he triumphed.

No 2 – 11 May 1983

For History

By Decree of the Military Government of the Malvinas, South Georgia and the South Sandwich Islands, dated 27 April 1982, the Military Government was placed under the protection of the Blessed Virgin Mary in her dedication as 'Our Lady of the Rosary of the Reconquest and Defence'.

No 3 – 14 May 1982

Editorial

Every soldier learns to use his weapons, comes to know them and handles them with care. However, above all he must know himself in order to live with himself; and know others in order to live with them. But there is something important, and that is he must know the TRUTH. Somone said that, 'He who does not proclaim the truth because he is ignorant of it is an accomplice of liars and cowards.' Therefore, the soldier will know first of all the Eternal Truths which are the principles of forgiveness and salvation. And then the truths which demand a full understanding of the facts, like the Argentine truth that the Falklands are Ours.

No 4 – 17 May 1982

What is the Enemy Like?

Radio, newspaper and magazine reports from the continent [mainland] give details of the different English units which approach on board the enemy's fleet. What are they like? The answer is simple – they are men like you and me. Tall, short, good-, bad-tempered . . . not one of them possesses the attributes of Superman – least of all that of being invulnerable to bullets. They are armed with FAL rifles identical to ours. MAG machine-guns, identical to ours. Rocket launchers identical to ours. Mortars identical to ours. But they don't have 120-mm mortars.

In short – you are not more poorly equipped than them. You have the same equipment and armaments. They are not immune to the fire of our weapons. You have a clear understanding of the reasons for your being here. You *know* why you are fighting. Therefore SHOOT TO KILL. Your fire will be effective.

The Difference Between Us and the Enemy –

The enemy does not know the reason he is fighting.
The enemy fights for his pay.
The enemy fights to defend Colonialism.
The enemy does not have the full support of a Nation behind him.

You know why you are fighting.
You are fighting for Sovereignty and National Honour.
You are supported by the entire Argentine Nation.
You fight for a just cause.

No 9 – 1 June 1982

To My Men

The hour of the final battle has arrived. All our efforts, the hours of waiting, the cold, the tiredness, the vigilance, have come to an end. The adversary is getting ready to attack Stanley with the audacious and odious intention of conquering the capital of the ISLAS MALVINAS. Every man must fully understand what his duty is. The enemy will be destroyed by the decisive action of each one at his combat post. If each man with his rifle, his mortar, his machine-gun, or artillery piece fights with the valour and heroism which has already characterised us, Victory is certain.

The gaze of all Argentina is on us; our parents, wives, fiancées and children, all our families have total confidence in us. In the supreme hour we have the duty not to defraud them. We have contracted a sacred responsibility before our comrades taken in action to convert their personal sacrifice into a page of glory for ARGENTINA, and we cannot allow their heroism to be in vain. Not only must we beat them, we must do it in such a way that their defeat is so crushing that they will never again have the impertinent idea of invading our land . . . *TO ARMS! TO BATTLE!*

Signed – MARIO BENJAMIN MENENDEZ,
Grl Br., Military Governor

No 10 – 3 June 1982

Editorial

Good examples are always very significant, in all aspects of life. But when these examples bear the mark of heroism the summit of man's achievement in life is reached. Luis, Class 2 soldier of an Infantry Regiment, was in a dug-out in the early morning hours, when his Company came under air and naval bombardment. Realising that it had ended, Luis suggested getting out into the open air. He receives a categoric reply – NO! Seconds later a bomb explodes near them. His companion is wounded in the arm and abdomen. He tells Luis that his injuries are painful, and Luis then leaves the dug-out to seek help. He doesn't find it because he is far away; it wasn't wise to distance himself from the dug-out. On returning he can't find his comrade. He had followed Luis, but after a few metres had fallen into a hole. Luis hears his name being called. His friend calls him and tells him to throw himself down by his side because the shelling is continuing. He throws himself into the hole, his body covering that of his companion at the very moment when a bomb explodes near them. Now Luis is injured, for a piece of shrapnel has penetrated his right thigh. Despite this, and when the shelling appears to move to another area, he pulls his friend from the hole, grabbing him by his sleeping bag and dragging him across treacherous ground. After a while he meets up with a Captain and a Soldier. As they are not able to reach the place where the Doctor is, two stretchers are sent, enabling the two wounded to be removed from the area. Luis is convalescing in hospital, hoping that God will help his friend, who has undergone an operation.

Perhaps, through lack of space, this narrative does not appear emotive, since it is neither sensational nor literary. However the scenes through which these marines lived and their actions give us the picture of the greatness of our soldiers faced with life and death.

No 11 – 7 June 1982

Editorial

It is likely that every reader of the Argentine Gazette is asking the same question as we are. What is really happening with the enemy? When is the promised attack coming? Why does he keep up a routine and boring action? Well, perhaps we can put forward some ideas to help us understand him.

THE ENEMY

Has learned that our soldiers are not easily driven back and that we have not lost faith.

His massive bombardments have not brought the results hoped for.

Weather conditions on the ground affect him.

The partial encounters with us have proved adverse for him.

The routine is beginning to worry him and make him lose confidence in his forces.

OUR TROOPS

We have ammunition for an indefinite time.

We have food for an indefinite time.

We have infinite faith.

Is not the enemy beginning to realise that he has mistaken the place, the adversary, and to realise that he is lacking in sincere and honest motivation?

Postscript

This concludes the portion of my Diary covering the Occupation. Two years have passed since that time. Stanley is gradually returning to normal; the wreckage has been cleared from the streets; the roads are being repaired; the troops are being moved out from the town into their own accommodation. Inevitably things will never be quite the same; that is a fact of life which has to be accepted. But as a result of these changes we have now the security which we have always wanted. The tranquillity is regularly shattered by the scream of RAF fighters as they go off on their patrols, but this is a small discomfort to endure if it means that we can go about our lives with confidence and in safety.

The relationship between the military and the local population is on the whole very good indeed. Naturally, with any large imbalance between military and civilians, there will be occasions when a bit of aggro on either side is likely to flare up, but in Stanley these occasions are remarkably and fortunately very few. One pleasing result of the military garrison being here is their interest and participation in local activities. As well as being a welcome social change it provides an opportunity for the Islanders to show their gratitude and help to make their stay in the Falklands a little more comfortable. The civilian population has been increased dramatically with the influx of people concerned with putting the town back on its feet again. Stanley is full and expanding. New houses are being built; a commercial bank has been established; new businesses and enterprises have been set up by emigrant groups from England – the pioneer spirit has obviously not disappeared altogether. New livestock has been brought in to replace that lost during the conflict. The minefields are slowly but surely being cleared. Travel between the Falklands and England is trouble-free on the MOD-chartered ships *Uganda* and *Keren*.

One result of the Falklands conflict is that it has provided a base-line or turning point in our history. A 'before-and-after' has emerged, creating the birth of what is becoming the Falklands heritage. Prior to April 1982 it was almost impossible to define our heritage – or even if we had one at all. As for the people of the Islands, some – because of where they happened to live – were affected more than others by the Occupation and the resulting upheaval. For many people in Stanley the harsh realisation of what has taken place during these past two years has just sunk in; it's almost a sort of delayed shock, especially among the older folk. Life used to be so quiet, so peaceful, so regulated, that for some it has been almost too much to absorb the sheer speed with which events have taken place: the body-blow of the Argentine invasion; the trauma of the Occupation; the joy and relief of the liberation; and the aftermath, with its influx of new people, new ideas, new projects, and help and aid of all kinds flowing in. Christmas 1982 gave everyone a breathing space, which was great while it lasted but left many people with a feeling of depression after having had time to sit down and sort themselves out. The feeling of anticlimax which prevailed in the early days of 1983 was shaken off and thrust away by the totally unexpected and unannounced arrival of Mrs Thatcher at five o'clock on the afternoon of Saturday 8 January, accompanied by Admiral Sir John Fieldhouse. Her visit was like a much needed injection of adrenalin for the people of the Falklands.

The future is bright. As has happened in the past and no doubt will happen again, there will be occasional bad patches, but these moments are small when compared to what might have existed now but for the determination of the British people who came to our aid without hesitation at a time when we needed it most.